David Stuart

THE HUNGRY JUNGLE

David Stuart

Thistle Street Books, Edinburgh

THE HUNGRY JUNGLE first appeared in 2002, as an illustrated book published by Frances Lincoln Ltd in London, and Harvard University Press in America. The original title was PLANTS THAT SHAPED OUR GARDENS.

As those editions are now out of print, and with the technology of publishing having gone through such immense changes in the subsequent years, it seemed that an 'author's edition', using some slight modification on the original text, with new illustrations, and a format designed for e-readers rather than the coffee table, would give my work an additional lifespan.

I hope you enjoy it (and please review it, either way).

Berwickshire 2013

For the latest information about other e-books by the same author, please check www.david-stuart.co.uk or www.thistlestreetbooks.co.uk

Reviews of the first print edition

The original editions were widely reviewed. Here are some extracts:

NEW SCIENTIST 13 April 2002
THE ORIGINAL GROUND FORCE

The Plants that Shaped Our Gardens by David Stuart, Frances Lincoln,

HOW many of us wandering round a local garden centre have any idea where the plants we choose originally came from, or how they reached us? David Stuart haa the answer: obsessive collectors on extraordinary adventures. Roses, tulips, magnolias, lilies. orchids, delphiniums, poppies and phlox - we owe these riches and thousands of other plants to a bunch of people who were prepared to endure hardship and danger in pursuit of new species. Many survived exttemes of climate, terrain and isolation, not to mention hunger, disease, wild animals and often hostile natives, only to lose their precious specimens and botanical notes in shipwrecks on the way home. David Stuart tells their stories with great panache in 'The Plants that Shaped Our Gardens, a beautifully written and well illustrated book. He reckons that the flood of new plants into Europe over the past five centuries has been the main drIving force behInd garden design. This abundance of choice cracked the rigid mould of Europe's formal parterres and landscape gardens. It encouraged the development of exuberant flower beds, herbaceous borders, rockeries, water gardens and hothousea - all of which draw the eye to the plants rather than the View.

GARDENS ILLUSTRATED October 2002 Penelope Hobhouse
EX LIBRIS
GARDENER'S BOOKSHELF
This is a triumphant book, detailing important plant introductions. It is written elegantly and with great authority, and the publishers have complemented the writing with fine production and some excellent illustrations. The subject – inevitably broader than the title implies – has entailed vast research, much of it assembled in new ways to illustrate and illuminate the author's thesis. A botanist and at one time a nurseryman, Dr Stuart is well-known for his previous works on both history and plants. His account is both informative and entertaining and includes anecdotal stories that illustrate the character of his heroes, as well as their gift for bringing back the most garden-worthy plants.

Dr Stuart is particularly fluent in enlightening the contemporary gardening and botanical world into which the plants were introduced.

Of course, the point of the book is to pinpoint those plants that have helped shape garden design over the centuries, and those that have become staple elements in our gardens. And the author does not forget the less desirable plants, such as Rhododendron ponticum, that have become invasive in Britain, and the many exotics introduced to American gardens that now threaten the wilderness. Dr Stuart also allows space to discuss the modern search for lost garden plants and the importance of saving plants in the wild.

During the four great periods of plant introduction, garden styles have evolved and adapted to make use of the new discoveries. The first major influx was the flood of bulbous plants from the eastern end of the Mediterranean in the last half of the 16th century, which awakened the Renaissance mind to scientific study and established the collector's instinct. The second planting revolution occurred when American trees, shrubs and woodland plants arrived in Europe in the mid-18th century: they provided specimens for growing experimentally in the new naturalistic landscapes, as well as an awareness of the need to provide suitable growing conditions. The third great era of plant introductions came with the discovery of highly coloured South American annuals in the early 19th century, hybridised in the new glasshouses to furnish the Victorian bedding-out craze. The Asiatic treasures introduced towards the end of the 19th century encouraged the establishment not only of great plant collections, but provided plants that were suitable for modestsized gardens based on Robinsonian principles of wildflower planting. All this is covered superbly in this book.

Intrepid explorers, often either loners by choice or social misfits, dedicated their lives to the pursuit of new plants and their tales are dramatic, relieving this serious book of any tedium. In the last few pages alone the story of the Austrian Joseph Rock and his 1922 Chinese expedition in search of the chaulmoogra tree (its seeds intended for the treatment of leprosy) is a good example. A brilliant young man, but also eccentric, paranoid and greedy, as well as foolhardy and brave, Rock accomplished his mission in the brigand-infested Yunnan. Although not mentioned by Dr Stuart, Rock lived on to introduce the coveted tree peony, now known as Paeonia rockii, to western gardens from seeds collected in the lamasery of Cho-ni.

There are, however, a few lapses that may be simple slips in the editing. The false acacia or black locust (Robinia pseudoacacia) mentioned has white rather than pink flowers, and Sequoiadendron giganteum from the Pacific Northwest – its seed collected in 1853 by William Lobb – is known as giant redwood not dawn redwood, the colloquial name for the much more recent introduction Metasequoia glyptostroboides, discovered in 1946 in China and a rare survival of a fossil tree.

The wonderful tales of the plant collectors in this book should appeal to every gardener, and hopefully awaken a greater awareness of where the plants that shape their own gardens have come from.

Penelope Hobhouse is a garden designer and writer.
COUNTRY LIFE Mar 21at 2002
KATHRYN BRADLEY-HOLE salutes the explorers
HUNTER GATHERERS
The Plants that Shaped our Gardens
David Stuart

CUTTING a bold swathe through the history of garden-making, the author makes a spirited case for putting the plants first: he argues that the garden as we know it was created not by garden designers but by ordinary gardeners responding to a discovery or influx of exotic and novel plants.

Much of the pleasure of a book like this comes from the tales of derring-do, the adventures and extreme hardships endured by men (it was usually men) in the quest for plants.

We learn that the 17th-century pirate William Dampier 'cheerfully broke off from robbery and murder to take delight in the exotic flowers of whatever landfall he made' – he travelled with his vasculum and plant presses as well as his weapons, and became the first European to collect plants from Australia.

Carl Thunberg's reward for enduring an unnervingly close encounter with a buffalo in the veld was the discovery of the bird of paradise flower, Strelitzia reginae, duly despatched to Europe. On his travels to France, Thunberg was disconcerted to note that 'the French language, held in such high esteem by the upper classes in Sweden and elsewhere, is spoken by both high and low members of society all over France'. Extreme naivety can be a useful part of an explorer's armament.

Spanning four centuries and ranging across continents, here is a thoroughly enjoyable romp through the intertwined relationship of plants, their gardens and the many intrepid people who deserve to be remembered alongside them.

Introduction

INTRODUCTION

The idea for this book first took root on a spring evening, in the garden-room
of a village house in a remote part of Scotland. It had been a hard winter.
The lemon tree, a Meyer's lemon, had lost most of its leaves, but the couple
of weeks of warmth had brought on a scattering of ivory-green flower buds,
and the first few of the resultant waxen starry white flowers had opened.
Skeins of their glorious perfume wound invisibly through other plants
coming into bud or leaf. It suddenly seemed so unlikely; brugmansias,
clivias, a wonderful epiphyllum whose flowering has been a great event for
decades now but whose ancestors must have flowered in the jungles of
Ecuador, have all somehow arrive here under the chill skies of the North. But
there were other plants too, like the bulbs of Hymenocallis, its flowers like a
daffodil designed by Aubrey Beardsley, from a canal boat in Amsterdam, or
the 'sambac' jasmine that once used to tumble over balustrades in the
'moonlight' palace gardens of Jahangir and Shah Jahan, or the expanding
sprays of glossy buds on the oleanders, the first white ones brought back to
France by Pierre Belon in the mid-sixteenth century, and gradually developed
into a myriad sorts of single and double, pink, yellows, orange, sultry reds.
Further along the shelves, buds were showing on more modern plants too,

like the tough orchid Coelogyne cristata first collected by Joseph Dalton Hooker in northern India in the late 1800's, or the elegant Begonia burle-marxii discovered in Brazil only a few decades ago.

None of these plants had arrived in the garden-room directly from the place of their origin. A few amongst them had been ardently sought and bought. Most had been given, or found, or arrived in some forgotten way, without any forethought on their owners' part. And if they had arrived without our determination, then they had, in a way, arrived on theirs. All plants are designed to colonise new territories, but some of these had taken that built-in urge to an extreme. In this unlikely, cold, northern place were plants from the hot deserts of South Africa, from the coastal beaches of Amazonia, from the forest branches of Brazil and central America, or the jungle floors of East Asia. And if they had used humans, whether our friends, friends of friends, school friends of many decades ago, or neighbours, as ways of getting here, then they had used their original collector, and all subsequent gardeners, as a way of expanding their geographic dominion.

The thought turned around and around. It placed the interaction of plants and gardeners in a more interesting light than that of our more usual human-centred interpretation of the relationship. It also put the possible interpretation of the changes in how our gardens have looked over the millenia in a new light too. If gardens are seen as possible places for the colonisation for ambitious plant species, then how our gardens look could be determined by what plants have colonised them, by what plants have managed to exploit the gardeners' instinct to collect. Consequently, plant collectors, whether great or minor, are humans who have acted as conduits for the expansion of plants' geographic range.

Major collectors then become completely central to questions of the garden's possibility for change and design. Only slightly less central are the gardeners who delight in crossing new species, or in the selection of new variants that can be derived from within a species. But enveloping them, and providing the real engine for the garden's change are all of us gardeners who are only too susceptible to a lovely plant's blandishments. Garden designers, long subject to adulation and critical scrutiny, become almost entirely marginal.

I began to think of the areas that go to make up many contemporary gardens. Some of the minor plant collectors slotted in easily, in the way that

the nineteenth century Scots gardener James Tweedie is central to the chapter
on half hardy bedding plants, and 'bedding gardens', because of his
collection of immensely influential South American verbenas and petunias.
For some of the major collectors, placing is more problematic. The twentieth
century Ernest Henry Wilson collected endless splendid plants from China,
alpine primulas, rhododendrons, aquatics, new species of maple as well as
old fruit trees and so on. Yet he is placed in Chapter Nine, where his lilies
and his ligularias proved to be some of the plants that drove the creation of
the 'marginal' gardens around pools recently created expressly to show off
the new hybrid waterlilies then pouring out of their breeder's, Marliac-
Latour, garden. And so on... I hope gardeners will forgive me if some of
their favourite collectors and plants appear in what may seem idiosyncratic
places.

For almost all gardeners, collecting plants for our gardens is a very
minor strand of our interests. Only for some of us does collecting become an
overwhelming obsession. All obsessions are dangerous, and their intensity
can create astonishing human stories. Some collectors have been strange and
complicated men like the pirate William Dampier, who cheerfully broke off
from robbery and murder to take delight in the exotic flowers of whatever
landfall he made.

The first European to see, let alone collect plants from, Australia, he
was born in 1651 in the tiny village of East Coker near Yeovil in Somerset.
He was swiftly orphaned, became ungovernable and, to everyone's relief,
soon ran away to sea. He prospered in a way that would have been
unimaginable in East Coker. At twenty two, he was under-manager of a
Jamaican sugar estate. Bored, he soon joined a band of lawless log-cutters in
the forests of Yucatan. When he took to the sea next, it was as a fully fledged

thug. With other buccaneers, he plundered and murdered his way across the Isthmus of Darien, then headed south down the Colombian coast. By now, he was entranced by plants, and travelled with his vasculum and plant presses, as well as his glinting weapons.

He became a pirate captain by seizing a Danish ship at Sierra Leone. Using the proceeds of that blood-soaked raid, he navigated an immense journey back across the Atlantic, round Cape Horn, to the calmer coasts of Chile. More blood later, he went northwards to Mexico, then on across the Pacific to China. Astonishingly, he went from there to what is now Australia. No European had seen it before. There can't have been much to plunder, and perhaps his botanising infuriated the crew. He was abandoned on the Nicobar islands in the bay of Bengal. His fickle pirates sailed off. Even more astonishing, with a few plants and a native canoe, he made his eastwards way across two hundred miles of open sea to Sumatra. From there, he managed to reach London.

Publishing an account of his travels, and being both charming and personable, he was soon lionised. With his experience of the South Seas, he also soon interested the Admiralty. For some reason unaware of his criminal background, they commissioned him to undertake an official journey to Australia, then called New Holland. This made him more popular still. Samuel Pepys asked him for supper, as did the aristocratic gardener John Evelyn. Both men asked him to bring back Australian flowers for their gardens. In 1699, he sailed off, collecting plants in Java, Timor, New Guinea, Brazil and Australia. After another astonishing trip, on the return voyage his ship, HMS 'Roebuck', foundered and sank 'through perfect age' at Ascension. Much of his collection, and all of Pepys' hoped for flowers, were lost. There was a darker side too. Once home, Dampier was court-martialed for extreme cruelty to his lieutenant, and stripped of his captaincy. In 1703, he was back in the South Seas, once more a pirate, though now with two ships crammed with rogues. He eventually died in London in March 1715. What remained to him of his plant material is still preserved at Oxford University.

Driven and tempestuous men like him have made good collectors. Lesser men are often destroyed; once plant collecting became a way of life in its own right during the nineteenth century, men went travelling who never really, even in the half-light of the rainforest, or the snow-light of a Himalayan cliff, managed to leave home. Augustus Margary was a young

man of considerable promise. As a young British consular official in mid-
nineteenth century China, he was detailed to travel over thousands of miles of
unmapped territory to see if it was possible to travel up China's great Yangtse
river, and connect with the Irrawady. The journey was terrible, though he
became increasingly fascinated by the plants he encountered. To remind
himself of 'home', every evening he treated his native bearers to a concert.
Standing erect in front of his tent, he sang songs like 'The Lass of Richmond
Hill' and always finished off with a rendition of 'God Save the Queen', first
heard in public at a dinner in 1740 to celebrate the taking of Portobello by
Admiral Vernon. That may have merely bored his servants. Alas, he
travelled with a beloved dog. Thinking it amusing in an English sort of way,
he let the dog be carried in his curtained litter, while he himself walked. In
China, the litter was almost a sacred object denoting the status of its
occupant, and of the whole travelling party. To put a dog inside it was
sacreligious. Augustus didn't notice the escalating discontent. Almost at the
end of his epic journey, his servants could take no more. He was murdered.
None of his plants made it to the garden, yet some collectors working in the
same areas allowed two, sometimes three, thousand species to colonise
gardens worldwide.

    There are extraordinary stories for the plants too. The first
bougainvilleas reached Europe from South America, as the remarkable result
of an incredibly romantic story. The glorious Magnolia soulei
commemorates a man who met an appalling end on a Chinese hillside at the
hands of Buddhist monks. I have chosen plants in this book for their
immense beauty, and for their significance in the evolution of our gardens. I
have chosen collectors for their significance for particular parts of the garden,
rather than for their overall careers. I have also chosen the ones who most

show to what lengths of desire the plant collecting instinct can drive a human being.

END

1

Chapter 1

THE COLLECTING INSTINCT

Constantinople. 1512. Ruthless, immensely energetic, Selim I ousted his father Bayazit II from the Topkapi fortress and became the Turkish empire's new sultan. Bayazit, once himself vastly powerful, had become absorbed with the future of his soul rather than the continuance of his immense empire. Its frontiers were beginning to crumble. He had many sons other than Selim, all with equal rights to inherit his endangered state. Selim needed to consolidate his gain at once. He began to have his many brothers slain, and all their sons killed. He also knew that on his own death, his empire might face collapse if all his own sons fought for his throne. While his brothers and nephews were being strangled or poisoned, he also had all but one of his own sons murdered. Even as all this violence was swirling through the pavilions and gardens of Constantinople, his immense military prowess was adding to his vast dominions. Soon he had control of all of every trade route that ran between Europe and the East. Unwittingly, he thereby changed Western gardens forever.

The very foundations of many European states shook as the wealth of their merchants took the impact of the Turkish empire's stranglehold on trade with the East. They had to do something at once. They sought sea routes around Africa in order to reach the spices, silks and medicaments that came only from China or India. They were so desperate that they also tried sailing due West from Europe, across the uncharted and dangerous Atlantic. By trying such an extraordinary journey to reach the East across that ocean, they had already discovered the Americas.

The colossal impact of that discovery was tempered by the great risks of the journey. The overland routes still seemed very much safer, and so the greatest of the European states sent ambassadors to Selim at Constantinople in an attempt to negotiate easier trading with and through his empire. Seeing a huge commercial advantage, he began to allow them some trading concessions. However, garden plants, as well as spices and drugs, can easily travel along trade routes. Selim's vast empire thus caused European gardeners to grow new plants not only from from Virginia and Mexico, but also species from his own rich lands, and garden variants developed in his own flower-loving culture.

Selim reigned until 1520, when his surviving son, sumptuously arrayed and jangling with gold, rode in through the great gates of the Topkapi fortress. Even more extraordinary than his ruthless father, he was a great military commander, a passionate builder of mosques, palaces, bridges and aqueducts. He was also a passionate lover of flowers. With fabulous power and fabulous wealth he was almost at once called Suleiman the Magnificent. European ambassadors were overwhelmed by the riches that they saw in his city. Suleiman's courtiers soon arranged for them to have, as well as greater treasures, lesser ones: bulbs and seeds to send home to their masters and friends. The English ambassador posted bulbs home to Lord Salisbury, who in turn handed them on. John Gerard, London herbalist and producer of the great 'Herball' of 1597, wrote of a magnificent new scarlet lily that it came from 'Constantinople, whither it is brought by the poore peasants to be solde, for the decking up of gardens. From thence it was sent among many other bulbs or rare and daintie flowers, by Master Harbran, Ambassador there, unto my honorable good Lord and master, the Lord Treasurer of England, who bestowed them on me for my garden'. William Harborne was the first English ambassador sent to Turkey, but though he sent a number of plants back to his own country, by far the most important ambassador was Ogier Ghiselin de Busbecq. A Flemish aristocrat, he was sent from Vienna by the Emperor Ferdinand I.

De Busbecq was fascinated by both the past, and the gardens, of Turkey. He almost at once sent home marvellous plants like the Crown Imperial (*Fritillaria imperialis*), and the very first cultivated tulip. The ambassador had noticed scarlet fields of it near Adrianople (modern Edirne), where it was grown to supply the huge flower markets of Suleiman's capital city, and which still functions on its original site. The new tulips were grown in Vienna in 1554, Antwerp by 1561, and in London by 1580. He sent home other marvels: the horse chestnut tree, the first lilac, mock orange, the Syrian rose (*Hibiscus syriacus*), and the first cultivated forms of *Hyacinthus orientalis*. Gardeners were fascinated.

More influential still, De Busbecq had also unearthed some ancient classical manuscripts, notably a wormy and crumpled copy of Pedanios Dioscorides 'De Materia Medica'. Dioscorides was a Greek-speaking citizen of Cilicia who served as a soldier, and probably as a physician, in the Roman army around 60 A.D. His book carefully described the plants used in contemporary medicine. Doctors in the northern Europe of the sixteenth century had left to them only the shadowiest and most corrupted traditions of what they should be using. The crumpled book De Busbecq saw was obviously sensationally important, allowing doctors to start using the real classical plants which they hoped would give real classical cures. Even so, it was still only a transcription made around 512 A.D. for Anicia Juliana, daughter of Flavius Anicius Olybrius, one of the 'phantom' Roman Emperors who ruled Rome after its sack by the 'barbarians'. Nevertheless, it was far closer to the original source than the murky traditions that survived, and in any case, all the original copies of Dioscorides' great work were eventually lost or destroyed. Anicia Juliana's copy had survived, finding its way to the eastern capital of Constantinople. Perhaps it reached there from one of the Arab cities conquered by Selim's expansion of his empire into Syria, Mesopotamia (Iraq), Arabia, and Egypt. Perhaps is had merely lain in the imperial library for more than a thousand years. However, eventually it came into the possession of one of the doctors of Selim I. Even though the manuscript was in very poor condition, De Busbecq urged his master Ferdinand I to acquire it. Its owners clearly knew its importance, and it took seven years of negotiation before it eventually reached Vienna, where it still remains. Rapidly copied and circulated, it allowed European doctors a chance to assess the similarities of the plants they were using on patients to the ones used in ancient times, and which were presumed to be more effective cures. Adventurous doctors soon wanted to see the real plants for themselves.

Ambassadors, finding the great city so well provided with flower and plant markets, found it easy to collect new things to send to their masters and friends. Finding the classical druggists' plants needed real exploration, and a much more adventurous spirit. One such was the redoubtable Pierre Belon. Like all doctors into modern times he was necessarily a botanist too. Born in 1517 at Cérans Foulletourte (Sarthe), he studied natural history and medicine with the great European scholar Valérius Cordus, with whom he had travelled in Germany and Bohemia. Once back in France he became apothecary to the bishop of Le Mans, René du Bellay. However, travelling had got into his soul, and he was soon restless. He got himself attached to a diplomatic expedition to the court of Sulieman the Magnificent, so travelled rather comfortably at the expense Henri II of France and of the Cardinal of Tournon. He reached Venice in the spring of 1547 and, sailing on, was robbed by pirates off Crete. Pirates often preferring not to have the guilt of murder on their head, he was left alone in an empty boat without food or money. Ever resourceful, he swiftly learnt how to sail it, and managed to find safe harbour on that enchanting island. His memoires noted for the benefit of other indigents visiting Crete that 'monasteries give such provisions as they have gratis to all travellers whatsoever, as pickled or dried olives, onions, bisquet, salted fish, sometimes fresh for they often go a~fishing, their vessels or boats being cut without great difficulty of the thick trunks of Plain (sic) trees; their nets for want of corks are supported by gourds'. Belon described several new species of garden plants, including a white form of oleander, the gorgeous *Paeonia clusii*, and the sticky leafed and aromatic *Cistus ladanifera*, a source of one of the sorts of laudanum.

Eventually re-financed, he sailed for Istanbul and, with a copy of Avicenna's 'Canon of Medicine' under his arm. Once in the city, he explored the druggists shops in the great dusty covered markets of the capital. The trade in medicines was colossally lucrative, and it's tentacles wound throughout all the great empires of the East. Both he and subsequent travellers noted that camels loaded with drug plants were far more carefully guarded than camels merely loaded with even the most sumptuous silks from Persia or China. Once out of Turkey, he revisited, then sailed on to Egypt, with its strange African crops of taro, sugar cane, bananas, and then on to Jerusalem, Aleppo and Lebanon. Loaded with plants, he set sail for home. Yet again he was raided by pirates, but they left him at least with seeds or plants of *Chelidonium majus, Helleborus niger, Cnicus benedictus, Mandragora autumnalis,* an as yet unidentified Egyptian paeony which was supposed to cure coughs, and dozens more. He tried to get Henri II to help him set up a botanic garden in which to grow some of the new things, but had to settle for the garden of his patron René du Bellay's château de Touvoie, Savigné-l'Evêque. There, holm oak, cork oak, spruce, arbutus, sicilian sumach (*Rhus coriaria*), the manna ash (*Fraxinus ornus*), *Platanus orientalis,* and his white oleander flourished for the first time. He published some marvellous and influential books, including "Histoire naturelle des estranges poissons marins etc." (1551), "De arboribus coniferis" (1553), "La nature et la diversité des poissons, avec leur description et naïfs portraits" (1555), and even the curiously diverse selection of animals and plants contained in "Portraits d'oiseaux, animaux, serpents, herbes, hommes et femmes d'Arabie et d'Egypte "(1557). It was his travel memoires that were most widely read. He died mysteriously, assasinated by thieves in the Bois de Boulogne in April 1564.

His travels were influential enough to be soon copied. One of his most adventurous followers was Leonhardt Rauwolf. An Augsburg doctor, his trip was financed by a merchant brother-in-law, who no doubt hoped for some commercial advantage from Leonhardt's voyage. He set off from Marseilles on the 18th May, 1573, aboard the 'Santa Croce'. Once in Constantinople, he soon discovered that 'in their gardens, the Turks love to raise all sorts of flowers wherein they take great delight, and use to put them in their turbants so I could see the fine plants that blow, one after another, daily without trouble'. He saw turbans sporting sweet violets in December, soon followed by tulips, hyacinths and narcissus.

However glorious and civilised the court at Constantinople, travel in remoter regions was rough and dangerous. In his memoires, published in 1582, Rauwolf writes: 'Yet I cannot but describe to you one more plant for the taking of which I and my two comrades fell into great danger... When I was busy about this tender plant and strove to get it out whole, which took me up the more time because I had no proper tools by me, a Turk, well-armed came galloping upon us to see what we were doing.' After a small bribe, the janisssary rode off apparently satisfied. Before Rauwolf could bag the plant the Turk came back at full tilt 'with his cymeter drawn and fetched one blow after the other at me, which I still declined running from one side of the tree to the other, so that they went into the tree and mangled it mightily.' The janissary was armed with a bow too, but the intrepid Rauwolf realised that if the Turk decided to make use it, he would have to put down the scimitar, making it possible, for a moment, to attack. However, for a few more coins, Rauwolf bought off the Turk, who nevertheless made off with Rauwolf's 'tablebook' of records which had fallen out of his wallet during the scuffle. The plant was a species of *Aristolochia*. He describes it thus: 'This is called by the inhabitants Rhafut and also Rumigi; it hath a strong yet unpleasant savour and about four stalks of a whitish colour and so tender towards the root and .so small as a pack thread wereon at each side grown seven or eight tender ash coloured leaves distributed like unto those of Osmond Royal, only they have round Ears towards the stalk like unto small Sage. . . . (It has) flowers like Aristolochia yet a great deal bigger and more brownish colour and hanging on longer stalks. The root striketh very deep and is very like to our Pellitory, of a drying quality and somewhat hot as the bitter taste intimates.'

Undeterred, Rauwolf and a friend, Hans Ulrich Rafft, travelled overland through the grey-brown hills to the Euphrates river. Intending to sail down it to Baghdad, they posed as Oriental merchants, wearing long blue robes buttoned right down to their feet, baggy white cotton trousers, collarless

shirts and blue brimmed white 'turbants' such as Christians usually wore.
Their shoes were yellow leather with nailed soles, and over their whole
ensemble, they wore a narrow sleeveless goat-hair tunic, reaching to the
knees. Rauwolf found the journey agonising (all botanists and plant collectors
will know the feeling), for their barge would often glide past tempting plants
he could see on the river bank, but not reach. Once back in Tripoli, more
janissaries arrested him as a spy, but once again a payment got him out of
trouble. However, impoverished, he began to practice medicine to make
enough money to get home with his botanical spoils. He was back in
Augsburg by 1575, the seeds and roots he'd managed to transport home
forming the basis for the botanical garden he set up in his home city. The
herbarium of pressed specimens he assembled can still be seen at the
herbarium of the University of Leiden in Holland.

As well as being the first European ever to see coffee being prepared, he
discovered what were to become important garden plants like *Acanthus
spinosus*, *Lilium bulbiferum*, and the ineffable butcher's broom (*Ruscus
aculeatus*). He saw in Aleppo gardens some of the varieties of tulips,
hyacinths and anemones that were yet to arrive in Europe, and created such a
stir when they did. He also found in the local bazaar the first Indian Shot
(*Canna indica*) collected by any European. He collected the smokebush
(*Cotinus coggyria*) now found in at least half of Europe's gardens. He also,
like Belon, came across its relative Rhus *coriaria* which gives the spice still
immensely popular in the Lebanon, but never much taken up in western
Europe.

His journal became the sixteenth century equivalent of a best-seller, and
determined gardeners lusted after the plants he described. It fuelled yet more
travellers to go and search these mysterious lands for their mysterious plants.

It fuelled gardeners' desire to collect tulips and fritillaries, to grow new lilies, plant acanthus and rhus.

Rauwolf's travels were read with excitement all over Europe, and, even more than Belon's, launched endless travellers' dreams. Richard Hakluyt, nephew of the Elizabethan explorer, wrote of tulips in 1582: 'Within these four years there have been brought to England from Vienna divers kinds of flowers called tulipas and those and others procured a little before from Constantinople by an excellent man called Carolus Clusius'. This was a Latinisation of the name of Charles de l'Ecluse, a prodigious scholar in the fullest Renaissance manner, having studied law at Louvain, philosophy at Wittenberg, and then travelled to Frankfurt, Strasbourg, Lyons. At the university of Montpellier, he discovered the delights of Flora. As well as a historian, a map-maker, a mineralogist, zoologist, philosopher, numismatist, he now turned botanist too. From Spain, he collected two hundred new plants. From Turkey, he introduced more fritillaries and tulips, many daffodils, the gorgeously perfumed and silvery flowered orris root *(Iris florentina)*, and brought in new forms of ranunculus and hyacinth. From a friend in India, he even introduced the sumptuous tuberose, though like all European gardeners found it hard to get to flower more than once. He got the scarlet runner bean from another in Portugal, who had it direct from Brazil. He couldn't stop collecting. Late in life he told his friends that no matter how cruel life could be, and his had indeed been, botany and gardening were everlasting solaces. Perhaps.

But these are great names in the history of botany and of gardens. Endless, though now unknown, merchants, navigators, diplomats, sailors, doctors, adventurers, even pilgrims, brought back pinches of seed, or a bulb, perhaps even a potted plant. Everyone, suddenly, wanted to collect a plant. For a thousand years, the collecting instinct of men and women had been almost in abeyance. The garden flora after the fall of Rome had, like much else in Western life, stagnated. The medieval gardens of Europe had been largely planted with native species and their variants, like double flowered buttercups, daisies, even the weedy plantain, and, where wealth allowed, with exotic greens like cherries, cabbage roses, or the bitter oranges introduced from the East by the Romans. But Mankind everywhere is subject to the collecting instinct, and other garden cultures were busily exploring their own and neighbouring floras. In the Middle East, gardeners were collecting and selecting or breeding tulips, hyacinths, narcissi, roses, anemones, apricots. In

China they were developing paeonies, chrysanthemums, plums, peaches, lotuses, and more roses. And in the Americas, the natives were exploring the its vast flora, finding plants to eat as various as *Lewisia* and *Camassia*. In the luxuriant subtropics, they had selected amaranths with edible seed and gorgeously colourful leaves, dahlias with edible roots and brilliant flowers, tropaeolums with edible leaves, flowers, and roots, maize with myriad coloured seeds, endlessly varied squashes with flowers perfumed enough to make a gardener faint, endless beans, potatoes, tomatoes, and several cornucopia brimming with tropic fruits.

It may often seem as if humans are exploiting the planet's flora, but that is an entirely human-centred viewpoint. All plants are desperate for territory. In their struggle to survive, and expand their range, many have evolved extravagantly beautiful designs. Sometimes these are designed to attract pollinating insects to the flowers, or to encourage a whole range of animals to distribute their seeds. Mankind has always rummaged through this astonishing abundance in pursuit of things of use or beauty and, imagining himself master, has been brilliantly exploited by huge numbers of plants. Verbenas and petunias from South America have found themselves niches, along with pelargoniums from South Africa, in bedding gardens almost worldwide from the 1860's onwards. Palms, aspidistras, even some orchids, adapted to life in the deep shade of the jungle floor, have discovered new niches in the drawing rooms of Moscow and New York. Flowers adapted to the prairies of Oregon or Nevada suddenly have a world-wide range once they reach the herbaceous border. Immense grasses that are designed to survive the ravaging fires of the pampas of Central America, go global as specimens on front lawns, or when fashion demands, as producers of dried flower stalks to decorate dingy parlours.

But the human collecting instinct can also focus itself in a minute area. Gardeners fall in love with auriculas or day lilies or tulips or carnations, indeed almost any genus or species that contains, even in the wild, a number of variants. These switch on the human need that must have 'all' of something. The need is even more strongly fired if the variants can be crossed to give new ones that are not found in nature. Species or groups of species can then explode, even over a few decades, into endless new things to feed gardeners' greed and envy, and a sometimes maniacle fascination with increasingly minute differences.

But the collecting instinct also changes the way we see our gardens, which is a way of representing part of how we interact with the world around us. The oldest way of doing this, vastly ancient and certainly from the dawn of civilisation, is to plant the garden as four quarters surrounding some sort of symbolic central feature, whether a pool, or a sacred tree, or a mount, even a statue of a god or goddess. This four-square garden, anciently a map of the known world, was an immensely stable unit of the garden, and is known incised into pottery shards from 3000BC., from the great palaces of ancient Mesopotamia, even in the city planning of the ancient capitals of China. In Europe, it was used in many Roman gardens as well as Roman encampmnets, and survived the fall of that empire in the plans of monastery cloister gardens, and no doubt private gardens too. By the late fifteenth century, it was becoming increasingly elaborated, and by the late fifteenth and early sixteenth century, the four squares had metamorphosed into elaborate patterns carried out in clipped plants, often evergreens like box, santolina, phillyrea, sage. Nevertheless, these 'knots' was merely an embroidered overlay upon the ancient garden plan. There were, of course, a few other garden elements; herb gardens of small rectangular beds, easily cultivated, with rows of various flavouring and medicinal plants; kitchen gardens with similar plans; turf seats (descended from the more informal sorts of Roman 'triclinia'), and orchards too.

But the flora of all of them was hardly developed from the Roman one, containing a few lilies, vervain, poppies, hyacinths as well as the roses and periwinkles that appear on the walls of the 'Casa di Livia' on Rome's gracious Palatine Hill. Pliny the Younger was delighted with the rosemary hedge and the violets that grew in his garden overlooking the Bay of Ostia. Perhaps he also grew *Hemerocallis fulva* and H. lilioasphodelus, once wild in the Orient but long grown in the West. Perhaps he like the several Italian *Gladiolus* and *Iris* species, and the Roman range of vegetables: onions, garlic, globe artichoke, cabbage, cucumbers, peas, radishes, and leek. Perhaps, like other Romans, he had on the fringes of his garden figs, walnuts, black mulberries, medlars and plums. But that was it. The only 'new' plants were some perhaps brought home by crusaders or their hangers-on, returning from the Middle East many hundred years later: the almost weedy Star of Bethlehem (*Ornithogalum umbellatum*), the Jerusalem flower (*Lychnis chalcedonica*), and a scatter of hepaticas.

The first major wave of new flowers that hit western European gardens in the sixteenth century was therefore quite overwhelming. There was

nowhere to put them. The knot garden was too tightly wound to let them in.
Other parts of the garden were too utilitarian to show off such treasures.
Clearly, the knot garden had to explode wide open to let them it. It did. It
rapidly developed into the parterre. The topiaried plants retreated to the
margin of the bed, still giving form to the design of the garden, especially in
winter, but leaving central areas of the bed open to allow growing space for
the new flowers. The old four square garden was capable of easy repetition
and expansion, with the quarters themselves quartered and variously
elaborated. The new scheme made a perfect system in which to display the
subtle shapes and colouring of the new Turks and Americans.

The first wave of introductions set the theme for all the subsequent
periods of gardening, including our own, whereby the change in design is
determined in a very real way by plant introductions. Fashion is secondary.
But though subsequent chapters deal with astonishing travels in China,
Australia, Chile, Peru, western North America, and the Indies, the original
first wave was perhaps the most overwhelming. Curiously, it is still running,
even if it is now more like the last swirl of a wave up a shining beach. The
late Professor Peter Davis' monumental 'Flora of Turkey and the East
Aegean Islands', finished in 1985, and following on from the E. Boissier's
'Flora Orientalis' of 1884, and the prodigious eastern travels of John
Sibthorp, revealed just how many new species remained in the country to be
described. Incidentally, Sibthorp, like De Busbecq, Belon and Rauwolf was
enthralled with the work of Dioscorides and the problem of identifying the
actual plants referred to by him, and which had been confused over the
course of the centuries with western European plants. In 1785 he travelled to
Vienna to study what had become known as the Codex Vindobonensis, and
having seen De Busbecq's find, set off eastwards. Professor Peter Davis, with
whom the author worked for several years on his massive 'Flora of Turkey',
had his own Turkish adventures.

However, let us return to the closing years of the parterre at the very end
of the seventeenth century, and to France. There, the formal garden,
epitomised by the immense schemes of Andre le Notre, beautiful but
botanically sterile, had its most grandiose triumphs. The traveller who closes
this chapter was a minor gentleman, vastly educated, immensely clever, and
epicurean in his enjoyment of life. He was also a rationalist who could laugh
elegantly at the superstitions of some of the natives with whom he came in
contact.

Joseph Pitton de Tournefort was born on June 5, 1656, at Aix-en-Provence, France. His father intended him for the church, and sent him to a Jesuit college in Aix. However, when his father died in 1677, Joseph at once turned his attention entirely to botany and medicine. He studied both at Montpellier, and medicine at Barcelona. He had his first experiences of the joys and hazards of a plant-hunter in the mountains of Dauphine and Savoy in 1678, and in the Pyrenees in 1681. Even that trip has its adventures, for he was robbed and stripped by local bandits. They treated him more kindly than they did some of their victims, and considering his distress and the extreme cold gave him back his coat. They hadn't noticed that there was some money tied in a handkerchief, and which had slipped inside the coat's lining. Tournefort, clad only in the coat, manage to walk to the nearest town, where he had enough to buy 'a Thrum-Cap, Linen Trowsers and a Pair of Wooden Shoes'.

He became, like many of the men in this book, a doctor. That proved immensely useful, but it was as a botanist that, in 1688, he received an appointment as professor at the Jardin des Plantes in Paris. Two years later he was despatched by Louis XIV on the same sort of journey as Belon and Rauwolf; 'to discover the Plants of the Ancients, and others, which perhaps escaped their Knowledge'. He was to travel with two friends; a German doctor called Andreas Gundelscheimer, and a young artist called Claude Aubriet (who was soon to give his name to the familiar rock garden plant – aubretia). The artist was essential, Tournefort wrote, for 'It frets a man… to see fine Objects, and not be able to take Draughts of them'.

Tournefort's splendid account of the voyage takes the form of a series of letters to the Secretary of State, M. de Pontchartrain. The result is one of the most engaging of travel-books, though "Relation d'un voyage du Levant" (Paris, 1717), only appeared after his death. It was immensely popular, being soon translated into English (1741) and German (1776). However, much of the book must have been recollection, for many of the actual letters that he did send home fell foul of the hazards of travel, and their bearers died of illness, or were drowned or assassinated. Tournefort himself also was to face similar risks, though not only did he survive, but he also collected 1356 species of plants during this one journey. Many were new. Many are still in our gardens.

He left on the trip in April 13 1700. After a voyage of nine days from Marseilles, the travellers landed at Khania in Crete, and started out with great expectations to explore the vicinity of the port. Perhaps he hit a poor season, for although even the immediate vicinity has some interesting plants, Tournefort wrote 'Discontent return' d at every step we took. . . . We ever and anon look'd at one another without opening our mouths, shrugging up our shoulders and sighing as if our very hearts would break, especially as we follow'd those pretty Rivulets, which water the beauteous Plain of Canea, beset with Rushes and Plants so very common, that we would not have vouchsafed them a look at Paris, we whose Imagination was then full of plants with silver leaves, or cover'd with some rich Down as soft as Velvet, and who fancied that Candia could produce nothing that was not extraordinary .'

They found richer pastures elsewhere, and ended up spending three months exploring of the island. He explored, too, many other islands of the Greek archipelago, encountering some lovely plants and some strange people. On Myconos, he even had a brush with the living dead. He wrote 'We were present at a very different Scene, and one very barbarous, in the same Island, which happened upon occasion of one of those Corpses, which they fancy come to life again after their interment. The Man... was murder'd in the fields, no body knew how, or by whom. Two days after his being bury'd in a Chapel in the Town it was nois'd about that he was seen to walk in the night with great haste... On the tenth day they said one Mass in the Chapel where the Body was laid, in order to drive out the Demon which they imagin'd was got into it. After Mass, they took up the Body, and got every thing ready for pulling out its Heart. The Butcher of the Town, an old clumsy Fellow, first opens the Belly instead of the Breast: he groped a long while among the Entrails, but could not find what he look'd for; at last somebody told him he should cut up the Diaphragm. The Heart was pull'd out, to the admiration of all the Spectators. In the mean time, the Corpse stunk so abominably, that they were obliged to burn Frankincense; but this smoke mixing with the Exhalations from the Carcass, increas'd the Stink, and began to muddle the poor Peoples Pericranies. ... Nothing could be more miserable than the Condition of this Island; all the Inhabitants seem'd frighted out of their senses... they knew not now what Saint to call upon, when of a sudden with one Voice, as if they had given each other the hint, they fell to bawling out all through the City, that it was intolerable to wait any longer; that the only way left was to burn the Vroucolacas intire; that after so doing, let the Devil lurk in it if he could; that 'twas better to have recourse to this Extremity, than to have the Island totally deserted: And indeed whole Families began to pack up, in order to retire to Syra or Tinos. ..'

Whether it was as a result of this strange episode, or whether they just thought local craft too flimsy, he and his companions soon got a pirate ship to take them on towards Turkey. He coolly informs Pontchartrain that the boat was 'one of those your lordship has forbidden pickeering from island to island for plunder. I promis'd the Master not to inform against him, and so he convey'd us to Argentiere, the first of August.' This tiny island, where, we are told, 'the Women have no other Employment but making love and Cotton Stockings', was a resort of the pirates, and being 'encumbered with our baggage, and reposing no great Confidence in the People of the Place' they soon moved on. Early in March 1701, they embarked on a Turkish vessel and a few days later arrived in Constantinople. Tournefort, as many travellers still are, was overwhelmed. He found Turkish customs and society immensely strange and fascinating, and couldn't help but describe them to his French audience.

However, Mount Ararat was his destination, and soon he tore himself away from the fascinating city. He arranged to join the caravan of the pasha of Erzurum. To go so far east in European clothes was dangerous, so he and his companions dressed as Armenian, though Armenians with Spanish leather boots. Thin Turkish slippers were not much use, he thought, for 'Persons who love to go a-simpling'. Their camping equipment consisted of tents, leather sacks for baggage, baskets, cooking and eating equipment and a good supply of 'Callicoe Drawers, which serve instead of Bed-clothes in this sort of Roads' The pasha was travelling with a wife, mother, daughter, majordomo and other officers. Such was his status and size of retinue, and such was the fear of brigands, that other merchant caravans joined them, and so the eventual company consisted of three hundred camels, six hundred

people, and many sorts of hangers on. In spite of the cleanliness of many of
the caravansaries, some important person amongst the six hundred was
always ill. Tournefort often used the opportunity to halt the entire caravan,
so that he could treat the patient, but collect plants at the same time. They
reached the ancient, spectacularly sited, and once beautiful city of Trebizond
(modern Trabzon), on 23rd May. The rhododendrons were in bloom, and so
Tournefort was the first botanist to see and describe the common purple
rhododendron (*Rhododenron ponticum*), and the incredibly perfumed yellow
azalea (*R. luteum)*. As it was the honey from the purple species that had
poisoned Xenophon's soldiers, Tournefort wrote that 'As beautiful as the
Flower is, I did not judge it convenient to present it to the Bassa ... but as to
the flower of the preceding species [the azalea], I thought it so very fine, that
I made up great Nosegays of it, to put in his Tent; but was told by his Chiara,
that this Flower caus'd Vapours and Dizziness.'

From Trebizond the caravan proceeded by the easiest rather than the
shortest route. This suited Tournefort, though 'The Merchants laught heartily
to see us mount and remount every moment, only to pick a few Herbs... At
the next Lodging we described our Plants while our Meat was in our Mouths,
and M. Aubriet drew all he could.' But Turkey is at the junction of three great
floristic regions. On the 6th or 7th June, they crossed the mountains of the
Pontic Range. They had journeyed into a new region, and one so rich in
flowers that 'we knew not which to fall on first'. After many new plants, and
expeditions into Georgia and Armenia, he ends:

'The 25th March, in returning from Samos, we went from Scalanova to
Ephesus. The next Day we departed to return to Smyrna, and we lay that Day
at Tourbale... a poor village, in which we see several old Marbles, which
please Strangers, for otherwise the Turks who inhabit it are not very civil.
... All this Part is is full of Leontopetalon, and Anemonies of a bright shining
Fire Colour . . .
Maunday-Thursday, the 13th of April, 1702, we set sail with the Wind at
South~East, in the Ship call'd the Golden Sun, commanded by Captain
Laurent Guerin of la Cioutad, carrying six pieces of Iron Cannon, and eight
Patereroes: It was laden with Silk, Cotton, Goats Hair and Wax for Leghorn.
The Wssel was of about 6,000 Quintals. After forty Days Sail, in which time
we had endured great Storms and contrary Winds, which oblig'd us to take in
Refreshements at Malta, we arrived at Leghorn on the 23rd Day, and went
into the Lazeres. The 27th we came out of the Lazares, and embarked on a

Felucca, which brought us to Marseilles the 3rd of June, being the Vigil of Pentecost, where we return'd Thanks to God, that he had preserved us thro the Course of our journey.' The stay in the Lazer house of Leghorn was a quarantine check that neither Tournefort not the ship's crew carried bubonic plague.

At last, still dressed a la Turque, Tournefort reached Marseilles, amidst great acclaim, in June 1702. The King himself acknowledged the great adventure. Tournefort went on to become one of the greatest of all botanists, and one whose concept of many genera we still use today. That we do is the result of a curious quirk of history related in the next chapter. One of his most important books was the sumptuously illustrated 'Éléments de botanique' (1694). In 1708, he and a professor friend were strolling along a sunlit street in Paris. A passing carriage, speeding, swerved. Both men were hit by the axle tree. The professor was killed at once. Tournefort died a few weeks later.

2

Chapter 2

The New Waves

David Stuart

UNRAVELLING THE KNOT

Once the parterre exploded with plants, loosening the bonds of the ancient forms of gardening, huge changes to how gardens looked and how they were used became inevitable. As trade with and through the East developed, and as settlement in the Americas increased, those who stayed at home, whether in Paris, Milan, London, or on their country estates, objects brought home from these distant lands were things of intense fascination. As the ability to read and write was also vastly much more widespread than it had ever been in previous centuries, avid collectors could write friends, relatives, even strangers, who were visiting or who lived in distant places, to send home anything interesting that caught their eye. All over Europe, networks of correspondents began to form, often centred on one, or a small number, of energetic individuals, commonly reaching across several continents, and quite commonly interconnecting. In cities, clubs and societies began to form, and in gardening these ranged from the modest florists groups formed to

develop perfect forms of tulip or anemone, to extremely high-powered clubs
like that held at, and named after, the Temple Bar Coffee House. Several of
its members appear later in this chapter.

By the end of the seventeenth century, the East was still the main source
of new plants. But the East wasn't just represented by the spring flowers of
Turkey and Persia. It included Russia too. Western gardeners were familiar
with *Iris sibirica* and others by the 1630's, but the Russians themselves were
as yet little interested in their own flora. Indeed, its first recorded
investigation was made by an English gardener. In 1618, negotiations were in
progress between James I and Tzar Mikhael, who wanted financial and
political help in his war against Poland. He offered trading concessions in
return, and as Russia was an important source of furs and timber,
ambassadors were exchanged. Two Russians visited London loaded with
sumptuous gifts. King James sent Sir Dudley Digges, of Chilham Castle,
Kent, to the Tzar. Sir Dudley needed a retinue of supporters, and a gardener
called John Tradescant applied to join the expedition. Tradescant was
already well travelled, having been gardener to the Earls of Salisbury at
Salisbury House in the Strand, London, and at Hatfield House. The gardens
at both great houses needed exciting new plants for the parterres and kitchen
gardens, and he had already been sent several times to Europe to collect new
sorts of vine and rose, to find black mulberry trees, and en route seems to
have visited the island of Cos, where he found the eponymous lettuce. In
those days he had been a bachelor, but marrying in 1614, he left London and
the Cecils for his own small property in Kent. However, he plainly enjoyed
travelling, and saw the Russian journey not only as a way of getting some
new species for his new employer, Sir Edward Wotton, but also in assuaging
his own highly-developed collecting instinct.

As a diplomatic mission, the journey was a waste of time. After six
weeks journey in Russia, Digges heard that the fearsome Poles were already
outside the walls of Moscow. The Tzar hardly needed another superfluous
ambassador. He returned to London. However, John Tradescant had set off
for Russia earlier, on a stormy six-week passage on the Diana of Newcastle.
The ship reached the port at Dvina on 14 July 1618, tying up 'befor the
Inglishe house' in the Bay of St Nicholas, a trading-post first established in
1591. He began collecting almost at once, and returned home with 'many
sorts of beryes, on sort lik our strawberyes but of another fation of leaf; I
have brought sume of them hom to show with suche variettie of moss and

shrubs, all bearing frute, suche as I have never seene the like.' Some of the
'beryes' were *Rubus chamaemorus*, an interesting amber-coloured raspberry.
More significantly for the British landscape, he also returned with a cone or
two of the common larch, lovely when yellowing in autumn, but otherwise so
dull. In spite of that, Tradescant had had the misfortune to alight on a
botanically poor part of that vast country, and he returned home without a
huge feeling of success. However, his career was soon filled with luckier
chances and, by 1625, he was gardener at Oatlands, an estate owned and
much used by King Charles I.

    With his much increased income, Tradescant bought himself a house in
what was then a village upriver from London, called Lambeth. He also started
collecting in a very serious way. The new house had a garden large enough to
hold his rapidly increasing collection of plants. Originally called Turrret
House, it soon became called 'The Ark', largely because, as with other
collectors in this chapter, John Tradescant couldn't stop collecting anything,
let alone plants. His treasure trove contained, amongst trees and shrubs from
distant corners of the globe, things as various as birds' nests from China to
Edward the Confessor's gloves.
    Many prosperous people were doing much same thing in assembling a
'cabinet of curiosities', but Tradescant was an indefatigable networker, soon
with contacts all over the civilised world. Working for the King at Oatlands
gave him access to anyone or any organisation he cared to bother. He
arrange for Edward Nicholas, Secretary to the Navy, to ask diplomats like Sir
Thomas Roe for plants. Sir Thomas was ambassador to the court of Jahangir,
the Mogul Emperor of Hindustan between 1615 and 1618, and an
enthusiastic garden builder. Sir Thomas had extensive dealings with
Constantinople too, still a source of good things. That was all looking

eastwards. Tradescant looked west too, and asked the Navy Secretary to ask the Chartered Merchants of the Virginia Company to search for new species to decorate both Oatlands and The Ark. The idea of Virginia obviously fascinated Tradescant, and, with his new income, he himself became a shareholder in the Virginia Company in 1617. Having paid for the transport of 24 settlers to the new colony, he had an entitlement to buy 1,200 acres of land there.

That particular move resulted in a flood of plants. Between 1617 and 1634, he added hugely to the Ark's garden, growing all sorts of fine things from the dazzling annual *Amaranthus (Celosia) hypochondriacus*, which he called 'The Great Floramour or Purple Flower Gentle', to the enchanting spring flowering *Dodocatheon meadia*, ineptly named the American Cowslip for although it is American it has no relationship to a cowslip. He was first to grow the still popular *Robinia pseudacacia*, sometimes called the Locust Tree, sometimes (wrongly), the acacia. Its fluttering translucent foliage half engulfing clusters of perfumed pink flowers can be one of the delights of early summer.

It was named after two of his correspondents; the other royal gardeners, Jean and Vespasien Robin, father and son, and both gardeners at the King's Garden in Paris. The Robins were gardeners for a succession of three French kings, and the Paris garden they established eventually became the Jardin des Plantes. In Paris, too, his other correspondents were the brothers Rene and Pierre Morin Influential nurserymen, they specialised in bulbs, and developed new plants, especially double hyacinths and sumptuous anemones for the immense bedding schemes at Versailles and other royal palace gardens.

But Tradescant's Ark was fruitful in other ways; John and his wife had had a son, also named John, and given, in the literature, the name of John Tradescant the Younger. He too turned out to be a man consumed with a collector's passion for plants. Once old enough, he decided to travel to Virginia himself, perhaps as much to look at his potential acreage as to look at the colony's flora. He ended up making three trips to Virginia in 1637,1642, and in 1654. These gave South Lambeth a whole new garden flora. His haul included the bald cypress, the first tulip trees (*Liriodendron tulipfera*), the delightful red maples (*Acer rubrum*) with tufts of scarlet flowers in spring and astonishingly brilliant autumn colours, the American black walnut (*Juglans nigra*) and its red mulberry; (*Morus rubra*), the shagbark hickory (*Carya ovata)*, with its long green pendulous catkins, and the amazingly successful Virginia creeper (*Parthenocissus quinquefolia*). He even brought back the poison ivy *(Rhus radicans*), though it seems not to have caught on. But orientals were still coming in to the London garden too: the Asian persimmon *(Diospyros lotus)*, the horse chestnut (*Aesculus hippocastanum*), the shrubby and now hardly grown bladder senna *(Colutea arborescens*), and even the mock orange or "syringa" (*Philadelphus coronarius*), in following centuries to be hybridised with species brought in from North American.

Naturally, even in the seventeenth century some plants in the garden met relatives from different continents and crossed. One of the first of these surprises remains immensely influential, and is now in cities across the globe. It is probably that the London plane (*Platanus x acerifolia*) originated in the Tradescants' Ark. Returning from his first trip to Virginia in 1637, the younger Tradescant had material, probably seeds, of the button tree or American sycamore (*Platanus occidentalis*). The Tradescants' garden had had the Turkish oriental plane (*Platanus orientalis*), since 1633. Once the American trees flowered, they set seed. Some of the seedlings looked very vigorous, were fast growing, and were easily propagated by cuttings. The Tradescants probably gave some plants to Jacob Bobart, at the Oxford Botanical Garden. He put one in the garden of Magdalen College. It survives, and is the oldest and largest of all London plane trees. Progeny from the Tradescants' seedlings now thrive in city centres across Europe and North America, and are even grown in China.

Curiously, Tradescant the Younger wasn't a list maker, and seems not to have listed his introductions until the appearance of a lovely book written by a friend of his. John Parkinson's 'Paradisi in Sole: Paradisus Terrestris' (A

Garden of Pleasant Flowers) appeared in 1629. In it, he assiduously tells the reader which plants he had had from the Tradescants' garden. Tradescant the Younger only began to list his plants once he had a copy, using the few blank pages at the back for his notes.

Parkinson was at the centre of his own network, and so the Tradescants were not his only source of American material. After all, the Dutch were in possession of New Amsterdam until 1667, and the French were still in Canada nearly a century later. Louisiana and Florida remained in French or Spanish hands until the beginning of the nineteenth century. Parkinson's new Americans may have come into his London garden from other collectors in Paris, Amsterdam or even Madrid. Some like *Rudbeckia laciniata*, the Cone Flower, and *Zephyranthes atamasco*, reached Parkinson via the Ark, which had been sent there by Vespasien Robin. *Solidago canadensis*, a good species of Golden Rod, travelled from Canada to Paris, and thence to London, in a few seasons.

John Parkinson was apothecary first of all to James I, but Charles I, impressed by 'Pardisi', made him Botanicus Regius Primarius (the King's first botanist). He too was an ardent collector, and his garden at Long Acre was packed with flowers. He wrote of some of the new anemones, perhaps some from Morin, via the Ark, that they were 'so dainty, so pleasant and so delightsome flowers that the sight of them doth enforce an earnest longing desire to be a possessoure of some of them at the leaste'. But the Tradescants also sent plants to Fulham Palace. This ancient estate had been the seat of the bishops of London since ..., and were so grand that they were once enclosed by the longest moat in England. The remains of Roman and medieval palaces lie under what is now the east lawn, though of the original thrity six acres of garden, only 13 acres remain today. The gardens were already famous in Elizabethan times, when Bishop Grindal introduced the tamarisk and other ... novelties. However, the Tradescants' patron was Bishop Compton, a man who had what was at the very least an extreme enthusiasm for growing rare plants. Indeed , towards the end of his life he suffered pangs of conscience about the large amounts of money he had spent on his garden. However much he regretted such frivolity, modern gardeners are much in his debt, for many of the rare species he imported from the East, but most especially the West, went on to become influential garden plants.

He was born Henry Compton, the son of Spencer Compton, 2nd Earl of Northampton, at the handsome Elizabethan house of Compton Wynyates. He had a conventional aristocratic upbringing, and was, in youth, for a while a Cornet in the Horse Guards. Turning to the church, he rose rapidly up the hierarchy, and became Bishop of London in 1675. Developing an interest in the spiritual and intellectual development of Britain's American colonies, he became the Chancellor of the College of William and Mary in Williamsburg, Va. and presided over the Church of England in America in the mid to late 1600's. He was so influential and popular that when the Catholic James II came to the British throne in 1685, the king deemed it impolitic to get rid of him. Compton was merely suspended of his duties, but left to live at Fulham Palace and keep his beloved garden. During his suspension between 1685 and 1689???, he set up a wide network of correspondents, and thereby mightily increased his collection. He also had a close friendship with George London, the most famous and influential of London nurserymen. London's assistant Stephen Switzer wrote in his won book 'Ichnographia Rustica', published in 1718, that Compton 'had a thousand species of exotick plantis in his stoves and gardens, in which last place he had endenizoned a great many that have been formerly thought too tender for this cold climate. There were few days in the year, till towards the latter part of his life, but he was actually in his garden, ordering and directing the Removal and Replacing of his Trees and plants...' Many of his trees survived into the late 19th century. James II must have ended up wishing Compton had stayed in his garden, for he became instrumental in inviting William of Orange to land on British territory, and ended up officiating at their coronation.

However, he was not only a networker by letter. He was also a member of the Temple Bar Coffee House Botanists' Club. Temple Bar, like other 'bars', controlled one of the main roads out of London. The botanists met weekly for conversation and no doubt more than coffee at the Rainbow Inn. Alas, there are no surviving records of any of its meetings, except that on May 11th 1691, there were forty members present at a Friday meeting, and that the membership include eminent men like Compton himself, and George London, hugely successful nurseryman and designer who had studied many of Andre le Notre's designs in France. He was responsible for the planting of some of the greatest parterres in the country, in the gardens of some of its greatest nobles. Coffee was also served to a number of members of the recently formed Royal Society like, Plukenet, Lister, Doody, Robinson, James Petiver, William Sherard. It also included men who had actually travelled in search of plants like the society doctor Hans Sloane.

Hans Sloane became one of the very greatest collectors of the age. Let's meet him aboard ship, returning from his duties in Jamaica. It is 1688, and he is accompanying the Duchess of Albemarle, the embalmed body of the Duke, 800 plant specimens and a surprising range of livestock. The Duchess, Mr Sloane, his plants all arrived safely in England. Some of the animals didn't; an iguana jumped overboard, a crocodile died after plunging into a tub that contained salt water, not fresh. A yellow snake, seven feet long and hungry for the ship's rats, escaped and took possession of the deck-house roof. A few of the passengers complained, and Sloane wrote that 'footmen and other domestics of Her Grace, being afraid to lie down in such company shot my snake' .

Sloane, for a young and unhealthy young man born in an obscure village in County Down, was doing well. Not only was he now personal physician to the duchess, but he had become romantically attached to a widowed heiress in Jamaica, and who would eventually become his wife. However well he was doing in 1688, Fortune continued to smile on him, and he was to become one of the most prodigious collectors of his age, his immense collection eventually being given to the State, and going on to form the nucleus of what was to become the British Museum.

He was born on, or around, the 16 April 1660, one of several sons of Alexander Sloane, tax-collector of Killyleagh, Co. Down. When he was sixteen years of age, Hans began to suffer from haemoptysis, a condition which caused him to spit blood. He suffered for three years, during which time he began to like flowers, though that interest was almost a family trait. Some of his rich relations owned elegant gardens. It may have been them too that spurred his economic and social ambitions. As with so many men in this book, medicine provided the ladder to success. Around 1679, Hans moved to London to study both it and chemistry. Botany was then an vital component of medicine, and in 1683, he went to France to complete his studies. After Paris, and working with Tournefort at the Royal Garden of Plants, he finished his studies at Montpellier, with its renowned medical school and famous botanic garden. As a Protestant, he couldn't graduate at either Paris or Montpellier, so moved to the e University of Orange, in the south of France, and graduated there on 28 July 1683.

He was already something of a star, and returned to London to work with Dr Thomas Sydenham. Sydenham was an extremely successful doctor, and Hans was soon introduced to some of the most fashionable and wealthy

patients in London. Perhaps with their help, he was elected a Fellow of the
Royal Society in January 1685, and a Fellow of the Royal College of
Physicians two years later. Better still, he became personal physician to the
young Duke of Albemarle, son of the enriched and ennobled General Monk,
who had helped Charles II regain his throne. However, the young man was a
rake, and was created Governor of Jamaica to keep him out of mischief. He
gave Sloane an initial payment of £300 and agreed a salary of £600 a year.
They set sail on 12 Septernber 1687.

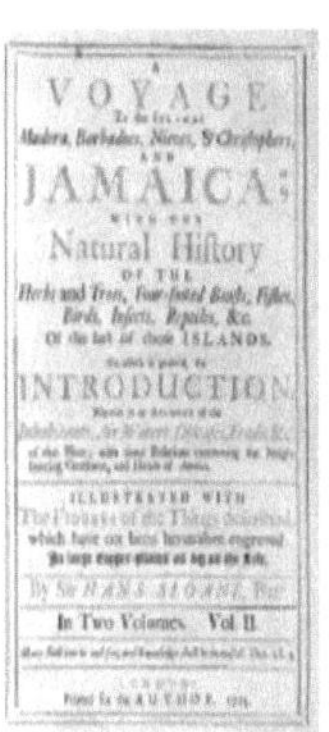

The four vessels reached Port Royal on 19 December 1687. After
County Down, even after Montpellier, the tropics had the young botanist
astonished. The flora was hardly known in Europe, and he realised he had an
enormous opportunity. He at once hired an artist to record the local flora and
fauna. He himself recorded his immediate locality with fascinated interest.
His duties or his inclination kept him fairly close to Spanish Town (Santiago
de la Vega) where his employer lived. Indeed, most of his plant collections
came from his own parish of St. Catherine and its near neighbours, and most
especially from the plantations bountied to officers of Cromwell's army
following the capture of the island from the Spanish in 1655. He was a
technically excellent collector, for the specimens survived the local, and all
subsequent, insect attack, and still today look remarkably similar to the
drawings made from the by his illustrator in 1700-1701. He collected some
splendidly exotic plants. Jamaica also allowed him a medical practice that
was unusually exotic. Though he happily treated both rich and poor alike, he
perhaps looked askance at one of his patients: the violent pirate (retired) Sir
Henry Morgan. Whether or not he helped Sir Henry overcome his
nightmares, he couldn't help the Duke, who died in 1688, after little more
than a year in the tropics. His wife decided to return to England with the

doctor and his menagerie, and the corpse of her late husband.

Once again in London, she retained Sloane as her personal physician and with such illustrious patronage, his clientele soon once again included the rich and famous. His practice grew by leaps and bounds and in 1695, he established it permanently in Bloomsbury, then the most expensive part of London. That same year he married his rich widow, Mrs Elizabeth Rose (nee Langley), and thereafter lead a life of domestic quiet, set against an increasingly glittering backdrop. He became an important member of the Royal Society, put the Chelsea Physic garden firmly in the hands of the Apothecaries Society, and put it in charge of Philip Miller. He began publishing his accounts of his West Indies trip in 1707, adding to his descriptions and illustrations of plants and animals, some fascinating sections on the lives of native Americans, and of the Caribbean and African slaves. He described the music and dance of African Americans and even included picture of their musical instruments. However great a collector, and however wide-ranging his interests, it isn't clear whether he was an talented organiser as well. Certainly, when the great Swedish botanist Linnaeus visited him in Chelsea in 1736, he wrote that 'Sloane's great collection is in complete disorder'. Presumably Linnaeus had no premonition that his own impeccably organised collection, demonstrating his sexual system of plant classification, would end up spending its future only a few miles away from Sloane's, at what is now the Linnean Society on Piccadilly.

Disordered or not, there was no stopping Sloane's collection, or indeed Sloane himself. In 1701, Queen Anne consulted him for the first time, and so his influence spread. His collection began to act as a magnet for others. In 1702, he was bequeathed the vast Charleton Collection. In 1718 he bought the Petiver collection for £4,000. He was left Sir Arthur Rawdon's immense holdings. These all made Sloane's collection the biggest in the world. Plant specimens were only a tiny part; Sloane's will lists '..my library of books, drawings, manuscripts, Prints, medals and coins; ancient and modern antiquities, seals and cameos, intaglios and precious stones; agates and jaspen, vessels of agate, jasper or crystal; mathematical instruments, drawings and pictures, and all other things....' The final inventory listed two hundred thousand items.

As to gardens, his greatest influence came from Miller and the Chelsea Physic garden, and the stipulation he had made that it had to present fifty new species of plant to the Royal Society every year. Even in the middle of the eighteenth century, fifty was a modest quantity. By the century's end, fifty new things was hardly anything at all. Miller we meet in a while, but as the momentum of plant collecting was swinging from East to West, another maniacal collector is more immediately important. This is Peter Collinson (1694~1768). Collinson was an ardent Quaker, a belief system which he combined with being a wholesale woollen draper and gentleman's mercer. He had his counting house in Gracechurch Street, London, with an enchanting postal address of being at 'The Red Lion'. Prosperous, he had a garden in Peckham, but also had a modest country estate called Ridgeway House at Mill Hill. Quakers, many of whom created successful businesses, had problems reconciling personal wealth with their austere religious philosophy. Collinson, who couldn't help but grow anything new he could get his hands on, found this especially hard in his garden, where there should not be 'too great a superfluity of plants and too great nicety of gardens' and that 'all Friends in planting gardens should do it in a lowly mind and keep to plainness and the serviceable part, rather admiring the wonderful hand of Providence, in causing such variety of unnecessary things to grow for the use of man than in seeking to please the curious mind'.

Collinson also suffered from having something of an artists' eye, and once compared tree planting to 'painting with living pencils' in wonderful shades of green. He couldn't even restrict his enthusiasm to trees, and received seeds of lesser plants from Jesuits like the priest Pierre Nicholas le Cheron d'Incarville and pere Jean-Denis Attiret. They sent him things from China. A Dr Mounsey sent him a hornbean from Persia. A Russian iron-mine owner sent him, in 1756, a lily 'as near to black as any flower' that Collinson had seen perhaps the small but sinister *Fritillaria camschatica*. Collinson was the first to succeed with the Iceland Poppy, *Papaver nudicaule* , which he got from Siberia in 1730 and more in 1759. He grew the first *Delphinium grandiflorum* that plays such a role in a later chapter, which he was sent by Dr Johann Ammann, the founder in 1736 of the Botanic Garden of the Imperial Academy at St Petersburg. He sent plants from his own garden out into the world too, notably tulips, carnations, auriculas, Crown Imperials, blue and white hyacinths, altheas, China Asters, Guernsey Lilies to John Custis, a planter whose daughter-in-law, Martha Dandridge Custis eventually married George Washington. He sent books to Benjamin Franklin for his Library Company of Pennsylvania, a sort of book club that grew out of Franklin's 'Junto' group. And Collinson endlessly bothererd a Pennsylvania farmer who is central to the next chapter.

His business helped his Peckham garden. He imported cloth worldwide, and so was perfectly able to ask his foreign agents to get him plants also. He also advised some of his grander clients on what to plant in their gardens, whether they wanted new plants or no. Gradually, by hundreds of letters, he began to create an interest, even a fashion, in new American plants. By 1733, he was getting increasingly excited about them. He wrote his Pennsylvania friend Dr Chew, asking for a potential collector. Chew suggested a farming acquaintance called John Bartram. It was an immensely influential piece of networking. Collinson and Bartram soon struck up a close working relationship that altered the lives of both men. Their correspondence lasted for more than thirty-six years until Collinsons death in 1768. While we meet Bartram and his son in the next chapter, in this one, we stay with Collinson. Expeditions then were, and sometime still are, often financed by groups of subscribers who, for their financial support, receive a suitable proportion of the resultant spoils. Collinson assembled groups of subscribers, often recruited from his clients and associates. As soon as shipments of seeds from Bartram arrived in England, Collinson would divide and distribute the collections to the various gardens. He himself began to germinate some new Americans in 1734 and 1735; he soon he had first skunk cabbage ever seen in Europe, *Aarisaemas* (called indian turnip by the American settlers), and more. A handsome cypripedium from American woodlands first flowered in Europe in Collinson garden in 1738.

Cypripedium acaule

New recruits to his subscriber groups poured in. The collections continued to arrive for the next three decades, and then, as now, the distribution made endless problems. Some subscribers felt they hadn't had enough material for their outlay, or not the things they had hoped for. In 1766, Collinson wrote that no sooner would the seed distribution be complete and sent off, than he would immediately receive requests from the subscribers begging, "Pray Sir how and in what manner must I sow them,- pray be so good, Sir, as to give mee some directions, for my Gardener is a very Ignorant Fellow.'

Yet, for all these new plants pouring into Europe from the Americas, from the Indies, from the Far East, from Russia and Southern Africa, gardening amongst the upper classes had been taking a very strange turn. For millennia, all gardeners had collected plants, and wealthy ones merely had more of the rarest to demonstrate their means. In France during the later part of the seventeenth century, the old plant-rich formal garden had developed fast into gigantic schemes, sometimes quite literally stretching to the horizon. The increasing botanical diversity of the age was certainly admired, but became restricted to great botanic gardens, or the wilderness areas of a few private ones. Some bulbs, especially hyacinths and tulips, had been taken up enthusiastically as parterre flowers, and huge planting schemes using splendid varieties of the were created for use at Versailles. However, the huge sense of 'state' in French gardens, of course especially in those for the Court and its greatest courtiers, often designed by Andre le Notre, were worked out using stone, water, grass, and an extremely limited number of hedging and tree species, most of them well known to the Romans. The horse chestnut was the only tree to break the classical barrier. Indeed, the simplicity of the garden materials gives gigantic gardens like Vaux-le-Vicomte much of their tremendous impact. Nevertheless, in them, order is created at the expense of chaos. Their serene unity is created at the expense of living diversity. Their tremendous formality replaces any expression of Nature. But the idea of emulating ancient Rome captivated the English rich too, and for much of the later seventeenth century, many wealthy gardeners had essentially followed the grand French style.   William Kent and his patron Lord Burlington, both members of the aesthetes' circles of the capital, but not especially interested in new plants, began a move away from the stupendous rigidities of gardens across the Channel. They wanted something of a landscape around great new houses being built much influenced by the 16th century villas designed by Italian architect Andrea Palladio. The landscapes they wanted were not derived from the real landscapes of Suffolk or Surrey, but from the dream-time paintings of Claude Lorraine, who frequently depicted views of a never-never land comprising ruinous Roman buildings, picturesque farm houses, meadows, forests and lakes, all fading into a slumbrous blue distance.

Though not a pursuit of plants, it was certainly a pursuit of nature, a concept now rendered far more attractive than it had ever been by the increasing knowledge of its riches over the rest of the planet. However, the idea of grandeur developed in France, and its simplicity of means, was taken over in England to make landscape. Lawns, clumps of trees, lakes, bridges and temples (fakes if need be), populated by herds of deer or cattle kept of the lawns by a sunken and invisible fence, made a scene every bit as artificial, and every bit as expensive to build, as anything by Andre le Notre. This landscape theme was taken up by a young man nicknamed 'Capability' Brown. He had an immense talent for making sculptural landscapes of great beauty and corresponding expense. The landscape garden became a fashion amongst those who could afford it, and great formal gardens were swept away to make room for 'Nature', at least a nature vitiated of anything untoward and unplanned.

Neither the canals and 'patte d'oie' of great French gardens, or the lakes and temples of English landscape ones were capable of compression into a couple of acres. In the past, almost any garden could have a even a tiny knot or a parterre in the latest fashion, complete with at least a few fine flowers. Now, the middling ranks of gardeners had become disenfranchised from fashionable 'garden taste' in a way that had never really happened before.

Nevertheless, they didn't stop gardening in a huff, even though, sadly, their gardens are rather little documented. The gardens they had must have been crammed with interesting plants. Nurseries flourished. Garden books, especially ones about the new plants, sold edition after edition. There were marvellous illustrated florilegiums popularising the new flowers. The most famous book of all, though, was written, endlessly updated, abridged, re-edited, by Philip Miller, Hans Sloane's appointee at the Chelsea Physic Garden. Miller, like Sloane, was himself at the centre of a huge network of correspondents and collectors, and participated in the syndicates formed from 1736 onwards to finance the introduction of new plants from America. He was also often amongst the first cultivators of new plants reaching Europe, and he had enormous success in keeping them going. The first edition of his great 'Gardeners Dictionary' appeared in 1731, with subsequent editions in 1733 1737, 1743, 1747, 1752, 1756-59 and 1768. A Dutch translation appeared in 1745, a German one in 1750, 1758, 1769, 1776. Even French gardeners had one between 1785 and 1790. The thick folio work, full of engravings, was so expensive that only grand gardeners could afford it. Realising that there was a far larger market beneath this, Miller wrote abridged editions, with only a few of the most utilitarian engravings, but essentially the same text. The first 'Abridgement' appeared in 1733, and was swiftly followed by others in 1741, 1748, 1754, 1763 and 1771. It was an extraordinary success. Large numbers of gardeners really wanted to know what new things they could grow, and how they should be grown. and even a few aristocrats like Robert James, Lord Petre, who was planning a fabulous garden at Thorndon Hall, Brentwood, Essex, wanted everything new he could lay his hands on. Intoxicated, he wanted lots of forest seed from Bartram, and organised presents and payment. Bartram was entirely happy with this, and even proposed that he be given an annual allowance to cover travel, clothing and provisions. Petre agreed to ten guineas. Miller himself stated in 1754 that 'there are many Persons of Distinction in England, who are pleased to honour the Art of Gardening, by making it a considerable Part of their Amusement; and who have been greatly assisting in the introducing of large Numbers of new Plants, Shrubs and Trees, into the English gardens'.

He can never have envisaged it, but his book is still of immense botanical importance. When Linnaeus came to London to visit Hans Sloane, naturally he went to see Philip Miller too. Both men liked one another, but Miller was absolutely his own man. He was not convinced by Linnaeus' classification of plants, but was eventually convinced of the usefulness of Linnaeus' 'binomial' system of making Latin plants names, and which, consisting of genus and species only, we still use today. Even so, he only began to use them consistently in 1768. Miller was also not convinced by Linnaeus' actual groupings of plants into genera. He thought that Joseph Pitton de Tournefort was a much better taxonomist than Linnaeus, and most often used his concept plant genera instead of the larger and more inclusive genera set up by Linnaeus. As modern taxonomy, which affects all gardeners, refuses to acknowledge any genera that pre-date Linnaeus' 'Species Plantarum' of 1753, Tournefort's genera are considered invalid. Miller, who continued using them in his Dictionary, is therefore, largely by chance, their first 'valid' author. The general consensus of contemporary botanists about many genera follow Miller, and therefore Tournefort, far more closely than they follow Linnaeus. Many modern taxonomists have to consult Miller's post-1753 Gardeners Dictionary almost on a weekly or monthly basis.

But to return to the eighteenth century. The great, green, formal gardens of the French magnates and the great, green, landscape gardens of English bankers and aristocrats were much closer to each other, in spite of their theoretical differences, than anything that had gone before. Whilst flattering the sense of power of their owners, they denied the riches of Nature. They denied, too. the collecting instinct of most of mankind. Neither Nature nor instinct could be held in check for long.

Chapter 3

The American Garden

David Stuart

THE AMERICAN GARDEN

For its first human inhabitants, the American continent was Eden. Meat, from the fish in the rivers to the mammoth and buffalo on the plain, was always to hand. The continent's prodigious flora was filled with edible plants that ran from lewisia roots and quamash bulbs to the seed kernels of gigantic conifers. Even the hazards of rattlesnakes, black bears, zigadenus lilies and other poisonous flowers hardly made America itself less of a garden.

While the nations of Central America built sumptuous gardens long before Cortez stumbled into them, the 'American gardens' of this chapter was a short-lived, but very important, garden element that arose in Europe in the late eighteenth century. A few examples still exist, but they evolved so rapidly during their heyday that they were hardly created after 1850. Nevertheless, we are still busily building the sort of gardens into which they changed. Their story is a vivid illustration of how garden design is driven by the collecting instinct.

In Europe, since the mid-seventeenth century, fashionable taste had seen gardens as either architecture or sculpture. In France, allees and rides, bosquets, topiary, were all architectural extensions of the house, and were designed to show the wealth and grandeur of the owner. They were not designed to show the riches and grandeur of Nature, and commonly made use of an extremely limited flora. The style, which has become almost entirely associated with Andre le Notre, was copied throughout Europe and Russia, and even made inroads into Middle Eastern gardening. It was eventually displaced by a style evolving in England from the 1720's. Though called the 'landscape movement', it aimed not at the Nature its name suggests, but at the serene Classical landscapes found in paintings, especially those of Claude Lorraine. It, too, was designed to show the wealth of the owner, and so make a sumptuous green frame for the owner's house. It, too, used an extremely limited flora.

While these two styles engrossed estate owners and their lesser imitators, Nature herself was busy subverting them. As European settlers spread out across America, American plants began to reach Europe in increasing numbers. Some were potential food crops, or could be smoked, used as dyes or medicines. Many more were none of these things. They were just beautiful, and were sent over simply to service collectors' instincts to collect. Many of these early collectors were drawn from the middle classes, and had modest gardens. They had no space to plant avenues that stretched to the horizon or to dredge new lakes. They turned their backs on the grand grand fashions of the time, and collected brand new plants instead of statues and architectural fragments dug from the mud of ancient Rome.

By the early 18th century, Nature's subversion began in earnest. The plants sent to Europe from America very swiftly began to include some magnificent trees and some even more magnificent shrubs. Soon even great landowners took notice and wanted to have at least the trees somewhere about them. Many of the new American species looked 'exotic', didn't fit at all well into the expensively designed 'landscapes' by William Kent or 'Capability' Brown, filled with native trees. Though some great gardens did have 'arboreta' in which to grow interesting things, it seemed to many owners that the new trees, shrubs and woodland flowers should all be put into a separate area in the garden. One overriding reason for this was their cultivation; a lot of the new plants had been collected from river banks or swampy ground, and so needed to be given the same growing conditions in

Europe.

When these new, wet, peaty, conditions were created for the new arrivals, the area became, unsurprisingly, called 'the American garden'. They were soon fascinating and fashionable places to be. Huge numbers were planted throughout Europe and Russia. The enthusiasm eventually became so extreme that it led to the extinction of a number of American species, like the Franklin tree, which are now only found in gardens, but not in the wild.

The first intimation of what was to come was the excitement over plants collected by the Rev. John Banister. He arrived in Virginia in 1678 and, within two years, had prepared a catalogue which provided the first printed survey of American plants. He illustrated the rarer species, and sent drawings and seeds back to the English naturalist John Ray, as well as to his friend Jacob Bobart the Younger, at the Oxford Botanic Garden. Into a garden culture obsessed with either ancient Rome, or with tulips, auriculas, myrtles and oranges, he let loose some extraordinary finds. One of his first was *Magnolia virginiana.* No gardener in western Europe had even seen a magnolia before, and this one, in America called 'the swamp bay', has huge glossy leaves and beautifully shaped flowers, creamy white and heavily scented. Gardeners swooned. *Lindera benzoin,* the Spice Bush, followed. Though only with greenish yellow flowers, they smell delicious, and the bush has leaves that glow buttery yellow in autumn. Even better was *Liquidambar styraciflua,* the Sweet Gum. It's autumn show was in scarlet, crimson and orange. No-one had seen such colours. But the list continued. Cornus amomum was a new species of dogwood with blue fruits; *Gleditschia triacanthos,* the Honey Locust Tree; *Chionanthus virginica,* the Fringe Tree, with tassels of scented flowers and dark blue egg-shaped fruit; *Rhododendron viscosum,* one of the first to be grown, with gorgeously perfumed pinkish flowers. And still it didn't stop: *Acer negundo, Rhus copallina, Aralia spinosa, Menispermum canadense, Quercus rubra, Ostrya virginiana, Abies balsamea, Nyssa aquatica* ... Gardeners' heads spun.

Banister was born into a rustic family at Twigworth, Gloucestershire, in 1650. Even with a modest start, it was soon clear that he was an exceptional and ambitious child. Even before becoming a scholar at Oxford university, he had become fascinated by plants. Not surprisingly, when finally at Oxford, he became a close friend of Jacob Bobart the Younger, then in charge of the Oxford botanic garden. However, the university gave him access to other worlds than those of gardeners and botanists. Close proximity to the wealthier students gave him great social ambitions and he determined to get himself an estate. America seemed the place where this could be most easily accomplished.

He arrived in Virginia during a politically unsettled time. Nevertheless, he was almost immediately entranced by the place, by its plants, by is sometime warlike and warring natives and their extraordinary crop plants. He even managed to get on with the narrow minded settlers who only wanted to grow huge crops of tobacco and make money as soon as possible. Banister wanted that too, but couldn't ignore the Indians' watermelons, brilliantly coloured maizes, the endless sorts of 'potatoe', musk melons, pumpkins, *Phaseolus* beans (only recently introduced to European gardens, but as decoratives not edibles). He even began to collect the endless varieties of tobacco grown by the Indians, making an early precursor of the seedbanks currently being set up in the modern United States, as part of the great heritage of native Americans.

His first loads of seeds sent to Britain, particularly those to Bishop Compton, caused a sensation. He was asked for more, for drawing of the mature plants, cuttings, living plants, herbarium specimens, anything he could send. The Temple Bar club sent him funds, and its member eagerly awaited each Virginia ship to berth at London's docks. Nurserymen like George London requested, and got, endless packets of seeds. Banister soon had American patrons too, notably amongst the fabulously landed Byrd family, with their huge tracts of Virginia. They eventually got hold of his library of botanical books, and it still exists as part of the Byrd Library, Westover.

Energetic and astute, his desire for land was soon abundantly realised. He eventually assembled an estate of nearly two thousand acres, manned by thirty five slaves, mostly captured native American, but at least two recently shipped in from Africa. The Fates smiled, so perhaps he should have gone more warily. On a collecting trip with some friends, exploring some ancient Indian trading trails, he went off into the vegetation looking for plants. As still frequently happens, and even twice more in this book, his movements were mistaken for those of a wild animal. One Jacob Colson fired, and Banister fell. Let's hope he fell among a patch of his favourite, and lovely, balm (*Monarda punctata*). The story was hushed up, and relatives and London friends were never given the real details. John Ray thought he had fallen whilst rock climbing, looking for plants.

But these first ripples of excitement, and it was only a ripple, were as nothing to what was to come. It took a while. Mark Catesby was born in 1682. John Bartram was born in 1739. Andre Michaux was born in 1746. Mark Catesby came on stream first. Though now famous in America because he drew the sketch from which Linnaeus named the so-called Bald Eagle, emblem of the US, he came from Castle Hedingham in Essex, though spent much of his childhood in the comfortable town of Sudbury in Suffolk. He seems first to have become interested in botany and ornithology through meeting Banister's friend John Ray, who lived nearby. He later wrote that he developed a "passionate desire of viewing ... the Animal and Vegetable Productions in their Native Countries; which are Strangers to England."

He soon got the opportunity. Catesby's father, a prosperous magistrate, died when Mark was 23, leaving him free of the need to work. However, he was an energetic and resourceful young man. A life of genteel ease in the provinces didn't attract him. His sister Elizabeth and her husband, a doctor, were already well established in Williamsburgh, Virginia, and he took the momentous decision to visit them. Arriving in April 1712, he stayed for

seven years. Once more Bishop Compton, Thomas Fairchild, the Hoxton
nurseryman, and John Ray's circle of enthusiasts had easy access to
American plants. Soon their gardens had *Ceanothus americanus*, the
enchanting *Porteranthus* (formerly *Gillenia*) *trifoliata*, and more.

When he got back to Britain, in the summer of 1719, he found that he
was much in demand. So much so that a group of grandees, including Sir
Hans Sloane, the Duke of Chandos, William Sherard, and the king's doctor
Dr Richard Mead, raised funds so that Catesby could immediately return to
America to find yet more handsome plants. He was to be given a post as
attendant to the Governor of Carolina, with Charleston (then Charles Town)
as his base. He arrived there in May 1722. He writes: 'With this intention, I
set out again from England, in the year 1722, directly for Carolina; which
country, tho inhabited by English above an age past, and a country inferior to
none in fertility, and abounding in variety of the blessings of nature; yet its
productions being very little known except what barely related to commerce,
such as rice, pitch and tar; was thought the most proper place to search and
describe the productions of Nature: Accordingly I arrived in Carolina 23rd of
May 1722, after a pleasant tho not a short passage. In our voyage we were
frequently entertaind with diversions not uncommon in crossing the Atlantick
Ocean, as catching of sharks, striking of porpoises, dolphins, bonetoes,
albacores, and other fish; which three last we regaled on when fortune
favored us in catching them; and even the flesh of sharks and porpoises
would digest well with the sailors, when long fed on salt meats.'

It was to be an extraordinary period in his life, and of immense impact
on European, as well as, later, American gardens. South Carolina was still not
far removed from its virgin state, and much less explored and cultivated than
the Viriginia he already knew.
He was there for four years, exploring Georgia too, sending home animal as
well as plant specimens, seed, even plants in tubs of soil. At that moment, the
Indians were not hostile, and often helped his expeditions. He was quite as
fascinated by them as them by him. Much of his time was idyllic, and only
occasionally hazardous. He writes: ' I was much delighted to see nature differ

in these upper parts, and to find here abundance of things not to be seen in the lower parts of the country; this encouraged me to take several journeys with the Indians higher up the rivers, towards the mountains, which afforded not only a succession of new vegetable appearances, but most delightful prospects imaginable, besides the diversion of hunting buffellos, bears, panthers, and other wild beasts. In these excursions I employd an Indian to carry my box, in which, besides paper and materials for painting, I put dryd specimens of plants, seeds, &c.as I gathered them. To the hospitality and assistance of these friendly Indians, I am much indebted, for I not only subsisted on what they shot, but their first care was to erect a bark hut, at the approach of rain to keep me and my cargo from wet.'

Sometimes he was ill. One morning he discovered he has spent the night sharing his bed with a rattlesnake, which slithered out only with the dawn. It was his travels that really set the scene for an early aspect of the 'American Garden'. Much of the time he collected by river margins or on flat swampy regions close to the coast. European gardeners, trying to make their new rarities happy, built them wet, peaty, places for them to grow. This was a complete break with all past gardening, when drainage had always been the first aspect to consider when gardening on new ground.

His haul, too, set European gardeners in a spin. The Carolina spicebush, or Carolina allspice (*Calycanthus floridus*), became an immediate hit. It flowered prodigiously in late spring and early summer, entrancing owners with their pineapple-like smell. That fruit was then the acme of luxury. Catesby liked it too, writing, "The bark is very aromatic, and as odoriferous as cinnamon. These Trees grow in the remote and hilly parts of Carolina, but no where amongst the Inhabitants". Later colonists used the bark as a substitute for cinnamon, but the whole plant smells pleasantly of camphor.

He also sent home, and popularised in contemporary Virginian and Carolina gardens, the Indian bean or common catalpa *(Catalpa bignonioides)*. He announces, proudly, that is wasn't known to any gardener, American or European, "till I brought the seeds from the remoter parts of the country." He continues, 'And tho' the inhabitants are little curious in gardening, the uncommon beauty of this Tree has induc'd them to propagate it; and 'tis become ornament to many of their gardens". He had found it amongst the fields of local Cherokee Indians, whose name for it was 'catalpa'. He'd also found autumn flowering *Wisteria frutescens* with its perfumed racemes of lilac-purple blossoms, the weird *Callicarpa americana* with tight clusters of berries the colour of crystallised violets, *Stewartia malacodendron*, with purple eyed flowers, and called 'Stuartia' in the 1830 catalogue of Conrad Loddiges and Sons, Hackney, London. It was named for Lord Bute, a Stuart.

Eventually his time in Carolina drew to a close. He dawdled rather, spending part of 1725 and 1726 collecting in the easy warmth of the Bahamas, where he became fascinated by the beautiful fish of the warm subtropical waters. Pulling himself together, and once in greyer and chillier London, he set about popularising the plants he had found. He went into the selling business, in association with a Fulham nurseryman called Christopher Gray. Needing more stock, Catesby began requesting additional seeds and plants from friends he had made in Carolina, as well as his long-suffering Williamsburgh sister. He realised that he needed to do some marketing as well, and decided to publish his notes, illustrated with prints taken from his own workmanlike watercolours. Getting plates made was even then an expensive business, and he didn't have enough of his father's money left to risk the outlay. Resourceful as ever, he taught himself how to engrave, and turned his drawings into handsome engravings. The black and white prints looked fine, but needed colour to sell. However, he found that he could employ colourists cheaply, and supervised the painting of the first edition of printed plates. The results, extemely desirable, appeared in batches as 'The Natural History of Carolina, Georgia, Florida and the Bahama Islands' between 1730 and 1747. They were a hit, and pages are still much sought after.

The work eventually comprised two large folio volumes, with two hundred and twenty of Catesby's vivid engravings, hand-colored. The plates were coupled with descriptions in Latin and observations in English and in French. He was modest about his artistic capabilities, and in his preface he declares: 'As I was not bred a painter I hope some faults in perspective, and other niceties, may be more readily excused, for I humbly conceive that plants, and other things done in a flat, tho exact manner, may serve the purpose of natural history, better in some measure, than in a more bold and painterlike way. In designing the plants, I always did them while fresh and just gatherd: and the animals, particularly the birds, I painted while alive (except a very few) and gave them their gestures peculiar to every kind of bird, and where it would admit of I have adapted the birds to those plants on which they fed, or have any relation to.' The plates are lovely, combining plants and creatures in a naive way that gives them great charm. The same year Catesby completed his massive undertaking, he also married Elizabeth Rowland, a widow with a grown daughter. He died just two years later in 1749, leaving two children and almost no money. His unfortunate widow was forced to sell the plates and the remaining copies of 'The Natural History' as her sole inheritance. Nevertheless, 'the American Garden' was truly underway.

Any emerging fashion, like the one for American plants, whets entrepreneurs appetites. In London, nurseries began to specialise. Auction rooms began to sell off consignments of new arrivals. This frenzy reached it highest pitch a few decades later, fuelled by the next two extraordinary collectors to emerge, one a true-born American, the second born in France.

John Bartram was the first of these. There were, of course, other botanists and plant collectors working in the US in the mid 1700s; men like John Clayton, Alexander Garden (after whom the Gardenia was named, though it's not an American plant), John Mitchell, and the splendidly named Cadwallader Colden. However, Bartram, an apparently modest farmer, was by far the most energetic, and ultimately by far the most influential. Indeed, he founded something of a plant dynasty, and his indolent son, of whom he despaired, is gradually becoming seen as even more influential in the story of American natural history..

The Bartrams, a Quaker family, had come the bleak hills of Derbyshire in northern England. Following William Penn out to New World, John's grandfather started farming immediately he arrived in the early 1680's. John's father, William, prospered too. His first son was a James, his second was our John, born in 1699. Their mother died when John was two, but his father soon remarried. He set out in 1709, with his new wife, to farm in North Carolina. His first two sons were left behind in Pennsylvania in the care of their grandmother. That was fortunate. Indians soon raided the North Carolina property, killing and scalping John's father, and taking his stepmother and her two children into captivity. Though she and her children were later ransomed, she seems to have faded from the story. The young John and the original Bartram farm continued to be looked after by his tough and tyrannical grandmother. John grew up as a most unlikely explorer. He was timid and fearful, often in poor health, and terrified of thunderstorms, an unhelpful fear he retained as an adult. Set free on his grandmother's death, he inherited a well-run farm of several hundred acres. In spite of his difficult childhood and its aftermath, he soon showed that he was an good and imaginative farmer. He advocated drainage of local marshes. He advocated copying the local Indian use of oyster shells as crop fertilisers. He used red clover as a ley, wanted the young state to replant its already vanishing woodlands to replenish timber. Indeed, he was an early 'green'. He was also very interested in child rearing, especially as regards to their diet and control. For the latter, he advocated the use of love, not fear.

Soon, he was a man of consequence in the local community, and counted as friends many of the leading citizens of Philadelphia, including Benjamin Franklin. It was an exciting time. Bartram was even instrumental in founding the American Philosophical Society in 1743, an organisation that still exists, and still housed in a handsome 18th century house. The Society was soon to have considerable affect on the American garden in Europe when it helped finance the next collector, Andre Michaux, explore vast areas of North America.

Farmer perhaps, but it was the American flora that eventually placed John Bartram at the centre of the scientific world. "I had always since ten years old, a great inclination to plants, and knew all that I once observed by sight, though not their proper names, having no person nor books to instruct me., he wrote to Collinson in 1764. Bartram's son, William, attributed his father's interest to his use of Indian herb medicines to treat neighbours who were too poor to for even for the cheapest Philadelphian doctors.

However, few botanist or plant collectors have any real knowledge of quite why they are fascinated by plants. Bartram, like Philibert Commerson, whom we shall meet in Samoa, and Andre Michaux, began his botanical travels to get over a great sadness: his first wifes death from an unidentified epidemic in 1727. Once home again, in the following year, John bought a small house and a hundred and seven acres of land in Kingsessing on the bank of the Schuylkill, about three miles from Philadelphia. He married again, and, living once more, began a major expansion of the house in 1729. In a five acre plot of ground between his new house and the river, John began, with his newly collected plants, to make a botanical garden. It was soon famous, and though often called the first in America., the city in fact already had a few others. His, certainly, is the only one to survive to the present day.

Eighteenth century 'networking' gave him his break. Amongst Bartram's friends in Pennsylvania was a Joseph Breintnall (d.1746). This gentleman had had the clever idea that, instead of pressing plant leaves for herbarium specimens, he would use the fresh material as a printing block to make 'plant impressions'. It was a 'craft' idea already popular amongst middle class ladies. Bartram had been finding him interesting plants to print, and Breintnall had sent a copy of his prints to the insatiable Peter Collinson in London. Collinson had been entranced, and at once latched on to Bartram, not Breintnall. Bartram was deluged with letters, often enclosing European garden plants, European gardening books, as well as advice, encouragement and money, all in the hope of receiving new American plants.

Whenever he could take time from his farming duties, usually after harvest, Bartram went into the wild, collecting plants for his new English patron and himself. Word of Bartrams collecting quickly spread in Europe, and Collinson, always the entrepreneur, was soon acting as Bartrams agent. Influential patrons poured in, and soon included botanist Philip Miller, whom we meet in the next chapter, and Sir Hans Sloane. There were grandees too, amongst them three earls and four dukes, even Queen Ulrica of Sweden. Eventually Linnaeus himself called John the greatest natural botanist in the world.. It was an amazing state of affairs for a modest Pennsylvania farmer.

Until his boys grew up to take his place, the farm took most of his energy. In slack time, instead of resting up, he was riding, head down like most botanists, through America's virgin territories, often in places where he was the first white man to go. Sometimes he travelled alone. Sometimes he used a little documented sort of folk as guides and translators: white men and women who had been captured by Indians and who had enthusiastically embraced the Indian way of life. Bartram did not like them. One, called Shicckalamy, professed to a chieftain amongst the Delaware Indians, though he was really a Frenchman from Montreal. Another guides with a strange life history was Conrad Weisser, a refugee from the Palatinate who tried being a recluse in the Seventh Day Cloister near Pennsylvania, but had somehow found belonging to the Maques Indians more to his taste.

Through Collinsons persistent lobbying efforts directed at the Duke of Northumberland and others, Bartram's scientific labours received official recognition when he was appointed botanist to King George III in 1765. The post's stipend of fifty pounds enabled Bartram to make a long-hoped-for collecting expedition to the Floridas, which had come under British dominion in 1763. Accompanied by William, John traveled through present-day North and South Carolina, Georgia and Florida, Ultimately, he was responsible for the introduction of between 150 and 200 new American plant species to Europe.

Not all the plants he sent to Europe were of his own collecting. The witch alder was first discovered in the Carolinas by Garden but only introduced into European gardens by John Bartram. Bartram suggested that this plant should be named Gardenia. It ended up being named *Fothergilla*, after Collinson's crony John Fothergill. Similarly, the gorgeous *Celtis occidentalis*, first introduce by the younger Tradescant in the previous century, had never established itself in Britain. Plants from Bartram did, and there was great excitement.

Not everyone thought Collinson a benign influence in Bartram's life. James Logan, a wealthy Pennsylvanian, felt that Bartram was being exploited. He felt that Bartram only managed to scratch a living from the land, and really needed proper patronage. Failing to do that himself, he did get as far as getting hold of a copy of Linnaeus' 'Systema Naturae'. Linneus had asked Logan to study pollen in American plants, but Logan was too busy, and so was hoping that Bartram would help out. There was a squabble, for Collinson was concerned that this would draw Bartram's attention away from collecting new garden plants. He needn't have worried. Bartram was a collector not a scientist. In any case, the Bartram-Collinson network was soon to be disrupted by the Wars of Independence. By its end, in 1781, the whole group were either dead or too old for collecting. John Bartram was dead, apparently killed by the worrying about the fate of his garden as the English troops approached. In the event, nothing happened to it.

Both the American and the French Revolutions, as well as the huge political and social changes that they enabled, had a tremendous impact in the garden. Not only did they augment the development of the American garden in Europe, but they had a profound effect on how Americans viewed their own gardens, and their own flora.

One of the plant collectors who became embroiled in both upheavals was Andre Michaux. He was born at Satory, near Versailles, France in 1746. Like Bartram, his father was a farmer, though as a tenant on the King's estates. The young Michaux at first followed in his father's footsteps. However, like Bartram, he was plainly a talented and energetic young man, and, via various strokes of good fortune, eventually began to study botany under the eminent Bernard de Jussieu. Well set on a good career, at 23 he married Cecile Claye. Then, just as with Bartram, something terrible happened: his beloved wife of eleven months died soon after the birth of their son. He did what Bartram did. He chose to travel. Working by now at the Jardin Du Roi in Paris, he set out under its auspices in February 1782. He was going to Persia. As with all his later travels, there seems to have been some element of politics and espionage. This time he was officially part of the entourage of Jean François Rousseau, recently appointed Consul at Teheran.

It was an exciting journey, crossing the stormy Mediterranean Sea in its worst season, journeying by camel caravan across whistling deserts, brushes with brigands and hostile tribes. Michaux soon left his nominal boss to attend to his own affairs. Setting a pattern that was to last through his life, he travelled alone, still sometimes a risky business in the Middle East. Captured by local Bedouins, he was stripped of horse and clothing, and left naked in the desert. Half dead, he was rescued by the English consul at Basra. In poor shape after the incident, he nursed himself back to health, and passed the time compiling the first French-Persian dictionary. Later, he cured the Shah of an illness that no court physicians could cure. He explored the ancient garden traditions of Persia; his reports back to Paris were filled with excitement. He had found his life's work.

The next three years were spent in the Middle East, finding new bulbs, new daphnes, oleanders, and collecting some of the ancient garden roses of Shiraz. He sent back local sorts of camellia, mimosa, pomegranates and olives. Among the hundreds of wild plants he brought back to France was a new genus, now named Michauxia as a tribute to him. He got back in 1785. Still restless, he couldn't settle. Then, a remarkable opportunity arose. The French navy was desperate for timber. As elsewhere in Europe, the forests of France had been decimated by the immense need for wood that wars caused. France built fleet after fleet during the long naval war with England and was running out of building materials. Wondering whether America might have species that would more swiftly replenish French forests, the government cast around for a suitable collector. Michaux was introduced to Thomas Jefferson, who was then in Paris. Everything, even Michaux's strange end, at once fell into place.

Andre Michaux was to visit America as a plant prospector, whose first duty was to find new American trees, and he was to send home wood samples to test new species for strength, durability and utility. He was was also to look for American species and varieties that would enrich French orchards, fields and gardens. He was also to import French plants to America; American gardeners might favour France over England if they liked French plants. Botany merged with political ends; he was to travel as a diplomat as well as a botanist. Ironically, he was sent out by order of the French king. But France espoused American ideals sooner and more violently that anyone could have forseen. Michaux would became Citoyen Michaux, working for an even newer republic.

That was in the future. Andre and his young son Francois reached New York on November 13th, 1785, only a year after the new Congress had ratified the peace treaty with England. They travelled at once to Philadelphia and presented letters of introduction to William Bartram. Exciting things like new liquidambars, tulip trees, american oaks, were soon despatched to the Jardin du Roi.

Wanting to experiment with sending young plants, rather than seeds, home to France he realised that he needed nursery ground in which to rear them. Though the new Republic forbade foreigners owning American soil, a special act was passed in 1786 by the New Jersey legislature to allow Michaux to buy about ten acres in Bergen (now Hudson) County, New Jersey. Clearly, the diplomatic aspect of Michaux's appointment was working as well as the horticultural one. The only stipulation was that the land be used solely for the purposes of a botanical garden. Today it is part of the Hoboken Cemetery.

Michaux didn't take long, though, to realise how rich the American flora was further south. The climate there was so different that he needed another garden for his young plants. This time the garden was almost the size of a farm, containing more than a hundred acres of land near Charleston, South Carolina. Michaux's purchase documents of 1786 are still in Charleston's city archives.There were no legal entanglements, but there was one difficulty, and one which powerfully affected Michaux's later life. Few French ships docked at Charleston harbour, and so plants bound for France had to be shipped to New York first. Transit times were longer, and plant survival was inevitably reduced.

However, the new southern garden was also to store plants from France; American gardens could soon boast mimosas, silk trees *(Albizia julibrissin)*, the crape myrtle *(Lagerstroemia indica)*, the tea plant and other camellias. Some of his introductions in that direction still survive, amongst them an ancient camellia tree still growing at Middleton Place, and now gradually being propagated.

However, mimosas and camellias were as nothing to the flow in the other direction. He found new magnolias in the Carolina Piedmont and Tennessee. A species he named *Magnolia macrophylla* created a sensation in France; Empress Josephine was among the first to have this new glory in her garden. He found new oaks, maples... During his eleven years in American, he shipped upwards of sixty thousand living trees and thousands of seed collections, first to the Royal Nurseries, and, after the fall of the Bastille, to the National Nurseries.

The political turmoil in France handicapped Michaux in America. To help offset his difficult financial state, members of the American Philosophical Society promised him backing in 1793. He had to agree to mount a western expedition that would take him across the Mississippi River, through vast Louisiana, and to the headwaters of rivers on the far side of the Rockies that flowed to the Pacific. Thomas Jefferson, then Secretary of State, drew up the proposals and subscription lists. America was wanting to explore its own vast flora.

The list of subscribers included George Washington, Alexander Hamilton, John Adams, James Madison, and Jefferson himself, as well many other less famous men. By this time, Michaux was clearly an ardent republican. On August 30th, 1794, he jubilantly recorded in his diary: Reached the summit of the highest mountain in North America... I sang the Marseillaise and shouted, 'Long live America and the Republic of France! Long live liberty!' Sometimes he took this enthusiasm to extremes; once, while nearly starving on one of his wilderness expeditions, he refused a meal from a frontier settler, a royalist, who insulted the new French Republic. Michaux wrote in his diary that he preferred to go hungry another night and sleep on his deerskin, rather than in the bed of a fanatical opponent.

Though he didn't make it over the Rockies, he eventually travelled over much of the continent, often making friends with native Americans, especially the Cherokee, whom he liked and admired, and whose language he learnt. Travelling was hard. On rivers, his skiffs and birch bark canoes were often swamped and overturned. Horses died, got lost, or were stolen. He was often ill with fevers and mysterious infections, often nearly starved. His son was partially blinded in a gun accident, and was sent back to France. His journals hardly mention any of this, often merely noting 'Gathered seed, Prepared seed for shipping. Shipped eleven hundred and sixty-eight seeds and plants'.

He sent home a huge haul of rhododendrons, azaleas, magnolias, many of the great American trees, asters, lilies, bignonias, twenty seven species of maple, balsam poplars, agaves, oconee bells (*Shortia galacifolia*), the yellowwood or virgilia (*Cladrastis lutea*), mountain stewartia (*Stewartia ovata*). In Europe, the gorgeous riches of America seemed inexhaustible, and room to grow them ever more important.

Ironically, during his journeys he was often dogged by the 'American garden' as it was developing in Europe. Such was the fashion now, that there was a huge market for almost anything green from American. He writes on one trip that he was being shadowed on the trail by a Scotsman called John Fraser... "Since Mr. Fraser took his last passage to England, Myself and my Son have promised for him at the Time approved of 4000 plants of the

Rhododendron chiefly of the Scarlet flowering Species and blue and red, and white & red speckled flowering Species... 1000 Magnolias & other plants..." Fraser was busy collecting specifically for the London market, following Michaux around America so that he wouldn't miss something special.

Michaux returned to France in 1796, but it was a difficult homecoming. The ocean passage had gone easily, and the ship was in sight of the Belgian coastline. Then the breeze turned to wind, and the wind to gale. They were in the middle of a terrible storm. His boat, the 'Ophir', was soon foundered and broke up. Michaux, swept away, nearly drowned. Unconscious, he was pulled ashore tied to a floating spar. Boxes of plant specimens were salvaged too. Journals, and every single living plant, were all lost. Apparently undaunted, in a day or two, he began drying his collection, and was soon on the road to Paris.

Once there, he found that the vast majority of the living plants he had shipped to France had perished during the revolution and its aftermath. While he himself was a revolutionary hero, there was no salary to pay him. Amongst these tremendous disappointments, he was at least reunited with his now fully grown son. Francois had trained as a physician but shared his father's passion for botany; one which was one day to take him back to America too.

Though Andre rejoined the staff of the newly named Jardin des Plantes, and began working on, and publishing his herbarium collections, he didn't settle. A monograph of the oaks of North America and the vast and important 'Flora Boreali-Americana', weren't somehow enough to keep him. Travelling light had caught his soul. He wanted new countries, new continents if possible. Australia beckoned.

He soon found the opportunity to join an exploring expedition to the South Seas sponsored by the French government under the command of one Captain Nicolas Baudin. Francois was detailed to see his manuscripts through the presses. Andre left France for the last time in 1800. Things at once began to go wrong, though he can't have know that Baudin was at least half mad, and would lead a ship almost constantly on the verge of mutiny. Andre couldn't bear it, and left the expedition when it dropped anchor off Madagascar. The island has a unique flora, and Andre was at once fascinated. He planned extensive collections. He planned another nursery garden. He built himself a primitive shack. Then, in November 1802, he died, perhaps of malaria, perhaps not. For all his work and enthusiasm, mysteriously, neither notes nor plant specimens were ever found.

His son went on to become a respected traveller and botanist. Returning to Philadelphia, he donated his father's remaining handwritten journals to the American Philosophical Society of Philadelphia, where they are still treasures. Michaux's botanical specimens are housed in Paris as a separate historical herbarium within the Muséum National d'Histoire Naturelle. The southern gardens of Andre Michaux are marked by a stone inscription set in the grass at Charleston Airport, a gift of the Garden Club of Charleston in 1954.

But to return to 'the American garden' and the Frasers. It was John Fraser senior, who kept crossing Michaux's path, and watching carefully what the Frenchman had found. John Fraser (1750-1811) was born in Scotland, but moved to London as a young man. Starting life as a mercer, plants caught him, and he switched businesses in the 1780's, to become a nurseryman, with his shop in Sloane Square, Chelsea. He was also smitten with an urge to travel and collect. Proposing a journey to Newfoundland, he was astonished to find funding from the Chelsea Physic Garden and the Linnean Society. Still surprised, he found himself in northern North America between 1780 and 1784. At that time the region was still British, but he soon realised that the flora was far richer further south. By 1785, he deemed it possible for a Scotsman to travel in the still anti-British republic, and headed south in the same year that Andre Michaux sailed to America from France.

Fraser had developed a new technique for transporting young plants, packing them with wet moss. Michaux should have copied him. Almost all of Frasers stock survived the return to England in 1788. He sold the plants off very profitably, and was back in the southeastern United States on three other trips between 1788 and 1796. By then Russia was also gripped by the American garden fashion, so he took stock to St. Petersburg, where he sold the whole lot to the Empress Catherine for an impressive sum. Even though she died the next year, the new czar and czarina, Paul I and Maria, appointed him their botanical collector. Fraser returned to America with a royal commission from the czar. By now, he was accompanied by his son, also named John. Together they tramped or rode across the wetlands of Carolina, finding dangers and new plants. Disguised as Americans, they even explored mountainous Cuba, then Spanish. Although their ruse was discovered , the Spanish governor allowed them to travel freely explaining, "My country, it is true, is at war with England, but not so with the pursuits of these travellers".

However, they had made a plant discovery that would allow the American garden to evolve into something much more colourful, and more suitable for small gardens. Of course, Michaux had actually first found it, but didn't get it back to Europe. In flower it was extraordinary, with trusses of bell shaped flowers five to six inches across, each flower with five petals joined together at the base, olive green spots on their inner surfaces. When in full fig, the bushes were an almost solid sheet of intense rosy red. First called 'the mountain rosebay', the botanists named it *Rhododendron catawbiense*. By 1809, every gardener in the country wanted it. More surprisingly, it turned out to cross happily with other rhododendrons growing in the American garden. There were soon hundreds of new varieties, referred to as "catawbiense hybrids". They were extremely hardy, and for that reason were called "iron clads." Flower colours ranged from creamy white and pink through crimson to deep, bluish purple.

The enthusiasm for them was so vast that a new sort of garden began to evolve out of the American garden. Though plant form and flower colour and shape of the 'ironclads' were rather limited, they did at least bring some showy glitter to the gloomy depths of most American gardens. Gardeners were mostly not geographically fussy, and were happy to slip in the occasional plant from other lands. From 1850, they all had to, Andrew Jackson Hooker went to northern India. Hooker's story is mostly in a later chapter, but his contribution to the development of the 'American garden' started with the Indian trips beginning in 1847. Though his father was by now at Kew, he himself was still unknown. He made some exciting trips into Antartica; now he wanted to look at the high mountain flora of tropical regions to see if they had similar plants. Sikkim was an obvious place to go, under British control, unexplored, and very mountainous.. He made four journeys to India; the third was the most important.

Hooker arrived at Calcutta in January 1848, too early in the season to think of going into the mountains. Instead, he joined a Geological Survey group going off to Sulkun, south of the Ganges. There Hooker hired some elephants, whom he trained to pick flowers for him, and in some style travelled to Mirzapur on the Ganges. He got to Darjeeling in April. He liked the place. It was often wrapped in what he called a' dear, delightful, double-distilled Greenock fog'. Even so, he was there longer than he wanted, held up by political difficulties in Sikkhim. However, he soon found that the local region had some astonishing rhododendron species.

He began to send home drawings and descriptions of his finds, to be published by his father as 'Rhododendrons of the Sikkim Himalaya'. In spite of the widely grown 'ironclads' developed from American species, it was a new revelation of the glories of the genus, and included species like *Rhododendron campylocarpum, R. ciliatum, the glorious R. cinnabarinum, R. falconeri, R. griffithianum, R. maddenii and R. thomsonii.* The gardening world fell in love with them, and planted them in their American gardens, where, in suitably wet examples, they thrived. As soon as they began to flower, hybridisers, finding that American and Indian rhododendrons crossed with great abandon, at once got to work. By the end of the 1850's, there were huge numbers of astonishing new hybrids. This coincided with a equally huge economic boom. Gardeners with wallets stuffed with new money and heads stuffed with romantic ideas culled from Walter Scott's novels, bought themselves Scottish or Cornish estates. The high rainfall, frequent mist, and mild air of these oceanic regions was hopelessly unsuited to the gaudy splendour of the popular 'bedding garden', all pelargoniums and verbenas. It did perfectly suit the tree species from Columbia and Oregon. It also perfectly suited the new rhododendron cultivars pouring forth from nurseries like Waterers and Hilliers. The American garden evolved swiftly into the magnates garden, a mix of evergreens shading a brilliant riot of 'rhodos', a sort of garden still widely admired and sometimes even still copied. The magnates garden, many still in existence, and all garishly colourful, became one of the modes of gardening for the rest of the century. Surprisingly, no designer emerged to tell the magnates how to plant them. There are still huge acreages of terrifying colour clashes as hundreds of gaudy rhododendrons compete to dazzle the onlooker.

But, to return to green America: the elder Fraser's collecting activities were curtailed when he suffered broken ribs and other injuries in an accident with his horse early in 1810. He died the following year. His son formed another nursery, devoted to the American flora, in Kent. He called it 'The Hermitage'. Father and son are commemorated in the Fraser fir (*Abies fraseri*

Poiret) and Fraser magnolia (*Magnolia fraseri*).

Seeing that the Frasers were making money out of America, other men tried to copy them. Some had terrible times. .... Lyon was another Scot. He collected, though didn't discover, the delicious Franklin tree. Indeed, such was its popularity in European gardens, though not British ones, he may have seen the species' last natural stand. In a journal entry for June 1, 1803, written in Savannah, Georgia, after a five day trip to into the backwoods where he found some Franklin trees: "It is sufficiently remarkable that this plant has never been found growing naturally in any other part of the United States as far as I can learn, and here there is not more then 6 or 8 full grown trees of it which does not spread over more than half an acre of ground, the seed has most probably been brought there originally from a great distance by a Bird of passage". He may then have dug them up. Certainly, he brought vast amounts of greenery over from America for auction in London. John Claudius Loudon reported in 1838 that: "He brought an extensive collection to England; the plants composing which were partly disposed of by private account, but were chiefly sold by auction in a garden at Parsons' Green, Fulham. The catalogue of these plants fills 34 closely printed pages, it enumerates 550 lots, and the sale occupied four days. Several of the lots were composed of large quantities of one year-old seedlings in pots; and ten lots at the end of the sale consisted each of 50 different sorts of seeds. This, it is believed, was by far the greatest collection of American trees and shrubs ever brought to England at one time, by one individual." Poor Carolina was getting stripped bare.

Though he made money, it wasn't easy. On one trip, he was bitten by a mad dog. Alone, he had himself to sear the three punctures in his leg with a burning-hot iron. Sometimes he his horse went astray, and he was forced to travel on foot. Many times he lost his way. Finally, in 1814, he came down with a fever in the North Carolina mountains and died.

All these collectors, great ones like Banister, Bartram, Michaux, even the Frasers and all the other hangers on, however passionate they were about America and its plants, were all rooted in the world of human affections and relationships. Whatever difficulties they faced when travelling, they were, somehow, just the difficulties of travelling in that place, and at that time. The strangest story of all and, in terms of the plants that resulted from it, the most extraordinary, needed another sort of man. It needed someone angry and affectionless, someone who would welcome every punishment that an untamed continent could provide.

A grim, humourless and violent stonemason in the village of Scone, in
Perthshire, had a second son born to him in 1799. The child was christened
David. He seems to have been justly named, and was soon willing to take on
his ogre-ish Goliath of a father. David's mother, frightened for his safety,
packed him off the the village school at the age of three to keep him from
harm's way. The young David Douglas' hatred of authority was already set;
he was intensely disruptive and expelled a few years later. At his next school,
regular thrashings by tawse seemed to affect his resistance not at all.
However, some other sort of teaching did take place; he developed a
consuming passion for natural history. He finally left when ten years old, and
went as apprenticed gardener's boy to Lord Mansfield's garden at Scone
Palace. Almost as once, he began to prosper. In 1818 he moved to Sir Robert
Preston at Valleyfield on the Firth of Forth, an estate which also still exists.
Sir Robert, sensing the promise of the young man, gave him the run of his
library. In 1820, he obtained a job at the new Glasgow Botanic Garden, and
went to the thrilling botany lectures being given by Dr W. J. Hooker, its
Regius Keeper. He prospered there too, and was plainly on the move.

The passion for American plants was at its height. When Joseph Sabine,
the secretary of the Horticultural Society of London (eventually to become
the Royal Horticultural Society), was looking for a collector in 1823, Hooker,
who seems to have been a perceptive and kindly mentor, suggested the young
David Douglas. The young man sailed for London, spent a bare three months
working in the Society's gardens at Chiswick, then set out on his first mission
to America on 6 June.

This first trip set the pattern of hardship. The voyage out from the
tumultuous city of Liverpool took fifty-nine days. On the second week, all

fresh water was rationed. Tobacco was so scarce that the crew used it twice: chewing it first around, then drying it in the sun to make it smokable for the second. He was relieved to arrive in New York on the 3rd. August. This first visit was to look for kitchen garden plants, and he spent much time visiting gardens and nurseries in the neighbourhood of New York and Philadelphia, with only one journey into the real backwoods.

He returned to England early in January of 1824. Through the generosity of American nurserymen, he had with him a wide selection of new apple, pear, plum, peach, and grape varieties that had been developed in America. That kept the Horticultural Society happy. He also had plants of the Oregon grape (then *Berberis*, now *Mahonia, aquifolium)* grown from seeds gathered by Lewis and Clark (see chapter XX). These created a sensation, and every gardener with even the smallest American garden, had to have some.

The Horticultural Society realised that the dour young man really would make a plant collector, and it decided that he could be sent out again in its service. He was soon at sea once more, though this time he was sailing towards great public acclaim. On July 26, 1824, he set out to reach the Pacific Coast of North America, not by going overland from New York, but via the wild Cape Horn. The great Meriweather Lewis (1774-1809) and William Clark (1770-1838) expedition had just finished exploring beyond the Rockies, and had found far more botanical riches that merely the *Mahonia*. It was those riches that the Society was determined to tap. The Pacific Northwest clearly supported coniferous forests of a complexity and magnificence only made possible by the mild winters and colossal rainfall. This cool rainforest stretched unbroken from northern California, up through Oregon and Washington state, and on into British Columbia. Douglas was soon to be astonished by the sheer variety of cone-bearing trees, from cedars and pines, to hemlocks, spruces, and firs.

It took him eight months to travel from Britain to the mouth of the Columbia River. If the journey had been terrible, Columbia was worse. At Cape Foul, weather was awful. He was travelling along with some other Scots adventurers, when they found that their food supplies were beginning to run out. To save them, they sent their porters home. Bivouacing on a beach, the wind became a hurricane, whipping the waves so high that they had to move camp twice during the night to avoid being washed away. The tents were long since blown down, and they had no protection from the storm other than wet blankets and a few pine branches. There was no food. The next day, they walked along the sandy beach for sixteen miles to a small deserted harbour. There was no food there either, and they had to resort to the roots of arrow-head *(Sagittaria)* and lupin. 'From continual exposure, I became much reduced.' Douglas noted. Starvation even reduced him to eating his own collections, using the berries and seeds for food. His herbarium specimens were left behind for there was no-one strong enough left to carry them.

The forests, though, were, and still mostly are, tremendous. Douglas, like all visitors, found them and their landscape overwhelming. He wrote that they are 'grand beyond description; the high mountains in the neighbourhood, which are for the most part covered with pines of several species, some of which grow to an enormous size, are all loaded with snow; the rainbow from the vapour of the agitated waters, which rushes with furious rapidity over shattered rocks and deep caverns, producing an agreeable although at the same time a somewhat melancholy echo through the thick wooded valley; the reflections from the snow on the mountains, together with the vivid green of the gigantic pines, form a contrast of rural grandeur that can scarcely be surpassed.'

The tree that most excited Douglas was the sugar pine, *Pinus lambertiana*, which reached 250 feet in its native habitat and had cones eighteen inches in length. He introduced this tree in 1827, together with the Douglas fir, *Pseudotsuga menziesii*, now one of Britain's tallest trees. Indeed, the flora was so incredibly rich, and so beautiful, that he decided to extend his stay for a second season of collecting. Back in Britain, gardeners chafed impatiently to get hold of seed, though it turned out that many of his plants only did well on the mild west coast of the island, and especially on the west coast of Scotland.

In the silent, eerie, green forests of Oregon, not all was going well for Douglas. He was beginning to have problems with his eyesight. He had several harrowing brushes with Indians, renegades, wild animals, and disease. He had suffered prolonged privations, quite often self-inflicted. He'd had enough, and wanted to return to England. Rather than round Cape Horn again, he waited until late March of 1827, he joined a party of trappers making their way up to Hudson Bay. Soon, he was once more East of the the Rockies. He must have looked a picturesque figure, for by now he was travelling with a live eagle caught for the London Zoological Society. That was an astonishing journey in itself. He finally sailed home on an English whaler, triumphant, but sick.

'Home' was a mirage. Of course, honours awaited him. He was elected a Fellow of the Horticultural Society, though, oddly, he was only allowed to avoid paying fees and subscriptions for three years. He also became a fellow of those great London Societies, the Linnaean, the Zoological, who had got their eagle, and the Geological. Arrangements were made for his journal to be published. He was lionised, even asked to fashionable dinners and balls. He probably hadn't ever been suited to that sort of life. He became discontented, ungracious, contemptuous, surly. None of these qualities were of use in the drawing room. His disgust had some cause. He found out that the salary he had from the Horticultural Society was less than the one that they were paying their doorman. Some of the animal skins he had also collected, at great trouble, had been badly looked after, and were now quite useless. He began to quarrel with almost everyone he came across, even those who could be most helpful to him. The only friend he seems to have made was with a fiery Scots terrier, whom he named Billy, and who was to survive him.

It was soon clear that the wilds were the only place he could be, if not happy, then at least functional. He, and those around him, were relieved when funds were put together, partly by the societies of which he was a fellow, to let him go off on another expedition to the west coast of America. This time, too, the British Colonial Office had an interest. They wanted accurate maps of what became British Columbia. He was shown how to be a surveyor, and provided with all needful equipment. This time, he had to sail round Cape Horn again. He left Britain, the faithful and loving Billy by his side, in October, 1829. This time he was sailing towards his destruction.

It took him eight months to reach the Columbia again, and begin surveying. His eyesight was getting worse. Old wounds ached. He hired a rough, tough, deckhand to carry his equipment. His collecting trips were less long than they used to be. Yet he could still hold out against a fever that wiped out whole Indian villages, and twenty-four of the fur company's men. He kept going by never giving in, treating himself badly by going on what he called 'healthful perambulations'.

At last he was finished mapping. He paid off his servant, and set a course southwards. His list of provisions included shoes, shot, cod line and candles, ten pounds of tea, nine gallons of brandy, two large black silk handkerchiefs, a large mooseskin, and a jew's harp. He and Billy sailed to the softer south, to California. He'd never been anywhere like it. The spring was unbelievably beautiful. He immediately began to find wonderful plants. *Garrya eliptica,* with its astonishing catkins, Monterey pine *(Pinus radiata)*, annuals like wild heliotrope, blazing stars, Californian bluebells…

Duplicate specimens of much of his material was being sent on to St Petersburgh. The Russians were as excited as the gardeners of London and Paris. The czar and the Russian governor of Alaska wanted Douglas to botanize Alaska, Siberia, and Russia. He would return to Europe overland, a journey of 1,150 miles. He set off once more. By now he was completely blind in the right eye and had to wear smoked spectacles to protect the left. His temper was far worse; he quarreled with a company trader, and had to refuse the offer of a duel. There were war parties of Indians ahead. He turned back, for the first time in his life, and disaster swiftly followed. Canoeing down the Frazer River, his party tried to shoot the rapids at Fort George Canyon. Douglas' bark canoe was gashed to shreds. He was swept off through the rocks and the foam, then carried into a whirlpool. He was there for an hour and forty minutes before he managed to scramble free. He lost a collection of four hundred specimens of plants and his volume of field notes. This contained all his collectors' information about what he'd found, and where. He was once again on the Columbia River, exhausted. He still had Billy.

He went south. Eventually he landed up at Honolulu. He did some desultory collecting, but realised that whenever a ship arrived that was bound for Britain, he would have to take it. It didn't come soon enough. Amongst various much stranger characters, he'd met a missionary who seemed to interest him. They were on the island of Oahu, but Douglas had said he's show the man some of the sights of Hawaii. After all, it was a glorious place, and he had written of his exultation on climbing its volcanoes: 'one day there, is worth one year of common existence.' Their boat to the main island got becalmed before it reached their destination. Douglas, impatient, got himself put ashore, saying that he would go by foot overland to meet the missionary at the town of Hilo. Setting off, carrying his own small bundle of clothes and collecting equipment, he stayed overnight at the house of a man named Davis. Early the next day, July 12th, 1834, he called on an English ex-convict called Ned Gurney. Gurney warned him that the trail ahead was set with cattle traps, big pits disguised with branches, leaves and earth, and often set with sharpened stakes.

A few hours later, two of Gurney's servants found that one of the traps had caught something. Inside, they found a trapped wild bull, bucking and snorting with fear. Beneath the bull, lay the gored body of a man. Beside the pit, a small black dog howled. There was eventually an investigation. It seemed impossible that Douglas could not have seen the trap, though he was partially blind. Some thought that Douglas' wounds weren't caused by the bull. Some said he'd quarreled with Gurney. No conclusion was reached. Douglas, some of whose plants must be in almost every garden worldwide, who had had a colossal impact not only on the 'American garden' but on them all, left behind just fifty pounds, and a bundle of plants he'd collected on the Sandwich Islands. He also left a dog. Billy was sent back to an uncertain future in England. Today, a simple memorial stands where Douglas died.

Overall, he introduced fifty species of tree and shrub, including *Abies grandis, Abies procera, Picea sitchensis, Pinus radiata* and *Pseudotsuga menziesii.* Some, like the Douglas fir, the Sitka spruce, the Monterey pine, became important timber trees. The flowering currant, *Ribes sanguineum*, can be found in every garden centre. The Snowberry, *Symphoriocarpos racemosus*, has become a serious weed.

But Douglas hadn't found everything that America had to offer. He had seen, but did not introduce, a tree which he described as 'the great beauty of Californian vegetation… which gives the mountains a most peculiar, which I was almost going to say awful, appearance, something that plainly tells us we are not in Europe.' This was the coastal redwood, *Sequoia sempervirens* .But the greatest of the all American trees eluded him, and remained undiscovered for another few decades. This was the dawn redwood, *Metasequoia glyptostroboides.* Albert Kellogg had studied medicine at Charleston, South Carolina, and at Transylvania College in Kentucky. He moved west to San Francisco, opened a pharmacy, and saw a few patients after hours. He was already hooked on plants, and was soon surrounded by a circle of other San Franciscans with similar interests. The gold rush city had, so far, hardly any institutions, so he and six friends met on April 4, 1853, to establish the California Academy of Sciences. The new organisation gave Kellogg some prominence, and plants were often brought to him to name, if that were possible, or to send on to John Torrey in New York or Asa Gray in Cambridge, Massachusets, if it wasn't. A prospector called A. T. Dowd had a claim in the Sierran foothills near Sacramento. One day he seems to have brought Kellogg parts of a strange, giant, conifer. Kellogg described this fabulous thing to the new Academy during the summer of 1853. There was a guest from England audience, someone they'd not heard of, called William Lobb.

Lobb, collecting for the London firm of Veich, both of whom appear later in this book, dashed off, breathless with excitement. He stood, stunned, when he reached the area now called the Calaveras Grove. The trees towered three hundred feet above him. Some had trunks thirty-five feet across. Saddle bags packed with seeds, cones, even seedlings, he tore back to San Francisco and booked an immediate passage to England. He had not a care about how his boss would react, for he knew just that he had found the ultimate tree for the ultimate American garden.

Two seedlings survived the journey, and rumour of this astonishing new plant soon spread. Seed was sown immediately and germinated quickly. By the summer of 1854 the Veitch firm was offering seedlings for sale at the rate of two guineas each, six guineas for four, or twelve guineas a dozen; eighteen months after Lobb had returned home, saplings of these potentially giant trees were being planted across all England. The plant was published in the Gardeners' Chronicle of 24th December 1853. First called *Wellingtonia gigantea,* Lobb's firsthand impressions made the front page. Astonished readers read aloud to their nearest and dearest, at once wanting a young plant. Lobb had written: 'From 80 to 90 trees exist, all within the circuit of a mile, and these varying from 250 feet to 320 feet in height and from 10 to 20 feet in diameter. . . A tree recently felled measured about 300 ft. in length with a diameter, including bark, 29 feet 2 inches at 5 feet from the ground; at 18 feet from the ground it was 14 feet; and at 200 feet from the ground, 5 feet 5 inches. . . The trunk of the tree in question was perfectly solid, from the sap-wood to the centre; and judging from the number of concentric rings, its age has been estimated at 3000 years. . . Of this vegetable monster, 21 feet of the bark, from the lower part of the trunk, have been put in the natural form in San Francisco for exhibition; it there forms a spacious carpeted room, and contains a piano, with seats for 40 persons. On one occasion 140 children were admitted without inconvenience. An exact representation of this tree, drawn on the spot, is now in the hands of the lithographers, and will be published in a few days. ... ' How could any gardener resist its lure?

The trees were, of course, a sensation everywhere. In California, the grove of giants became a tourist wonder, with hotel, dance floor on the stump of a felled tree, a bowling alley along a trunk. Its bark was even shipped around Cape Horn for display in New York to feed the burgeoning American appetite for scale. The bark of another was shipped eventually to London, and exhibited at the Crystal Palace at Sydenham. It must have considerably added to the heat when that building burned down in December 1866.

Fortunately, for such an amazing plant, it was, and remains, very liberal with its seed. One entrepreneur shipped a snuff box full of seed to George Ellwanger's nursery business: Ellwanger & Barry at the Mount Hope Nursery in Rochester, New York. Mr Ellwanger re-appears in a later chapter. The collector paid twenty five dollars shipping, but eventually got well over a thousand dollars back. The nursery had raised thousands of seedling, and shipped them to nurserymen in England and throughout Europe. The 'Wellingtonia', whether as single specimens now dwarfing country cottage or rectory gardens, or as whole avenues now making an impact on the biggest of estates, are the result of this collecting. It's a shame that Kellogg wasn't faster off the mark, and a more confident botanist; he wanted to call the plant Washingtonia. However a botanist called Buchholz seems to have been first into print, and even Lindley's name of Wellingtonia had to fall to the earlier *Sequoiadendron*, showing the trees relationship to other huge redwoods growing in the same region.

Most of the redwoods were perfect for 'the American garden' as then constituted, most growing in a 500 mile region of wet, fog-drenched forest along the Pacific coast, from northern California and southwestern-most Oregon. They grow especially well in the wet western parts of Scotland. The new giant preferred hot, dry summers, and was much better suited to eastern Britain and mainland Europe. In their native land, most were felled for fence posts, vineyard stakes, roof shingles, and general building. In later life, Lobb returned to San Francisco to live, and must have sorrowfully watched his trees' destruction. He died there on May 3, 1864.

In spite of the American excitement about the tree, gardeners did not seem keen to grow it. This is surprising. Already, big collections of native plants were springing up, initially in the eastern states. Bartram's garden survived the Revolution, in spite of John Bartram's worries and marauding English troops.. It became famous. His son continued to collect for it, and though he collected whatever attracted him, he was most interested in plants that had pharmacological uses in the native American culture. Another member of the family, Humphry Marshal (1723-1801), farmer and stone mason, inherited his father's considerable estate in Pennsylvania. He moved to what is now called Marshalltown, in 1773, and laid what was to become another celebrated botanical garden . He also wrote about plants, and his 'Arbustum Americanum: The Americaa Grove or an Alphabetical Catalogue of Forest Trees and Shrubs, Natives of the American United States' was eagerly read by owners of American gardens in Europe, as well as many gardeners in North America.

The greatest early collection in America was at The Woodlands, the three hundred-acre estate of William Hamilton, on the banks of the Schuylkill River. Unlike the nearby Bartram gardens, The Woodlands was decidedly patrician, landscaped in the European manner. Hamilton liked all sorts of plants, and while there were every American he could lay hands on, he imported plants from Europe too, and had the largest collection of foreign shade and fruit trees in the country. Some of his imported trees, like the Lombardy poplar and the Norway maple, eventually became important throughout America.

However, he could find plant contacts at the highest level. Lesser gardeners needed nurseries, but plenty of these existed too. Following the Lewis and Clark expedition, Bernard M'Mahon sold the Oregon grape (*Mahonia aquifolium*), from his nursery in Philadelphia, and plants soon became wildly fashionable. He got staggering prices for what is really quite a modest species. By 1825, the Prince Nursery firm of Flushing, New York wanted twenty-five dollars each. Other New York nursery gardens like Ellwanger's soon followed. Indeed, the establishment of nurseries and seed merchants near the fast expanding cities of America moved hand in hand with the increasing awareness of the riches of the American flora.

The American garden had at last arrived in America.

4

Chapter 4

The Bedding Garden

David Stuart

THE BEDDING GARDEN

We are at Mr Stevens' splendid auction rooms at 38 King Street, Covent Garden, London, on a misty Thursday afternoon in October 1825. Thursday is plant day. Going under the hammer in an hour or two is an extraordinary collection of lemon and orange trees, and dozens of their relatives. Many of the finer plants, especially some of the rare 'Hand of Buddha' lemon trees, have long been coveted by a number of knowledgeable London gardeners.

The trees' owner, fallen on hard times, is hoping for a good price. Auctions like this are common, and this room has recently seen collections of auriculas, orchids, recently imported oriental chrysanthemums, 'Indian' azaleas and florists tulips going for a good price. The rooms will play, over the next few decades, an influential role in garden development, seeing, for instance, in 1861, the auctioning of the first consignment of ten bushels of Monkey Puzzle tree seed just arrived directly from Chile.

The orange trees' owner has ensured that catalogues of his collection have fallen into the hands of two rival ladies, both with fine gardens and fine glasshouses, and who might well compete for some of the more delectable specimens. He's also ensured that many of their friends are also present.

The rival ladies are the Dowager Duchess of Bedford and Lady Grenville. Their quarrel is already two seasons old and started on a warm afternoon in the spring of 1823. The grander of the ladies had noted with impatience the increasing fame of a nearby garden, and she decided to make a visit. To ensure she had an expert on hand, she took with her her head-gardener, John Caie. Lady Grenville's splendid gardens were at Dropmore Lodge, in Buckinghamshire. Her husband was William Grenville, now baron, and younger brother to the Marquess of Buckingham. Described by contemporaries as astonishingly handsome, he was also 'cold and unbending, even to great people'. Perhaps that was why his wife, very much younger and very much richer, had so taken to gardening.

Lady Grenville specialised in the new 'rustic' style, a chic development of the Picturesque mode of gardening. This itself was a reaction away from the chaste smoothness of the classical English landscape garden style. But it wasn't that that the Duchess Alice wanted to see. Lady Grenville was especially famous for constructing rustic flower baskets out of garden and household detritus. These were said by catty contemporaries to be very beautiful, if also very numerous. However neither these floral baskets, nor the marvellous roses nor the rare trees were the reason for the duchess' visit. What she wanted to see was Lady Grenvilles' remarkable new ways of planting flowers. In Mr Caie's pocket was a new notebook

The 'landscape' mode of gardening familiar to the duchess, and splendidly displayed at Woburn Abbey, hardly allowed for flowers. Grass, smooth or shaggy depending on whether the garden was meant to be Classical or Picturesque, surrounded all her houses. 'Flowers', and most colours, were banished to out-of-the-way places, very frequently the kitchen garden. Yet marvellous new flowers had been pouring into European gardens from the Americas and from Asia for much of the previous century. The duchess and most of her contemporaries were desperate to grow them, but had nowhere to put them where they could easily be seen. When Lady Grenville, in exasperation, cut some large circles out of the lawn in front of her drawing room windows, and filled them with scarlet bergamots, blue salvias, or yellow cosmos, she broke a century's taboo, and started a colossal new movement.

By the time of their meeting in King Street, two seasons later, it had become clear to the grand gardening world that the duchess' gardener Mr Caie had not only taken detailed notes of the revolutionary new flower beds at Dropmore, but has copied them in detail at Bedford Lodge. He was even beginning to claim that the new way of planting flowers originated with him, and that Lady Grenville, and her gardener Philip Frost, were the copyists.

The duchess, catalogue in hand, made a grand entry into Mr Steven's auction room. Lady Grenville was already there. The entire room turned to watch. The great lady paused for a moment, imagining that the lesser one would dare do nothing untoward. Lady Grenville at once turned her back on the greater woman and went to look at the plants. From the astonished bystanders, there was a sharp intake of breath.

At least, that's my story. There is, alas, no evidence that the ladies really met in this way. Mr Steven's auction room was real, and the two women, also real, did indeed have a real quarrel about who originated the new way of planting flowers. It was important.

When whichever spade first cut the turf at whichever garden, it was a completely defining moment. At one thrust, gardening was returned to all ranks of gardeners. The dull green grandeur of Le Notre and Brown were finally laid to rest. All the precious and convoluted theorising about canons of chaste beauty, about the Picturesque, about the Gardenesque, were sliced through like a Gordian tangle of worms. It was as if, through that first cut, gushed a vast arterial rainbow of flowers. The brilliant deluge was to wash away the chaste landscape garden, all greens, greys, misty blues. A moment later, it washed away the shaggy greenery of the Picturesque. In its undisciplined exuberance, it made pompous marble temples and pavilions or faked-up cottages look as foolish and empty as they themselves had once made Chinoiserie pagodas and Gothick towers seem trivial and silly.

The gaudy riot of flowers swept over every country garden, swept through every city plot, poured out of London, taking over Paris in a season, New York and St Petersburgh only a season or two after that. In a riot of cut-out stars and ribbons, plaited guilloches of colour, copies of parterres and magical Persian carpets, it greedily embraced the thousands of new flowers pouring into European gardens. At one moment the flood spawned strange pyramids of begonias and lobelias, at another, borders with drifts of asters and Japanese anemones. In some gardens, plaster Matterhorns arose as rock gardens far gaudier than Nature can ever have intended. Sometimes, it produced gardens that approached the heights of civilised taste, and sometimes it produced some of the most ghastly.

And what new flowers they were: brilliant annuals from the dry lands of Texas and Mexico; verbenas and petunias and a host of other half hardy tropic roadside weeds from Brazil and Chile; geraniums from the veldts and mountainsides of South Africa, and echeverias and strange succulents from its deserts.

These amazing plants were all pouring into London, Paris, Stockholm, even St Petersburgh almost at the same moment as Lady Grenville was handed a perfectly polished spade. The year of my fictional meeting of the duchess and Lady Grenville, 1825, saw another, and real, event that, over the next few decades, further fuelled its brilliance. It began in Glasgow, in that autumn, as a last mooring rope hissed across the greasy cobbles of the quay, and slipped into the murky green-ness of the river Clyde. A ship began its journey to the open sea. On board, watching his ungrateful homeland sliding away, was Mr John Tweedie, gardener. He was bound for Buenos Aires, and though he was already fifty, and something of a disappointed and frustrated man, he must have been completely unaware that he was also bound for at least one of the variants of immortality.

Some of the plants he was soon to send home from South America would dominate the astonishing changes in gardening allowed by Lady Grenville's cut in the grass. Indeed, in 1850, the dowager's gardener Mr Caie, still trying to establish his old employer and himself as the great experts on flower bedding, published detailed planting plans of the flower beds at Bedford Lodge. For the summer plantings, and probably unwittingly, he used almost entirely flowers produced from Mr Tweedie's astonishing new South American material.

John Tweedie, though he became one of the most important collector of Brazilian and Argentinian plants, was not alone. There were hundreds of other European collectors scattered over the globe also sending plants home. Partly, they were searching for commercial products. Some were travelling for purely scientific ends. Most, though, were collecting to assuage ordinary gardeners' almost frantic desire to grow new plants. It was no longer just the great who wanted to collect them. Everyone with access to a piece of ground wanted the latest chrysanthemum from China, or the lastest calceolaria from Chile. It was a huge revolution, and working class gardeners, who had for a century or two largely populated the old 'florist' societies specialising in breeding plants that had been in the 16th century wave of Turkish and Persian flowers, especially tulips, hyacinths, pinks, and anemones, took up new introductions every bit as quickly as dukes. Indeed, they often found themselves centre stage in the new gardening. Many began collecting some of the sumptuous new verbenas. By 1849, only a decade or so after Tweedie sent the first ones back to Europe, there were show classes devoted to it even amongst the humble Cottage Garden Societies. Colours ranged from purest white, through an infinite number of pinks, rose and scarlets, to lilacs so deep as to seem almost black. In stature they soon varied from the minute 'Boule de Feu', to immense and vigorous variants like 'Robinson's Defiance'. Big commercial nurseries started propagating vast quantities of plants. In 1861, John Scott of Merriott stocked one hundred sorts of verbena, and took thousands of cutting of each every season. Similar establishments were selling rooted verbena at two shillings and six pence for a dozen. Another had eighty thousand verbenas for sale to suburban Londoners.

The verbena was, even by contemporaries seen as being central to the whole bedding movement; William Thomson, head gardener at Dalkeith Palace near Edinburgh, commented "Looking at Verbenas, I cannot help recording my conviction that the present principle of arranging plants in masses owes them very much... [its introduction] had a very considerable share in the advent of the grouping style, and helped to establish it'. The verbena had gone a long way in twenty five years.

The collector of the first verbenas was an interesting man. James Tweedie (1775-1862) was born in Lanarkshire where there was already a great deal of horticulture going on to supply the rapidly expanding city of Glasgow. Of very humble birth, he worked his way up through the garden's ranks, eventually getting a job as head-gardener at the Edinburgh Botanic Garden. He took rather to design, and left that institution to work as a landscape-gardener on several Scottish estates. That seems not to have worked, and he decided to emigrate. He settled at Santa Catalina near Buenos Aires, turned shopkeeper, but also landscaped a number of local estates.

He began travelling in 1832, first sailing sixty miles up the River

Uruguay, then returning to the sea and the sailing north to Rio. He next tried
for Patagonia, but first starved, then became ill, and, when better, was trapped
for weeks inside a fort by hostile Indians. For a third journey, Tweedie took
lesser risks, by joining a 'tropa', a caravan made up of seventeen waggons,
240 cattle, forty-four horses, thirty-five mules and thirty-two persons, all
bound for Tucuman. The journey that was expected to last forty to fifty days
but took very much longer. It was a hard trip and, at first, yielded almost no
plants. One river was full spate and they had to wait a fortnight for the
waters to allow them to the far bank. Passengers and baggage were loaded
into crude canoes each made of a single ox-hide with the corners tied
together. These were towed across the torrent by Indian girls holding the tow
ropes in their teeth. It took the expedition eight days to get entirely across.
This gave Tweedie time to botanize, but it was already the dry season and he
found little. Travelling all night to make up time, Tweedie dozed on a
waggon loaded with bales of cloth. Towards morning the driver fell asleep
and the waggon overturned, and Tweedie fell from a height, the bales of cloth
on top of him. Perhaps not surprisingly, the only surviving photograph of
him shows a remarkably depressed looking man, and even the eventual
discovery of some exciting new plants didn't prevent him from 'falling into a
sort of melancholy fit'. He wrote on the day of his sixtieth birthday, when he
was nine thousand miles from home and among people far removed in style
from the couthy folks of his homeland. He depression lifted sufficiently to let
him send a box of seeds back to Dr W. Hooker in Glasgow. He wrote; 'being
from a strange country, they may be in request for your Botanic Garden'.
One of them turned out to be a new species of passion flowers (Passiflora
tucumanensis). He also began sending seed back to nurserymen friends in
Edinburgh, one of which, Handasyde of Musselburgh, was one of the first in
Europe to start crossing some of the new species of verbena to produce
brilliant hybrids.

Tweedie continued to correspond with Hooker, who described many of
his new species and genera. The one which bears his name is the beautiful
twining *Tweedia caerulea* (illustrated above), with speckled torquoise
flowers that are like nothing else in the garden. He sent back dozens of
verbenas. He found, too, the Petunia violacea that became one of the main
ancestors of all the petunias in the garden today. He introduced
Cyphomandra betacea, the Tree-Tomato, which combines fragrant flowers
and edible fruit. Most dramatic of all, though, and still increasingly popular,

is the great grass that gardeners either hate or adore: the silvery, rustling
Pampas Grass (*Cortaderia selloana*). Seeds were first germinated at
Glasnevin Botanic Gardens, Dublin, in 1840, The plants flowered two years
later, and caused a sensation.

A writer in the Journal of Botany of 1834 described him as 'unassuming
but indefatigable'. It would have been interesting to know what he made of
another collector he met on his travels. This unnamed Prussian lady insect
collector is one of only two women collectors in this book who travelled to
far off places. She was obviously rather a wild one too, commonly wading
into dangerous lakes up to her armpits to collect something she thought
interesting. Tweedie noted in a letter home that she would cheerfully do this
in lakes so filled with alligators that the local people wouldn't even go near.
Tweedie was far less adventurous, though was shipwrecked several times,
including once when 400 miles up the Paranha river. In another storm, off
Montevideo, his brigantine was completely destroyed and he saved himself
by clinging to some riggging. He faced starvation on several occasions, once
surviving for weeks on end eating the seeds of a new species of pine. His
letters make rather little of these incidents. Finally, at the age of 87, the
'Weekly Standard' of Buenos Aires reported his death. In Britain, his
obituary appeared in the Jun 28 1862 issue of 'Gardeners Chronicle and
Agricultural Gazetter', amongst the lists of bankruptcies: Noah Hodges,
Tailor; Thomas Tandy, needle maker; Robert Philips, wireworker.

As Thomson noted, Tweedie's new verbenas, and the hybrids that were
rapidly developed from them, allowed a completely new sort of gardening. It
was a rather ambiguous sort of gardening too. On one hand it ransacked the
globe for plants that would suit it, and produced huge numbers of hybrids,
many of beauty and some of cost. It seemed to be on the side of diversity.
On the other, it reduced the plants it adopted to a single quality, mostly
flower colour, but sometimes shape or form of leaf. Uniformity was all.

These great bedding genera of mid-19th century gardens, calceolaria,
petunia, verbena and geranium (pelargonium) were popular not only were
they brilliantly colourful, assuaging the contemporary taste for gaudy and
intense effects. They were popular because, being from the sub-tropics, they
were 'seasonless'. As soon as the plants were growing, they also began to
flower. They offered no temperate nonsense about a burst of flower in late
spring or early summer, and then a flowerless pause as seed production
started. The plants were also very easily propagated. Huge swathes of

entirely uniform colour were easily possible. They were also mostly sub-shrubs, with relatively flexible stems. That meant that they could be pegged flat.

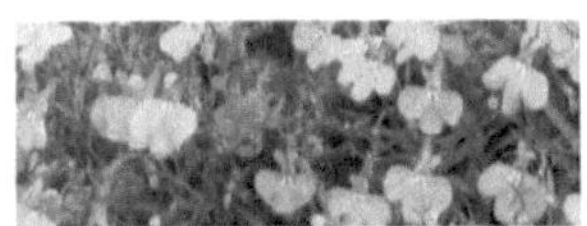

When Lady Grenville started off the new movement, there was, at the start of the bedding craze, no fuss about plants not all being of the same height. As she largely planted a single species or variety as the only occupant of a bed, the effect was reasonably natural. However, a few decades later, gardeners wanted things to be more complex: in beds sufficiently large, why not have bands of different colours, if need be supplied by entirely different plants? Circular beds could have concentric bands, the long beds bordering paths and walks could have stripes, and be called ribbon beds. For this to work, the plants showing the different colours had to be of uniform height. Victorian gardeners managed this either by constantly clipping and pinching out their plants, or by pegging down any branch that wanted to go its own way. Obviously, some plants refused to be so treated, and went on to form the herbaceous border. But the four great bedding genera were entirely amenable and thereby hugely successful.

Gardeners are a diverse tribe though, and some felt that the blazing displays of colour were too vulgar. They wanted something subtler, and, if possible something without the nuisance of fleeting flowers. They developed what became called the carpet bed, the word 'carpet' being used as if it referred only to faded rugs from Persia. Grey-greens, soft browns, sages, bronze, earth reds and dusty purples were the colours they wanted. They tried planting with new sempervivums and sedums, echeverias and new aeoniums. However, the plant group that gave them everything they could possibly ask were the latest hybrid geraniums, not because of their flowers, which were suppressed, but because of their foliage. Hybrids developing in mid-century had leaves patterned in the most extraordinary manner, with horseshoe markings of bronze upon a base of livid green, or white on emerald, or yellow on tan, and infinitely more. Bedding schemes of the utmost subtlety of tone and colour were easily built.

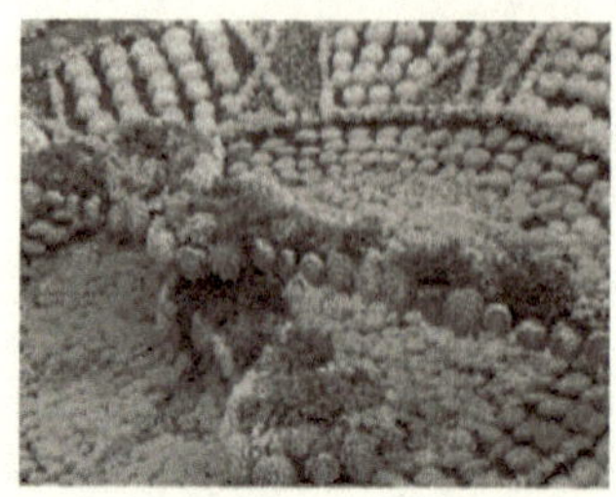

As with verbenas and calceolarias, most of the old geranium varieties are lost. It is hard to remember that their huge diversity was scarcely more than a century and half old. It is hard too, now that the bedding garden has relaxed it's domineering hold on most gardeners' imagination, to realised to what extent the genus underpinned gardening from London's Great Exhibition of 1851, for almost the next century. And not just London, but Paris and Prague, New York and Toronto.

The genus' first association with the garden began in the seventeenth century. It was restricted to the dingily flowered, but attractively perfumed, *Pelargonium triste* which had travelled from South Africa. Once evening falls, the green and brown striped flowers pour out a clove-like perfume, and one that at once attracted European gardeners. A few decades later, the Dutch botanist Paul Hermann sent home from the Cape *Pelargonium cucullatum*, and the ivy leafed geranium *P. peltatum*. *P. inquinans* and *P. zonale* soon followed. Several of these species crossed, and by 1732 *Pelargonium. x hortorum*, the garden geranium, began appearing in reference books. The 1754 edition of Miller's abridged Gardeners Dictionary lists twenty one sorts, but says there are many more. Miller, a man of his time, especially liked the ones related to P. triste, whose flowers only began to smell delicious after sunset. Thomas Jefferson liked them too, but it was only twenty years later that he managed to take seeds home to America from France. Development continued slowly into the next century, but until glass became cheap in the 1820's, pelargoniums remained plants for prosperous gardens. However, once greenhouses could be owned by anyone with the tiniest garden, they took off.

By 1838, grand gardens had several varieties of scarlet flowered zonals, some with variegated leaves. Ivy-leaved sorts were making an appearance in fashionable rustic baskets. By the 1840's, there were prize lists for new varieites at many local flower shows, though decent new sorts were expensive at two shillings a piece. This seems to have acted as a spur to growers, breeders and collectors alike, and the genus spawned the first of the new florists clubs. The Pelargonium Society was set up on June the 18th. 1842. By 1852, geraniums were used for every aspect of bedding. Leaf colour often clashed nastily with flower colour, but once the flowers had been pinched out, the leaf markings were often exceptionally subtle. Some matched the more interesting mid-Victorian colour sense almost exactly. 'Lass 'O Gowrie' had, and still has, a white margin surrounding a jade green leaf with a reddish 'zone'. The lovely 'Crystal Palace Gem' had, and has, a green zone on a yellow leaf. Numbers were as prodigious as for verbenas. Scotts of Merriott overwintered several thousand plants of at least fifty sorts of the latest geranium. At the vast private garden of Shrubland in , the gardener and writer David Beaton regularly overwintered five thousand geranium 'Punch' cuttings, and several other varieties on top of that.

None of this would have been possible without an extraordinary pair of men: Francis Masson (1741-1806), and Carl Peter Thunberg (1743-1828). Masson was a gardener by training, and was born in Aberdeen. Thunberg was a medical man, and was born in the same province of Sweden as his great teacher Linnaeus. Masson was quiet, stoical, even wise. Thunberg was excitable, foolhardy, boastful, rendered paranoid by rivalry, tiny, strong. Masson was later to die, frozen in the wastes of North America. Thunberg died at home in his own bed, loaded with honours. Both men made huge contributions to gardening and botany, though Thunberg's were less important than he claimed. Both made the largest contribution to gardening during the time, from 1772 to 1775, and so ensured that their lives were entwined.

The Cape was already famed for its wildflowers. Officers of visiting ships often purchased collections of rarities to take home as souvenirs for their gardens in Europe. There had been other botanists there before Thunberg; the earliest was Paul Hermann (1646-1695). A Danish pupil of Hermann's developed the botanic garden at Cape Town, and sent much of the early South African material to Europe. Things then went quiet until Johan Andreas Auge (1711-1805) was appointed assistant-gardener at Cape Town's garden, which he went on to turn into a proper botanic garden. However, Auge was a gardener, not a botanist, and mostly made collections for sale. He sold much to Governor Tulbagh (commemorated in the charming bulbs *Tulbaghia*), and he sent material on to Linnaeus and others. However, some of the plants he collected were extremely beautiful, and whetted the appetites of gardeners, especially the great scientific entrepreneur, Joseph Banks. On returning to London from his famous voyage with Captain Cook, he suggested to the king that a collector should be sent to South Africa to collect for the king's own garden at Kew.

He must have been remarkably, if only sporadically, clear headed, for he had just become entangled in an extraordinary piece of foolishness. He returned from Cook's first voyage to great acclaim, and the acclaim seems to have unhinged him slightly. He at once began to make plans for a second expedition, but the plans became increasingly grandiose. He wanted to have an entire entourage of naturalists, musicians, and the best artists of the day. Zoffany was a candidate. Cook wanted to sail in a handsome and stable Whitby collier called the 'Resolution'. It didn't suit Banks, who, partly at his own expense, had it torn apart and almost rebuilt. The captain's Great Cabin was extended into a room to house his naturalists, and was bigger even than the accommodation thought suitable for an Admiral of the Fleet. Captain Cook was to make do with a small shack built on the poop. Banks had a new deck built above the original main deck of the collier, and the new space was intended for Banks's party. The ship's officers were made to reside in dark quarters lower down, and packed 'as close as herrings in a barrel'. Cook tried to sail the resulting and improbable ship to Sheerness, but the boat was now so top-heavy that it nearly keeled over and drowned her crew. Cook refused to have anything more to do with Banks, and the Admiralty agreed.

Banks, furious, retreated to his house in Soho. He must, though, have recovered himself fairly quickly, for he ensured that Cook's replanned expedition should have a botanist sail with it as far as the Cape. The King was to have the best that the Cape could offer. Banks' prescience, and the energy of a young Scottish gardener, was to change not only the king's gardens forever.

The young man was the thirty-one year old Francis Masson. Though he later claimed that he was the only applicant for the post, he had already been working as a gardener at Kew. He must have impressed Banks, who towards the end of Masson's life, was to call him 'indefatigable'. Banks must have impressed Masson too; Masson sent regular letters and specimens to Banks on all his subsequent travels. Many are now in the Mitchell library in Melbourne, Australia. With a salary of £100 a year, payable on his return, and an expenses budget of up to £200 a year, Masson set sail on Captain Cook's next fateful voyage. After six months at sea, the 'Endeavour' anchored at Cape Town on 30 October 1772. Masson, wasting no time, at once set out on a two-month excursion, accompanied only by a Danish interpreter and guide. Instantly, he began finding marvels. He was hooked.

After this first trip, he met up with the extraordinary Thunberg. Carl Peter Thunberg was born in the city of Jönköping in the province of Småland on November 11th, 1743. The inhabitants of that part of Sweden are noted for frugality, as are Masson's Aberdonians. That may have been at the root of their bond. Carl's father was a bookkeeper for a local iron-foundry, and also had a small shop. The father died early, but Carl's mother manage to keep the shop going well enough to give him an education. It was worth the doing. Thunberg was soon recognized by his teachers to have great abilities. At the university of Uppsala he studied theology, law and then philosophy. Moving to study medicine, he spent the next two years working with Linnaeus. Linnaeus got him a tiny travel grant, in 1770 he set off for Holland and France. Thunberg seems to have made some fortunate meetings. In Amsterdam, he visited the Burmans, a wealthy family fascinated by botany. They then engineered a post for Thunberg with the Dutch East India Company, a commercial organization of immense wealth and power. Feeling that he was 'on the way' he began a diary, added to each day, and the source of his published memoires. These contain some oddities. He noted, for instance, of Holland "that water is the element that has permitted the Dutch to develop their shipping". Of France, he wrote, aghast, that "It is highly disconcerting to note that the French language, held in such high esteem by the upper classes in Sweden and elsewhere, is spoken by both high and low members of society all over France". In Paris he attended lectures in medicine and botany. Here he was astonished that the French were not permitted to bring their swords into the laboratories. He also disliked their habit of applauding during dissertations and autopsies.

The Dutch East India Company thought that Thunberg should go looking for horticulturally or commercially important plants in Japan. The Japanese were, with just cause, highly suspicious of all foreigners. Only Chinese and Dutch traders were at that time allowed in. Thunberg was not Dutch and so needed camouflage. He was asked to learn Dutch, and the Dutch colony in South Africa was chosen as the most suitable place in which he could study it.

In 1772, he set sail as ship's surgeon on the East India windjammer 'Schoonzicht', destined for the Cape. Many of the crew had been 'shanghaied' or 'press ganged', were miserable and in poor health. In spite of Thunberg's efforts, 115 of the crew died during the voyage. Thunberg and the other officers almost died too when the cook baked them pancakes that used white lead powder for half the flour. Once recovered and on land, Thunberg was not pleased by the arrival of another of Linnaeus's students, the brilliant, extravagant, stylish Anders Sparmann, after whom the lovely and popular houseplant *Sparrmania africana* is named. They did some collecting together. Rather than be overshadowed by him, Thunberg cast around for other less showy travelling companions.

In August, Thunberg made preparations for a long excursion with three men he thought might be suitable. They weren't. They were away for four months, travelling along tracks from farm to farm. Their baggage was on an ox-waggon, heavy, cumbrous, and with a maximum speed of eight miles an hour. Lions were ever-present. Water was scarce. By 7 September 1772, they had a saddlehorse each, and the cart had three yoke of oxen, driven by two local Africans. On 3 November the party was attacked by a rogue buffalo. It charged the sergeant's horse and slit its belly open. It turned to do the same to the second horse, and didn't notice Thunberg's arrival. Thunberg leapt up into the branches of a tree. The buffalo, feeling mollified, wandered off. Thunberg clambered down and went to look for his companions. He found them 'sitting fast, like two cats, on the trunk of a tree with their guns on their backs, loaded with fine shot, and unable to utter a single word. . . the sergeant at last burst into tears, deploring the loss of his two spirited steeds; but the gardener was so strongly affected, that he could scarcely speak for some days after'. The troupe eventually got safely back to Cape Town by 2 January 1773. The star turn of Thunberg's collecting on that trip was the Bird of Paradise flower (Strelitzia reginae), which he sent back to the botanic

gardens of Leyden and Amsterdam. He still hadn't found a travelling
companion. As to the fabulous plant, ironically, it was Masson whose
scientific name for it now survives, honouring Charlotte of Mecklenberg-
Strelitz, king George III's wife.

    How Thunberg and Masson met isn't recorded by either man.
Thunberg's salary hadn't arrived, and he was in financial difficulties. He'd
set up a small medical practice in Cape Town, but didn't want it to to get too
big. There would be no time for botanising. Patients' fees kept him alive, but
he had to beg a loan from the secretary of the police to purchase a new
waggon, and medicines to distribute in the interior. Masson, financially sound
as King's Botanist, was in a much better position, and soon was 'well
equipped with a large and strong waggon, tilted with sailcloth, which was
driven by a European servant upon whom he could depend'. Thunberg felt
that Masson was only a gardener, and not likely to upstage him. Masson was
also much better equipped.
    They started on 11 September 1773. At first they travelled through the
veldt. Masson was again enchanted. 'The whole country' he wrote, 'affords a
fine field for the botanist, being enamelled with the greatest number of
flowers I ever saw of exquisite beauty and fragrance.' Amongst them he
found dimorphothecas, ixias, lachenalias, gazanias, ornithogalums, romuleas,
and the white arum lily (*Zantedesciia aethiopica*). He started collecting some
of the ever-present shrubby pelargoniums. However, the veldt didn't last,
and they began the climb into the Blue Mountain range. Going was hard.
'We climbed over the mountain's ... even being obliged to lead our horses
for three hours amidst incessant rain which made the road so slippy that the
horses, stumbling among the loose stones, had their legs almost stripped of
skin. And the precipices were so steep that we were often afraid to turn our
eyes to either side. Towards sunset with great labour and anxiety we got safe

to the other side where we found a miserable cottage belonging to a
Dutchman, but however cold and wet as we were, we were glad of
anything... There was only one room and the Dutchman gave us one corner
to sleep in. He hung a reed mat and he and his wife slept there in the other
corner. Just beyond a number of Hottentots lay promiscuously together.' The
rough terrain exhausted their animals, shook the ox-drawn carts to pieces,
broke axles, yet was incessantly producing new plants. Whenever possible,
Masson and Thunberg let the carts shamble along whilst they, on horseback,
wandered off to see what new things they could find. Sometimes they got
lost. Sometimes they themselves had alarming accidents. At one point, they
were told that with no guide and only one pass [Mosterts Hoek], which was
very dangerous, '...we should run the risk of losing our lives, having a rapid
river to cross several times by fords which were dangerous by late rains. We
were a little intimidated by this information but fortifying ourselves with
resolution we proceeded and in an hour arrived at the first precipice which we
looked down with horror at the river, which formed several cataracts
inconceivably wild and romantic. This passage, which took us three hours, is
at the broadest a quarter of a mile, but generally not more than one-eighth.
The mountains on each side rise to steep, perpendicular heights and are now
snow-covered. We crossed the river four times. The fords were exceedingly
rough, the beds being filled with huge stones tumbled down from the
mountain, and though this was laborious and difficult we were repaid by a
large number of plants. The banks of the river were covered with a great
variety of evergreen trees and the precipices are ornamented with erica and
other mountain plants described before.' They found many more
pelargoniums. Thunberg found the orchid *Disa caerulea*. Masson found,
amongst the many new sorts of Cape heath, *Ixia viridiflora*, a gorgeous bulb
with sea-green flowers.

At one point on the way, on November 19th, riding back through the
astonishing land, they had to cross the Duivenhok River. 'Thunberg, without

making inquiry', wrote Masson 'took horse and suddenly disappeared. He and his horse plunged head over heels into a pit made by a hippo, deep and steep on all sides, and for a few minutes I thought he might be dead, but his horse managed to get a foothold and scrambled out.' Thunberg wrote of the same occasion that 'I, who was the most courageous of the company and consequently always in the lead, had the misfortune to plunge into a deep hippopotamus-wallow, which might have proved fatal if I, who have always had the good fortune to possess myself in the greatest dangers, had not with the greatest calm and composure, guided the animal... and kept myself fast in the saddle.'

After further hazards, the two men got safely home. Thunberg sent huge amounts of material back to Linnaeus in Sweden. Masson sent plants seeds, bulbs, and dried specimens home to Kew and Joseph Banks. Amongst these were more than fifty species of Cape pelargoniums. They were soon distributed to the nursery trade in London, and tried out for hybridisation. Nurseries like that of Edward George Henderson (ca. 1782-1876), in London's Edgware Road, or the French firm of Jacques Calot were soon producing plants that immediately began altering the look of gardens throughout Europe and America.

Both men soon went their own ways, having with just two pairs of hands immensely enriched the world's gardens. In March of 1775, the Dutch East India Company decided it was time for Thunberg to go on to Japan. The journey went by way of Java, then a Dutch colony, where he had some smart uniforms made for his forthcoming stay in Japan, and also did some speculating: he bought up a supply of narwhal tusks which he knew would sell well in Japan. Japanese men thought them an aphrodisiac. On August 13th, 1775, after a stormy seven weeks crossing from Batavia via Macao, the triple-decker 'Stavenisse' anchored at the harbour entrance of Nagasaki. Thunberg was launched on a new career. He is still sometimes hailed as the Father of Japanese Botany, though he made less of a contribution to it than a later visitor, whom we meet in a later chapter. He was there for three years, returning once more aboard the 'Stavanisse', to make his way slowly back to Sweden. Calling once more at the Cape, he learned that he had been appointed lecturer in Botany at Uppsala. He got home in 1779. After his return, Thunberg hardly left, and then only to travel to Stockholm. He was appointed to the Chair of Botany in 1784, and held it for 44 years. His huge collections are still at Uppsala University, and they include 36 immense volumes of letters, to and from well over a thousand other naturalists and botanists. Thunberg was busy writing his autobiography when he died, August 8th, 1828, at the age of 85.

Masson, on the other hand, couldn't settle in once place ever again. He kept collecting, but it was never to be the same. A few years later, he sailed to the Azores and the West Indies. Once, while he a very unwilling British conscript into the army, trying to halt the fall of New Granada in the West Indies, he was taken prisoner by the French in their attack on Grenada in 1779. Joseph Banks seems to have engineered a release. Masson went on to lose all his collections in a hurricane on St. Lucia, though he did manage to hold on to material of Cineraria cruenta, the ancestors of the showy cinerarias that were such popular pot plants in the mid 20th century. He even returned to South Africa in 1785, but things had changed and it was not safe to travel more than fifty miles from Cape Town. Even closer to the settlement, Masson had some frightening times. On once occasion, a chain gang of escaped convicts tried to capture him and use him as a hostage. They swept, chains extended, through the vegetation. He spent the night in the open, too terrified to move, crouched in hiding with a clasp knife in his hand, while the desperate convicts kept hunting him through the bush. They tired by dawn, and he escaped. On that trip, in spite of the difficulties, he collected he found over a hundred new species.

In 1795 he was granted permission to return to England to work on his most important work, a book on stapelias. Considering what astonishing plants he had found, and how influential some of them had already become, it was an odd choice. He could have chosen gladioli, or aloes, or even pelargoniums. Stapelias are succulents, with strange finger-like stems, sometimes velvety or serrated. When they flower, their putrescent stink can as quickly clear a greenhouse of humans as fill it with blowflies. The five petalled flowers, in browns, yellows and maroons, are often velvety, sometimes dotted with weird filaments that move in the breeze and resemble maggots. However uncongenial, they plainly fascinated Masson. His monograph was called 'Stapeliae novae: or A collection of several new species of that genus, discovered in the interior parts of Africa. ' and published in London, 1796. It was dedicated to the King, and started '

Sire,

Compelled to leave the Cape of Good Hope, lest I should lose, in an unexpected invasion, the Collection of living Plants that I had made, during

ten years residence there, I returned to England; and was indulged, on my
return, with your Majesty's gracious permission to remain a year at home.
Unwilling to waste so much time in idleness, I resolved to render this
vacation somewhat profitable to the science of Botany, by publishing
observations made on that subject, in the interior deserts of Africa.

Twenty-four years I have enjoyed the honour of being, by your
Majesty's commmand, attached to the Royal Gardens at Kew, as a collector
of exotic plants. I have had the satisfaction of seeing several hundreds of
those, collected by me in various climates, flourishing there, more
beautifully, in some instances, than in their native soils. . . .

Let these circumstances, Gracious Sire, plead some excuse for the
ambition that induced me to solicit the honour of laying my little work at
your Majesty's feet.

Penetrated with gratitude for the uniform protection I have unceasingly
received from your Majesty's bounty–anxious to recommence my
employment as a collector, and still enjoying, though in the afternoon of life,
a reasonable share of health and vigour, I am now ready to proceed to any
part of the globe, to which your Majesty's commands shall direct me. Many
are the portions of it that have not yet been fully explored by Botanists–all of
them are equal to my choice.–To extend the science of Botany, to enrich the
Royal Gardens at Kew, and to obey your Majesty's gracious commands, are
the only objects of ambition that activate the breast of

Your Majesty's
most humble,
most dutiful,
and most grateful Servant,
FRANCIS MASSON.

At last, 'Stapelia Novae' written, he was sixty five. With no personal
life and but a few close friends, he found no home. Banks obtained a
commission for another journey. Masson sailed for New York in 1797. 'We
arrived here' he wrote, in his usual neat hand, 'in great distress after a
passage of four months from Gravesend during which period we experienced
many difficulties. Regarding the Western Isles, we were stopped by two
French privateers, one of which boarded us, examined our papers and let us
pass. Nothing happened until the 5th of November towards night when we
saw three sail bearing down upon us, one of which was a French privateer
belonging to St Domingo who fired several shots and a volley of small arms

into our ship and soon after boarded and took possession of us. The passengers were then put on board a Bremen vessel bound for Baltimore, and after having suffered many hardships from weather, want of water and provisions, were ultimately taken on board another ship and so to New York.'

He travelled on from New York to Niagara, and then to the shores of lake Ontario. From there, he went west to Queenstown, then to Fort Erie returning to Niagara and Montreal. Amongst the plants he sent home to Banks was the glorious *Trillium grandiflorum*. He died in Montreal, killed by the winter's cold in 1805.

END

Chapter 5

The Herbaceous Border

David Stuart

CLASSIC HERBACEOUS BORDERS

The great age of the herbaceous border is largely over. Though virtuosic Edwardian designers like Gertrude Jekyll could play with the splendid colour schemes that became possible as plant breeders developed wider and wider ranges of colours in delphiniums, asters, phlox, dahlias, very few gardeners now have the means to plant and maintain huge borders. Gorgeous flowers like Oriental poppies, Japanese anemones, Russell lupins, astilbes, and the rest have had to find new roles in the garden. Nevertheless, the great Edwardian herbaceous border has a fascinating past, and has been resilient enough to evolve into new forms relevant to contemporary gardens. The story of the delphinium, almost the archetypal flower of those great banks of colour, shows the border's rise and transmutations. It also shows, yet again, how the history of plant introduction drives change in the garden.

Most gardeners now think of delphiniums as towering spires of gorgeous blue, dove grey, soft pink or white, yet splendid plants like these

are only of the most recent origin. Perhaps the highest point in their
existence came in 1910, when Amos Perry, a famous British nurseryman,
staged an exhibition of new delphinium hybrids, displaying thirty thousand
spikes of flowers. Astonishing as it was, a few decades before that show,
there were almost no hybrids at all.

In European gardens, some of the native species of delphinium had been
growing at least since the fifteenth century. It's an enormous genus, with
species scattered over Asia as well as North America. Probably still evolving
fast, it isn't clear how many species there really are; estimates vary between
three and five hundred. The genus encompasses species with scarlet or
yellow flowers, as well as ones in endless shades of blue. It is just the sort of
genus to intrigue collectors and breeders.

Probably the first into the garden was *Delphinium staphisagria*, the
'Staveacre', or louse grass, first grown to keep those creatures away from the
gardener. Another species, *D. elatum*, from central Europe and central
Russia, has had more influence on modern flower gardens. The seventeenth
century collector and author John Parkinson admired it. He notes that 'the tall
and upright single kindes have been entertained but of late years. The double
kinds are more rare'. With muddy blue flowers, and at most a metre high, it
found a place in eighteenth century wildernesses. There were no other kinds
until new species began to pour in from America and China in the early
1800's. At first the most exciting of these were the closely similar *D.
chinensis* and D. *grandiflorum*. Both would grow to six feet high if heavily
fed, and caused great excitement.

By the late 1830's, a famous Manchester florist, called Sam Barlow, had
started crossing some of the more dramatic of the new species. He described
the first true garden hybrid, known as *D. barlowii*, in the Botanical Register
for 1837. That august work stated 'It is a most ornamental and beautiful
herbaceous plant and very easy of cultivation: it appears to flourish in any
soil and situation. We have had plants in bloom throughout the whole

summer and autumn, the principal stems sometimes attaining the height of 7 and 8 feet and many branches.'. The flowers were semi-double and intensely blue.

By 1850, a Norwegian nurseryman had a vast collection of species in use as parent material. Some of the more interesting hybrids were taken up in 1860, at Kelways nursery at Langport in Somerset, where delphinium breeding still takes place. French nurserymen, like the vastly influential company of Lemoine of Nancy also did much of the early work. Though the firm is best known for its tremendous development of numerous woody plant cultivars including *Syringa, Hydrangea*, and *Philadelphus*, they did huge amounts of work on herbaceous genera too. Their delphiniums astonished gardeners; they were all of double or semi-double form, and in shades of lavender, sky-blue, mauve and various combinations. Exhibited in London, one even got an Award of Merit from the Royal Horticultural Society in 1908.

Though gardeners were enthralled, the plants all had one awful drawback; none were reliably perennial. The first truly perennial one was British, and called 'Millicent Blackmore'. Launched in 1910, she had a branched flower spike and individual flowers three inches in diameter. Naturally, the flower was soon called 'The Queen of the Border'. Everyone wanted her,or something as grand. Breeders in France, America, and Britain were happy to oblige. Amos Perry obliged on the grandest scale, whilst also producing magnificent daylilies, Oriental poppies, asters, kniphofias, huge numbers of herbaceous-border irises, as well as his delphiniums. His nursery became one of the most celebrated in the world, and his hybrids almost underpinned the whole of the development of the herbaceous border

He was was born on Sept. 22, 1841. His obituary says he 'started life in

the scholastic profession, but after serving his apprenticeship as pupil teacher, his health failed and his medical adviser advised him to leave this country. Instead of doing this he secured employment in Messrs. Wingfield's Nursery, Gloucester, adopting the profession of his forebears – his grandfather was a foreman at Messrs. Veitch's Nursery, Exeter, and his father was Rose-grower at Messrs. Ware's nursery, Tottenham.' He plainly had plants in the blood. He had independence in it too, and working for others didn't suit him. He believed that a new market was forming as wealthy gardeners got bored with bedding plants. Perry started to collect hardy herbaceous plants, ones that would never fit into the bedding schemes of the day.

While a number of his finds were half-forgotten plants that had been in gardens for several centuries, far more of them were either recent introductions from America and China, or were hybrids of recent introductions. And if there weren't interesting varieties to be found, well, he bred them himself. No 'establishment' gardeners were interested; when he tried to exhibit them at one of the meetings of the Royal Horticultural Society, the Show's superintendent almost refused to let the plants in, eventually letting them be shown in an out of the way corner, amongst gardeners' sundries. Perry persevered. He began collecting suitable plants in Europe, especially white flowered variants of native species. He rummaged amongst the new things coming in from abroad. Finally, he set up on his own in 1894, and started growing alpines and herbaceous perennials. Some of his most famous herbaceous plant include things like *Echinacea purpurea* 'Winchmore Hill'; *Phlox canadensis* 'Perry's var.'; *Spiraea rivularis* 'gigantea'; *Chrysanthemum maximum* 'grandiflorum', *Achillea* 'Perry's White'; *Sparaxis pulcherrima, Anchusa italica* 'Perry's var.'; *Spiraea venusta, Helenium pumilum* 'magnificum'; *Aster Amellus* 'Perry's Favourite', the first pink variety of this flower. Even when he 'retired' from business, handing it on to his children, he couldn't stop hybridising, and his garden was filled with thousands of seedling *Lilium, Sparaxis*, delphiniums and poppies.

Delphinium breeding hasn't stopped. Flowers get larger. Petals get more frilled. New strains are produced that don't need staking, or are good as cut flowers, or are resistant to mildew. However, the big lure in delphinium breeding eluded Perry, Blackmore and Langdon, Lemoine and the rest: scarlet delphiniums. Red flowers are found in two Californian species, Delphinium cardinale, discovered in 1885, and the orange-red D. nudicaule, discovered a few years later. Both species are worth growing in their own right.

America breeders like Luther Burbank, an enthusiastic crosser of plants and avid promoter of their progeny, or N.I. Vanderbilt, a President of the now defunct American Delphinium Society, don't seem to have tried using them, or if they did, got no seed. Frank Reinelt, a Czech gardener who emigrated to America in 1925, also tried. Although he was able to achieve a cross by artificial means between *D. cardinale* and the *old D. elatum*, there were no reds amongst his seedlings. Good purples were the best he could do. More recent attempts have taken place at Wageningen University in the Netherlands. So far, only pinkish-red semi-double delphiniums have been produced. Ultimately, scarlet delphiniums will arrive, and perhaps spark a rebirth of the border.

What was happening amongst delphiniums wasn't unique. Many other plant groups were also, almost literally, exploding, as species newly in from China, America and India, began to swap genetic material in the garden. That great standby for autumn flowers, the Michaelmas daisy, is an example. *Aster novi-belgii, fir*st identified in 1687 by a Belgian, had been introduced into England in 1710. Philip Miller, in the 1733 edition of his Gardener's Dictionary, gives three 'species', probably only variants of the 1710 species, which he says will flower till mid-November. The 1830 catalogue of the London firm of Conrad Loddiges lists the same ones, yet one hundred years later there were at least four hundred varieties of *Aster novi-belgii* alone.

The autumn flowering asters in our gardens are American, and many that contributed to the vast increase in variation came from the parts of America still, in the early 19th century, unexplored by botanists. These, and some of the new delphinium species too, were collected on the amazing journeys undertaken by a strange young man. He was incompetent, innocent, almost a 'holy fool', and yet seemingly protected by a zealous and extremely patient guardian angel. The young man was Thomas Nuttall.

Though he fell helplessly in love with the wilds of America, its plants and its birds, Thomas Nuttall (1786-1859), was born in England, at Settle, near Skipton, in Yorkshire. Life there was simple and safe. He couldn't swim, shoot, or cook. He didn't need to. He didn't even need to consider a career', for his uncle who owned a prosperous printing business. Thomas became a printer. Perhaps he and his uncle didn't get on, or Thomas wanted wider horizons. In any case, he set sail for America, landing at New York, then moving swiftly on. He arrived in Philadelphia on 23 April 1808, and soon set himself up in his accustomed trade.

Even in Yorkshire, he had had an intense love of nature. In Pennsylvania, the story goes, he began to walk the local countryside soon after he had found somewhere to live. He came across a flower he had never seen before, and a companion suggested he take it to Dr. Benjamin Smith Barton, a professor at the University of Pennsylvania and author of the first American botany text. It was a momentous meeting between an Old World innocent and a New World cynic. It ended up creating a new Thomas Nuttall, and the botanist he became collected more new kinds of American native plants than anyone else. No naturalist, which he also became, saw so much of America in its almost primeval condition. Barton, who was both too busy and too weakly to explore the unkown parts of his own country, seems to have, almost jokingly, suggested that Nuttall become his surrogate voyager into that unknown. Furnishing a letter of introduction to the governor of the Northwest Territory, where Dr. Barton hoped Nuttall would explore, he described him as 'a young man distinguished by innocence of character."

Barton sent the young man on two collecting trips in 1809. The first was to the coasts of New Jersey and Southern Delaware, and was a disaster that haunted Nuttall for the rest of his life; he got so badly bitten by mosquitoes that he was 'all but driven away' from a house he approached for lodgings. The owners thought he had smallpox. From those bites, he also caught malaria. It recurred throughout his live, and several times almost killed him. The second journey took him to the shores of Lake Erie and the Niagara Falls. That journey was exciting. He was hooked.

These first two trips he financed himself. The next, in 1810, was financed by Barton. Nuttall was to have a salary of eight dollars a month and

expenses. He was given a double-barrelled gun, a pistol and a dirk; Nuttall
eventually used the gun for digging up plants and storing valuable seed in its
barrel. Progeny from some of these we still grow in our gardens.

This time, Nuttall's proposed itinerary was completely impossible, and
it isn't clear whether Barton knew this. On 12 April 1810, Nuttall left
Philadelphia by stagecoach for Pittsburgh. That was the last of comfort; the
rest of his time he travelled on foot or by boat. His new malaria kept
appearing. His trunk got lost. A week later, he set out into the unknown,
'very weak and burthened', with the contents of his trunk on his back. He
struggled through to Erie, until he at last got a boat for Detroit, and arrived on
26 June. Half dead, he holed up there for a month, then found a surveyor with
a birch-bark canoe, who was going up the coast of Lake Huron, to a
settlement called Michili Mackinac. This place must have been a shock after
Skipton, Yorkshire, and the genteel life of Philadelphia. It was a fur-traders
encampment, and one of the wildest and most raucous places on the
Continent. It was also headquarters to John Jacob Astor's fur-company, and a
new expedition, the Astorian, was ready to leave. Thomas joined it. His
education had begun.

Nuttall left St Louis on 13 March 1811, with the leader of the Astorians,
Wilson P. Hunt, to join the main body of the expedition, camped about 450
miles up the Missouri River. The sixty men proceeded upriver in four boats.
Thomas collected plants along the river banks whenever he could, causing
everyone else delay. He can't have cared, for he'd soon found some notable
things. These included important garden plants like *Penstemon albidus* and *P.
grandiflorus*, the white-flowered evening primrose *Oenothera caespitosa*, a
silvery saltbush called *Atriplex argentea*, various milkweeds like the
Artemisia longfolia and the now widely grown *A. ludoviciana*. The voyageurs
shook their heads but tolerated him. One described him 'as engaged in a
Pursuit to which he appears singularly devoted and which seems to engross
every thought to the total disregard of his own personal safety and sometimes
to the inconvenience of the party he accompanies. When the boat touches
shore he leaps out and no sooner is his attention arrested by a plant or flower
than everything else is forgotten. The inquiry is made: Ou est le fou? (Where
is the fool? – He is gathering roots). He is a young man of genius and very
considerable acquirements but is too much devoted to his favorite pursuit and
seems to think that no other study deserves the attention of a man of sense'

If that's what he was like in company, by himself he was far worse. Far up the river, walking toward what he called 'the northern Andes', meaning the Rockies, he ran out of food and water a hundred miles from the nearest trading post. Turning back too late, he lay exhausted on the ground, unable to go farther. He would soon have died had not a passing Indian found him, and recognised him as the mad medicine man who gathered plants that were of no use. He loaded Nuttall into his canoe, and paddled him down to the post. On another occasion, still with the fur trappers, he set out alone and got terribly lost. He seems, by now, to have been held in some affection. His companions sent out some Indians to bring him back. The Indians tracked him down, but fearful of his medicine making powers, they dared not approach too closely. Nuttall, however, seeing them around him, was terrified. He tried to escape, ducking into ravines and hiding in the brush. The puzzled Indians followed. It took three days before he staggered back to the post, still herded by the faithful Indians.

For all the humour at his expense, he plainly knew the value of the plants he'd found. Once the expedition was over, he sailed homewards to Yorkshire from New Orleans. Before sailing, he sent most of his herbarium material to Barton, but he took with him a large quantity of seeds and living plants. Once in Britain, much of this was planted at his uncle Jonas Nuttall's garden at Nutgrove, near St Helen's, Lancashire. Parts of the collection were given to the Liverpool Botanic Gardens, but the rest was sold on by the Frasers, whom we have met already in the previous chapter. Their 1813 catalogue was written by Nuttall, and many of the gorgeous new plants, many herbaceous, were illustrated in the Botanical Magazine. They included *Oenothera missouriensis, O. caespitosa, O. Nuttallii,* the subtle blue-green *Penstemon glaber, Camassia Fraseri (now C. scilloides), Rudbeckia columnaris.* Bigger things included *Yucca glauca,* than golden flowered and perfumed *Ribes aureum* and *Shepherdia argentea.*

He returned to Philadelphia in May 1818, and soon published his 'Genera of North American Plants', a book which he mostly typeset himself.

This was the third American flora, Andre Michaux's being the first. Nuttall's one was naturally the most complete, but left him unsatisfied, and he set out on his travels shortly afterwards, this time financed by friends who were presumably going to get seeds or plants in return. It was to be yet another hair-raising voyage. On the banks of the Ohio, he bought a ramshackle boat, and hired a ramshackle old man and his young son as crew. They were at once engulfed in troubles: ice floes, sand bars, floods, sunken trees, river Indians. Almost by chance they found the junction with the Arkansas River, and proceeded up. 'Nothing could at this season exceed the beauty of these plains,' Nuttall wrote, 'enamelled with such an uncommon variety of flowers of vivid tints, possessing all the brilliancy of tropical productions. I delayed behind the party for the purpose of collecting some of the new and curious plants interspersed over these enchanting prairies.'

Once again he got lost. He lost his horse. 'My botanical acquisitions in the prairies proved so interesting,' he wrote, 'as almost to make me forget my situation, cast away amidst the refuse of society without money, unprovided with every means of subsistence.' He set off once more, walking over prairies, 'gilded with millions of *Rudbeckia amplexicaulis*'. Amazing.

With a new companion, he explored more. Malaria and depression were never very far away. Green blowflies filled their blankets and personal linen with maggots. 'To compensate for these disgusting and familiar visitors,' he later wrote, "we had the advantage of the bee and obtained abundance of excellent honey, on which, mixed with water, I now almost entirely subsisted.' Later, they almost wandered into a hostile Cherokee Indian camp, but escaped just in time. The trip yielded new portulacas, new eriogonums, grasses and gentians. The prairies were now 'enamelled with innumerable flowers... and charming as the blissful regions of fancy' ; these flowers included *Coreopsis tinctoria, Oenothera speciosa,* yet more penstemons and rudbeckias. He got down to New Orleans on 18 February 1820, and returned to Philadelphia by sea.

His botanical knowledge brought him the appointment of Curator of Harvard University's Botanic Garden at Cambridge, Massachusets, a post that he held from 1822 to 1834. He made a few small sallies into the unknown, and revisited England several times, taking seeds, especially of Arkansas flowers, to be grown on by friends and nurserymen. Finally, he went on a joint trip with some naturalist companions, and crossed the Rockies, as well as finding the lovely shrub that remains his widely planted memorial: *Cornus nuttallii. He* was so eager to go travelling again that he resigned his chair. The party went over what was to become the Oregon Trail. One of the party wrote that they 'traveled over one of the most arid plains we have seen, covered with jagged masses of lava and twisted wormwood bushes. We saw not a drop of water and our only food was dried meat... in these regions, the air feels like a sirocco, the tongue becomes parched and horny, the mouth, eyes, and nose are incessantly assailed by fine pulverized lava.' Even in this desert Nuttall found new plants. Finally, he reached California. He was the first botanist to visit the region, and found some more delphinium species, though neither of the red ones.

The boat he had chosen to take him back to the East Coast was the 'Alert'. It was the same one on which the former Harvard student Henry Dana was serving his celebrated 'Two Years before the Mast'. Dana at once recognised Nuttall. He was astonished. 'I had left him quietly seated in the chair of Botany and Ornithology in Harvard University' he wrote, 'and the next I saw of him, he was strolling about San Diego beach in a sailor's peajacket, with a wide straw hat and bare-footed, with his trousers rolled up to his knees, picking up stones and shells....' Like the Canadian boatmen years before, the sailors did not know what to make of the white-haired naturalist; they called him 'Old Curious', but thought his madness harmless.

However, without his comfortable professorship, on his eventual return, via a wild rounding of the Cape of Good Hope, he was without income, and now ageing fast. Fortunately for Thomas, his old uncle Jonas had died. Thomas was left his estate of Nutgrove, but on the inconvenient condition that Thomas live on it for nine months of the year. Thomas was in no position to do anything else, and so sailed once more to England. In his new garden, he grew his favourite American plants in memory, perhaps, of the extraordinary escapades during which they had been collected. He died in 1859. Almost every European garden, and many American ones, still grow many of his flowers.

Nuttall was a naturalist not a geographer. Routes through the Rockies were becoming increasingly of interest to new Americans. Maps were needed. A collector who carried out some immensely important mapping of 'the wild west' was a surprising and complete contrast to the crotchety bachelor Thomas Nuttall. Unlike Nuttall, he was fabulously handsome but also a rascal, a catastrophic speculator, an estate owner, a gold miner, a pauper, completely 'au fait' with civilised society as it was developing in

America, he was also once court marshaled, and once was even in the running to be a President of the United States. He was also exceeding tough in the field and found nearly a thousand new plants. One of his guides on an early expedition said of him: '[he] morally and physically was the most complete coward I ever knew, and if it were not casting an unmerited reproach on the sex, I would say that he was more timid than a woman. As an explorer, I knew more of the unexplored region fifteen years before he set foot on it, than he does today. They tell me that Stonewall Jackson whipped him in a battle, and it was no credit to Jackson, for an old squaw could whip [him]....' This extraordinary personage, eventually widely hated, was John Charles Fremont.

Fremont was born on Jan. 21, 1813, in Savannah, Georgia. It was not an auspicious start, for he was the son of a "dashing French emigre of the town" named Charles Fremon, and a Mrs. John Pryor, described as 'an ardent and beautiful young woman, the picture of animation and energy.' She was, perhaps because of those qualities, a discontented wife with an elderly husband. Her beautiful young son, intelligent, seems to have worn his illegitimacy lightly, and found approving patrons with great ease. Supported by a number, and particularly the diplomat Robert Poinsett (after whom the familiar plant is named), he entered Charleston College in 1829. He was expelled two years later 'for irregular attendance' but, having done well in mathematics, soon talked himself into a job teaching mathematics on a warship. He rapidly left the navy to become second lieutenant in the United States Topographical Corps, later the Army Corps of Engineers. He started his travels in 1838, and in 1839 was mapping terrain around the upper Mississippi and Missouri rivers. By 1841, he headed his own expedition into Iowa and along the Des Moines River. The expeditions weren't primarily for plants. Settlers were moving west in increasing numbers, some to Oregon, where the United States had a legitimate claim, and others to California, where the claim was less clear. There were, as yet, were almost no decent maps to facilitate this movement.

Nevertheless, science was important too. The first expedition yielded more than twenty new plants, but in the second, the number was nearly eight hundred. The final tally was over one thousand. The expeditions themselves were constantly beset with problems. Staffed by rough and ready Creole and French Canadian adventurers, paid around a dollar a day, the recruits were young, but had already spent time in the difficult lands of the western frontier. They knew how to survive in primitive conditions, could shoot and ride, and were already selected for hardiness. That was as well; during the course of the journey they needed to be able to eat anything. At one point, all they could find for the pot was a dead skunk. At another, the expedition dog Clammet got cooked at a bivouac in Sierra Nevada in 1844. The expedition surveyor, squeamish at first, eventually realised that even a mule's head, stewed gently overnight, was fine if it had plenty of salt. The rest of the mule wasn't much good, for it, like the men, was starving. At least there were good smoky fires when cooking; the men spent as much time as they could wrapped in the smoke. Whatever it did for their lungs, as least it freed them from the ever-present clouds of biting flies and mosquitoes. On parts of some of the expeditions, conditions got so bad that the carcasses of starved and dessicated cattle and horses, all no doubt headless, acted as waymarkers of the exhausted expedition.

Still, Fremont responded to the magnificence of the continent. Though one of his party wrote crossly that 'Fremont is roaming through the mountains collecting rocks and is keeping us waiting for lunch. I am hungry…. That fellow knows nothing about mineralogy or botany. Yet he collects every trifle in order to have it interpreted in Washington and to brag about it in his report. Let him collect as much as he wants – if he would only not make us wait for our meal.' Fremont was oblivious, for he was finding 'The depths of this unexplored forest were a place to delight the heart of a botanist. There was a rich undergrowth of plants, and numerous gay-colored flowers in brilliant blossom….. We wandered about among the crags and ravines until dark, richly repaid for our walk by a fine collection of plants' many of them in full bloom'. During the summer of 1845, on 20th July, he wrote 'We continued our march up the stream, along a green sloping bottom, between pine hills on the one handy and the main Black hills on the other, toward the ridge which separates the waters of the Platte from those of the Arkansas. As we approached the dividing ridge, the whole valley was radiant with flowers; blued yellows pink, white, scarlet, and purple vied with each other in splendor. Esparcette was one of the highly characteristic plants, and a bright-looking flower *[Gaillardia aristata]* was very frequent; but the most abundant plant along the road today was *Geranium maculatum,* which is the characteristic plant on this portion of the dividing ground. Crossing to the waters of the Platte, fields of blue flax added to the magnificence of this mountain garden.'

The men slept in a single large lodge of buffalo hides. Fremont had his own smaller version. Camps were surrounded with all the mess of a plant hunting expedition: drying paper hung in any available breeze, open plant presses, press straps, boxes of dried material. Not all of it got back to the relevant institutes and their botanists. A pack mule carrying some of the plants fell into a chasm in the Siege Nevada on the second expedition, and its entire cargo was lost. A camp and all its materials was swept away down the Kansas river during a sudden flood.

For the men and beasts, things were often very hard indeed. Fremont noted that the Indian members of the expedition were often tougher than the whites. Winter 1854: 'The Delawares all came in cold, but the whites of my party were all exhausted and broken up, and more or less frost-bitten. I lost one, Mr. Fuller of St. Louis, Missouri, who died on entering this valley. He died like a man, on horseback in his saddle, and will be buried like a soldier, on the spot where he fell.'

The party was attacked by hostile Indians. On 25 October 1853 Fremont's artist Richard Kern, and botanist Frederick Creutzfeldt were both slain. Two seasons later, an expedition member wrote that the whole party was on foot. Lack of food made them weaker each day, and the cold was killing men and animals. They decided to dump part of the baggage to lighten all their loads. The men could at leat all ride again. Whenever a horse or mule died, or was killed for food, the man who had been riding it had to walk. Killed animals were divided into 20 parts, 10 for the Indians and 10 for the balance of the party. Each portion had to last for two days. The hungry consumed theirs in one day, then had to go without until the next horse or mule was killed. Each day the surviving men and animals became more gaunt and nearer starvation.

The tough travelling didn't diminish Fremont's social charm, and on leaving Iowa, he he secretly married Jessie Benton, the headstrong and intelligent 17-year-old daughter of Senator Thomas Hart Benton. Over the next few years, she took over the writing of his expedition reports, several of which sold well. They bought an estate at Mariposa in the Sierra foothills. By chance, it had good seam of gold, and Fremon (by now further Frenchified into Fremont) was suddenly a millionaire. With both money and contacts, he became a senator for California in 1850 and later even became the first Republican candidate for president. The American Civil War dislocated his life, as it did more terribly for so many others. He got a command in the Western Department of the Union Army, but his incompetence and his wife's rash actions forced President Abraham Lincoln to get rid of him.

Worse was to come. After the war Fremont lost his fortune through ill-conceived promotions of railroads, and his wife had to support the family with her writing. Finally, her connections got him the job of territorial governor of Arizona. He tried to use that position to regain his fortunes, and spent most of the time in his own personal mining schemes or land development. Nothing worked, and under some opprobrium, he returned to poverty and California. A few months before his death he was restored to his army rank of major general and was granted retirement pay. He died on July 13, 1890, in New York City.

His contribution to the garden included some notable shrubs like *Carpenteria californica*. The herbaceous border has blood from many of his plants. The bicoloured flowers of lupins are indebted to species he found. Sidalceas, liatrises, oenotheras, penstemons, mimuluses, cleomes, salvias, all have more. He found the silvery yellow *Lysimachia ciliata*, the smoky red *Sphaeralcea coccinea*, many sorts of milkwort, and the lovely golden foliaged *Carex aurea*.

Meanwhile, in Europe, the bedding garden was evolving fast. All sorts of plants were being forced into its over-riding need for uniformity of height. Recalcitrant plants were clipped to size, ruthlessly pruned, or had their sprawling branches pinned tightly to the ground. That was fine for verbenas or calceolarias. Even pelargoniums could be reduced in this way. The new clematis hybrids developed by Mr. Jackman were grown on horizontal frameworks of wire. But huge numbers of plants simply couldn't be treated so scurvily.

As gardeners wouldn't give them up, they had to be grown somewhere

else. This area devoted to recalcitrant plants was the herbaceous border.
Something similar had sometimes been planted around the perimeter of early
18th century parterres, often in a long bed against the surrounding walls, if
the garden were grand enough to have them. They'd survived into the early
19th century, when John Claudius Loudon in his 'Gardeners Dictionary'
wrote of their 'promiscuous' planting schemes. He uses that word to mean a
planting scheme where no two plants of the same sort were planted next to
one another. However, some of his suggested plants include the very latest
arrivals: *Anemone japonica, Zauschneria californica, Dicentra spectabilis.* It
was soon plain that every garden had to have a herbaceous border. All that
was needed was some way to make them look less of a mess.

At the same time, the bedding garden began to look, at least to some
enquiring gardeners, lurid. It was artificial, a system that reduced plants to
being merely the providers of undifferentiated colour. The tiniest gardens
had stars and scrolls of scarlet pelargonium, purple verbena and yellow
calceolaria, lobelia and petunia. Stylish gardeners shuddered and hoped for
something different.
William Robinson was to be the most audacious critic of the bedding garden.
In his book 'The Wild Garden' of 1870, he inveighed against what gardening
had become, with its insistence on intense maintenance and colour saturation.
He began to push the sort of plants that were hardy, wanting the reader to
grow thalictrums, anemones (like *A. appennina,* as well as the new *Anemone
japonica* 'Honorine Jobert'), and a vast list of hardy herbaceous flowers.
The new herbaceous border needed space. It had to display eupatoriums,
plume poppies, and the increasingly tall delphiniums. Borders needed to be at
least two metres deep to allow sufficient space for banks of colour, and they
could hardly be less than ten metres long to register at all. Their plants
needed spraying, staking, dividing, manuring; all endlessly time consuming
and very expensive. Their season only ran from midsummer to mid autumn,

which was insufficient in small gardens where it was the only element. The herbaceous border swiftly became one of the great artifices of the garden, hinting at the abundance of nature, but also at the abundance of the owner's purse. It allowed the wealthy to differentiate their sort of garden from the gardens seen on seafronts or in front of boarding houses. That it was also becoming increasingly wealthy in botanical terms too merely added to its attractions.

This wealth was not just derived from the flora of North America. The Treaty of Nanking of 1842 had opened China to foreigners for the first time. Botanists already knew that the seabord of China was filled with exciting and economically important plants. They wanted to see. What they didn't at first realise was that western China, with its colossal system of mountain chains and narrow valleys, was infinitely richer still. If that area took another few decades to be explored, and turned out to be exceptionally dangerous, even the coastal regions were hazardous. One explorer's tale, of a trip made in the late 1840's ran:

'About four o'clock in the afternoon the captain and pilot came hurriedly down to my cabin and informed me that they saw a number of Jan-do [pirates] right ahead, lying in wait for us.... I therefore considered it prudent to be prepared for the worst.

I got out of bed, ill and feverish as I was, and carefully examined my fire-arms.... I also rammed down a ball upon the top of each charge of shot in my gun, put a pistol in each side pocket, and patiently waited the result...

...All was now dismay and consternation on board our junk, and every man ran below except two who were at the helm. I expected every moment that these also would leave their post; and then we should have been an easy prey to the pirates. "My gun is nearer you than those of the Jan-dous," said I to the two men; "and if you move from the helm depend upon it I will shoot you". The poor fellows looked very uncomfortable.

The pirates now seemed quite sure of their prize, and came down upon us hooting and yelling like demons, at the same time loading their guns, and evidently determined not to spare their shot. This was a moment of intense interest....

The nearest junk was now within thirty yards of ours their guns were now loaded, and I knew that the next discharge would completely rake our decks. "Now," said I to our helmsmen, "keep your eyes fixed on me, and the moment you see me fall flat on the deck you must do the same".... We had scarcely done so, when bang! bang! went their guns, and the shot came whizzing close over us, splintering the wood about us in all directions.... "Now, mandarin, now! they are quite close enough", cried out my companions, who did not wish to have another broadside like the last. I, being of the same opinion, raised myself above the high stern of our junk; and while the pirates were not more than twenty yards away from us, hooting and yelling, I raked their decks fore and aft, with shot and ball from my double barrelled gun.

Had a thunderbolt fallen amongst them, they could not have been more surprised. Doubtless many were wounded, and probably some killed...

They were so completely taken by surprise that their junk was left without a helmsman... and, as we were still carrying all sail and keeping on our right course, they were soon left a considerable way astern.... Another was now bearing down upon us as boldly as his companion had done.... I determined to follow the same plan with this one, and to pay no attention to his firing until he should come to close quarters. The plot now began to thicken; for the first junk had gathered way again, and was following in our wake... and three others, although still further distant, were making for the scene of action as fast as they could. In the mean time, the second was almost alongside, and continued giving us a broadside now and then with their guns....

My poor fellows who were steering kept begging and praying that I would fire into our pursuers as soon as possible, or we should all be killed. As soon as they came within twenty or thirty yards of us, I gave them the contents of both barrels, raking their decks as before. This time the helmsman fell and doubtless several others were wounded.... their junk went up into the wind... and was soon left some distance behind us.... Two other piratical junks which had been following in our wake for some time, when they saw what had happened, would not venture any nearer; and at last, much to my satisfaction, the whole set of them bore away.'

The explorer in question was Robert Fortune, and his herbaceous plant haul included the marvellously beautiful white-flowered form of *Anemone japonica* that he'd found growing on the graves of Shanghai. Over several journeys in China and Japan, his contribution to the herbaceous border was enormous. From China alone it included, apart from the anemone, *Adamia versicolor, Arundinaria sinensis, Callistegia pubescens, Chirita sinensis* (later to win awards as a great garden plant), endless chrysanthemums,

Dielytra (now *Dicentra) spectabilis, Platycodon grandiflorum and P.grandiflorum* 'Album', huge numbers of paeonies, many ferns including the handsome *Cyrtomium fortunei, Statice Fortunei*, as well as campanulas, farfugiums, *Aster turbinellus, Eupatorium Fortunei, Gentiana scabra var. Fortunei* and more. From Japan he introduced yet more chrysanthemums, a variegated lily of the valley, the parasitic *Lastrea Standishii, Lilium auratum and L. lancifolium, Saxifraga Fortunei*, the gaudy leafed *S. stolonifera* 'Tricolor', and *Primula japonica*.

    He was born on September 16th, 1812, near Duns in Berwickshire, the son of a hedger on the Kelloe Estate. Showing plenty of talent, he went to work at the Royal Botanic Garden, Edinburgh from 1839, then sailed for London to become Superintendent of hothouses at the Horticultural Society's garden at Chiswick in 1842. As that was the year of the Treaty of Nanking, the Society was eager to obtain its rumoured botanical riches. By February 1843 Fortune got the job of Collector for the Society at a salary of pounds 100 a year. He was 31 years old. Then as now the Society was divided up into committees. The minutes of the Chinese Committee for 1842/3 drew up a job description. He was 'to collect seed and plants of an ornamental or useful kind, not already cultivated in Great Britain… and to obtain information upon Chinese Gardening and Agriculture together with the nature of the Climate and its apparent influence on vegetation'. He may already have seen a 'Wardian case' in a house overlooking the Botanic gardens in Edinburgh, and he was to make extensive use of them throughout his career. They were, in essence, small glasshouses. Young plants could be shipped around the globe, scarcely needing watering, and being free of sea spray, rats, and over-attentive sailors. They were kept in the light, on the poop if possible, or on deck, or failing that, more dramatically, 'in the Main or Mizzen-top'. The Society asked him to find all sorts of exotic plants, some entirely mythical like 'Peaches of Pekin', and the famed yellow flowered camellia. He was also to find 'Plants that yield Tea of different qualities', 'the plant which furnishes Rice Paper' and 'The Orange called CumQuat'. The Society issued him with the firearms that saved him from the pirates, and many letters of introduction.

Fortune's own story of his first visit to China was published in 1847 as "Three Year's Wanderings in the Northern Provinces of China", and was very popular. He took some remarkable risks for his plants. As no foreigner was allowed to travel more than 30 miles from the main ports of Amoy, Fuchou, Ningpo or Shanghai, Fortune took to disguise. He had his head shaved, wore a wig and tail, dressed in local clothes and, he writes, "made a pretty fair Chinaman". British officials certainly knew of this, and approved. It was astonishing that he wasn't discovered, for he visited endless Chinese nurseries, got followed around by Chinese children, even Chinese thugs, yet must have remained mute through all these encounters. Still, his collections grew, though at one point, near Ningpo, he tumbled into a pit dug to catch wild boar. He managed to grab a twig on the way down, and saved his life. Had any Chinese been near, his cover would certainly have been broken. He later mused that had the twig not held, he would have suffered the "fate of my predecessor, Mr Douglas, who perished in a pit of this kind on the Sandwich Islands.... his melancholy end naturally coming to my mind at the time, made me doubly thankful for my escape."

To make certain that his material reached Europe, he divided the collections into three or four consignments, sending them home on different boats, and by different routes. Travelling home with one of them, he wrote" As I went down the river I could not but look around me with pride and satisfaction; for in this part of the country I had found the finest plants in my collections.' When he returned from Japan, he turned out to be on the same boat as another soon-to-be-famous collector, John Gould Veitch. He was amused to see the boat loaded 'so that the whole of the poop was lined with glass cases crammed full of the natural productions of Japan. Never before had such an interesting and valuable collection of plants occupied the deck of any vessel, and most devoutly did we hope that our beloved plants might be favoured with fair winds and smooth seas.'

Many of his and Veitch's plants had long been known, even domesticated, in Chinese gardens. The great centres of Chinese culture were all in the eastern parts of the country. The far reaches of the west, where the mountainous terrain made communication and cultivation so difficult, were

the home of strange indigenous peoples with strange languages. China raised
what taxes it could, but left the inhabitants otherwise to themselves. Christian
missionaries had had, over several centuries, mixed fortunes in China.
However, towards the end of the 19th century, French missionary societies
sent substantial numbers of priests to China. These men, some of exceptional
energy and imagination, fanned out through the country, some into the
country's remote western regions.

That area of the country, bordering on Myanmar (Burma) and Bhutan,
is part of the eastern system of mountains thrown up as India crashes
formidably into the great tectonic plates to the north and east. The Yangtse
river penetrates to their very centre. As with all new mountain chains, the
valleys formed are deep and steep sided. The climate in them can often run
from humid and sub-tropical at the base, to plantless and permanently
snowed-up at the top. This change can be encompassed in less than a
kilometer of horizontal difference. The plant communities even in adjacent
valleys are genetically completely isolated from one another as pollinating
insects cannot easily cross the topographical barriers. Either through
haphazard events, or through environmental and climatic pressures, plant
species change rapidly. Without the stablising influence of large amounts of
their original genetic material from distant populations, plant populations
soon alter to become, as far a plant taxonomists are concerned, new species.
All new mountain chains are rich in species. Western China is astonishingly
rich for it also lies at the junction of three huge floristic regions, those of the
tropic south, the Indian continent, and the Middle East.

When the French missionaries interested in Chinese plants began to
send material back to Paris, it was at once clear that they had stumbled into a
treasure trove. The first to send material home was Abbe Armand David. The
Chinese had been forced to agree to allow missionaries to travel throughout
their entire land in 1860. In 1862, Abbe David received a posting to the
Mission of Lazarists in Peking, where he was to teach science and natural
history. By now he was a man of thirty six. Born in Espelette, a small
Pyrenean town, he was one of the three sons of Fructueux David, the local
doctor, mayor and magistrate. Fructueux had three passions: medicine, good
food and natural history. He had a son for each. Young Armand became the
natural historian, walking the Navarre foothills for eleven or twelve hours in
a day hunting for interesting things for his collection. It was a good training.
Once in China, he couldn't help but continue. His beautifully prepared

specimens from remote regions of Mongolia, central China and the Tibetan border caused a sensation in the scientific circles in Paris. He was given leave from his missionary duties so that he could concentrate on collecting.

He made three huge journeys in the late 1860's. All of them were undertaken with a remarkable disregard for comfort or safety: he said that if he took notice of such things he would never get anywhere. He was often ill, often caught up in local wars, was almost always in places where he was the first westerner ever to be seen, and the object of intense suspicion by local monks. He found transport hard to find, and difficult to keep. Once, having found an obliging donkey, he discovered that the local wolves were so hungry at night that he had to share his tent with the donkey for its protection. There were huge compensations. He was the first westerner ever to see a panda. He found rare wild silkworms. He saw an astonishing new tree, with white bracts the size of handkerchiefs. It was to become named *Davidia involucrata*. He saw endless other new plants. Sometimes he was so weak and exhausted, he fainted and couldn't go on. Sometimes he was stuck on a riverbank for months waiting for a spate to subside. Even when rivers were navigable, conditions were hard; once on the upper reaches of the Yangtse, in a region of rapids and gorges, it took eighty hauliers to get his boat up through the current. The tow rope broke several times; the gorge's shallows were littered with the ominous remains of previous wrecks. He got malaria, severe bouts of 'intestinal irritation', even symptoms of typhus. With terrible pain and swelling in the legs, Chinese doctors called it 'bone-typhus' and treated him with ginger and onions moistened with brandy. He was obliged to cut short his visit and leave for more civilised regions. After years in the field, he journeyed back to Shanghai in a sedan chair, but his malaria got so bad that he was given the last rites. He didn't die, and made it back to Paris, where he was to find over eighty species of plants growing in the garden of the Natural History Museum, from seeds he had sent home.

Even so, these were but a fraction of his botanical discoveries. Many were eventually brought back to European and American gardens by others. However, his botanical collections were published as 'Plantae Davidianae', in sumptuous volumes, the first of which contained forty-five illustrations, hand-colored in some copies. It appeared in 1884. A second volume, devoted to the plants of eastern Tibet, followed in 1888. Whatever ills he had suffered in China, he lived to see his seventy-sixth year, lecturing to prospective missionaries in the rooms of his own museum.

Many of David's plants were trees and shrubs. However, here is an astonishing list of sumptuous plants from the same region, and all now widely grown: *Thalictrum delavayi, Thalictrum dipterocarpum, Anemone delavayi*, huge numbers of delphinium species, *Paeonia delavayi, Paeonia lutea, Meconopsis betonicifolia*, huge numbers of corydalis, dozens of *Draba, Rogersia pinnata*, huge numbers of *Saxifraga*, huge numbers of *Sedum*, the lovely *Primula delavayi, Primula malacoides*, the wildly coloured and popular *Primula vialli* (named after a M. Vial), huge numbers of gentians, *Clematis chrysocoma*, dozens of Androsace, Lilium, the first *Nomocharis* species, *Roscoea*, several sorts of *Trollius*, and, of course, *Incarvillea delavayi*.

The list gives the clue: their collector was Pere Jean Marie Delavay (1838-1895). Little seems known about his early life. Born in Abondance, Haute-Savoie, France, he doesn't emerge from the shadows until he is already a missionary priest, and reaches the Chinese region of Guangdong. He must have been interested in plants before he arrived, for hunting them soon became an obsession. He had first started collecting in a small way in order to oblige Dr Henry Fletcher Hance, a member of the British Consular Service in Canton and Hong Kong. However, in 1881, Delavay went home to France on leave, and while in Paris he met Pere David. David introduced him to Adrien Rene Franchet, the Director of the Natural History Museum, and immediately Delavay agreed to send his future collections to Franchet. Franchet had no idea what he was setting in motion. He proved unable to cope with the flood of material that Delavay soon started to send.

Franchet had managed with David's plants, describing more than 250 new species and ten or eleven new genera. He had even managed to publish 'Plantae Davidianae'. But Delavay sent him some 200,000 beautifully prepared specimens, constituting 4000 species, about 1500 of them new. Overwhelmed, Franchet tried to write a short list of Delavay's plants in 1885, but got no further than the letter 'A'. He tried to start on a 'Plantae Delavayi' in 1889, but died before it was finished. Some consignments of Delavay's material were not even opened for another few decades.

Unlike Pere David, who was released by his order from any attempt at gaining Chinese souls for Christianity, Delavay had missionary work to do as well. He seems to have managed both strands of his life by exploring a relatively small area of China with great intensity: he is said to have climbed Mt. Tsemei Shan, which he called 'his garden', sixty times from all sides and at all seasons. Contemporary plant collectors increasingly find this an important approach, for the flora of the region is so rich, that even a month can bring into flower an entirely new range of species. Even with such an intensive cover of a small area, Delavay realised that he had hardly tapped the resources of the rich Chinese alpine flora.

He, like David, seems not to have noticed any dangers, even though a few years later, two colleagues of his were to meet the terrible ends described in Chapter XX. He couldn't, though, avoid one of the scourges of Asia. In 1888 he contracted bubonic plague, and though it didn't kill him, he lost the use of his right arm and was in bad health for the few years he had left to live. He got home to France once more, loaded with specimens and seeds, then returned to China in 1893. He reached Yun-nan-sen in February 1895, and died in December. Few of the seeds did well, though *Deutzia purpurascens, Incarvillea delavayi, Iris delavayi, Paeonia lutea* and *Rhododendron racemosum* soon reached the garden. His herbarium material entranced gardeners. It launched a dozen collectors, anxious to be the first to bring home, and establish, marvellous herbaceous plants like *Meconopsis betonicifolia, Primula malacoides, Thalictrum dipterocarpum* and the genus *Nomocharis.*

Of course, once many of the plants were established, gardeners were overwhelmed by such marvels. They had to grow them, they had to find somewhere to put them. The herbaceous border was, for the larger plants, the obvious place. Some of the new genera and species allowed new effects. No-one had ever seen anything like the purple haze of the *Thalictrum delavayii* before, or wondered what to plant with the exotic pink trumpets of *Incarvillea.* Using new marvels from China, and the new hybrids fast developing in dozens of other genera, designers like Gertrude Jekyll were able to start playing with painterly ideas. She could invent the colour scheme for a border, then look for plants to fill the roles needed. Many of her plans survive, but are often so sumptuous that they can hardly be recreated today. Other designers used much simpler schemes which are much more relevant to contemporary gardeners.

One excellent designer was Miss Hope, a spinster of Edinburgh, who wrote frequently for the magazines of the day, notably the 'Gardener's Chronicle' and 'The Garden'. She liked combining some of the new red or creamy white paeonies with the perfumed lemon yellow flowers of *Hemerocallis lilio-asphodelus*. For smaller plantings, she combined *Delphinium formosanum* with the greeny pink and thread-like petals of *Tellima grandiflora*. For larger ones she mixed white spires of *Aruncus sylvester* with the cold yellow *Aconitum vulparia* and the cream variegated leaves of gardeners garters (*Phalaris arundinacea* 'Elegantissima'), or glittering rust red *Papaver orientalis* with straw coloured irises.

However, many plants created for the herbaceous borders of the early 20th century today face extinction. Purism amongst gardeners is on the increase, and fancifully named and flamboyantly over-developed hybrids are seen as less admirable than pure species collected from the meadows of the mid-west USA, or the valleys of Yunnan. Yet what has happened to the flowers in the garden, and at the hands of the gardener, is only what can happen in nature, but vastly speeded up. Continents no longer need to collide, or valley systems erode, or be scoured clean by glaciers. We gardeners bring plants together. We gardeners get hooked by our plants. Their evolutionary possibilities are hugely enhanced by our weakness for them. They win.
END

Chapter 6

The Glass Garden

David Stuart

THE GLASS GARDEN

On a frozen late afternoon in December 1843, at the Duke of Devonshire's stupendous garden at Chatsworth in Derbyshire, England, the Great Conservatory's vast central aisle was lit by twelve thousand tiny lamps. Their light shone softly on the foliage and flowers of plants gathered from the jungles of Guatamala and Gabon, from the dripping foothills of the Himalayas, and from the swamps of the Malayan archipelago. Footment rushed to the great glass doors, opened them, and in clattered an equipage of jet black horses harnessed to an open carriage. The landau bore the young Queen Victoria and Prince Albert. They had come to look at one of the most astonishing glasshouses ever built, and one that contained one of the greatest collections of fabulous rarities ever assembled. Yet, in spite of the orchids, many of which had been collected especially for the duke, the twining palms from South America, gaudy bougainvilleas, the colossal ferns, the new begonias and pandanus and passionflowers, the Duke's glasshouse was going

on to hold more extraordinary plants still. What he had growing in his
epitome of glasshouses, everyone soon wanted. They soon were to have a
good part of it.

    Houses for exotic 'greens' had appeared in the gardens of the rich in the
sixteenth century, but they were little more than a spare room in the garden
quarters, with minimal heating, usually an open fireplace, for winter.
Lemons, myrtles, oleanders were amongst their winter inhabitants. The
orangery, popular well into the eighteenth century, was hardly much of an
advance. Even Botanic gardens, like those at Leiden in Holland, and at
Oxford in England, where heated 'green' houses were built between 1680
and 1687, had glazed roofs, but apart from that advance, were scarcely more
sophisticated. Plants sent home by seventeenth century collectors like Dr.
Paul Hermann, from his voyages to South Africa and the Far East, had little
chance of survival.

    Things changed gradually. The growers of exotic greens looked to the
kitchen garden, where gardeners had long been aware of the heat given off by
fermenting farmyard dung. They had used it to to bring on early vegetables
like asparagus and peas, or to induce melons to fruit in northern Europe. Bell
jars, glass cloches, or even whole frames, were placed on hotbed built of
horse manure, and the plants grown in pockets of soil. Glass became
gradually cheaper through the eighteenth century, and glasshouses of the sort
we would recognise today were built in the kitchen gardens of the wealthy.
At first, they were still heated by fermenting manure beds. Even in northern
climes, the technology could give prodigious crops of pineapples, early
cherries, strawberries, asparagus and so on. The dung gave off large amounts
of water vapour, as well as heat, and a certain degree of smell. Glasshouses
were clearly not suited to all plants, nor all people. Alternatives were
needed. At first, the back walls of lean-to glasshouses were built containing
winding chimney flues. With a furnace fed from the back of the house, hot air
and fumes wound up through the wall, heating the air in which the plants
grew. The level of heat depended on the skill of whomsoever fed the
furnace. The heat was very dry, which encouraged pests like red spider. Any

leakage of fumes into the glasshouse rapidly killed the plants. Again, alternatives were needed. This was becoming more and more urgent, as tropical plants were beginning to be sent to colder climates in increasing numbers, and gardeners were getting the itch to grow them.

Finally, in the early nineteenth century, and especially during the Napoleonic wars, the art of casting iron became far more refined, and very much cheaper, than it had ever been. Iron stoves became efficient. Iron tubing to hold hot water or even steam became cheap. Coal was plentiful. The scene was set. The repeal of Britain's glass tax in 1845 was, in that country at least, the trigger to a huge increase in the ownership of glasshouses. It enabled the them to move from the kitchen garden, and attach themselves, as conservatories, to ordinary homes. Suddenly, there was a colossal market for the exotic vegetation of the tropics.

Soon glasshouses ranged from backyard leantos for the culture of calceolarias from Brazil, to Decimus Burton's Palm House at Kew or the the private jungles of great princes like Prince Potemkin's vast conservatory at the Tauridian Palace in St Petersburg. This his gardener, Mr Gould, had heated the with hot-water pipes. 'Great emulation now exists in this department of horticulture not only among country gentlemen but among commercial Gardeners,' wrote John Loudon in the edition of his Encyclopaedia of Gardening published in 1828. In London, the firm of Conrad Loddiges was renowned among the nurserymen for its palm house, 45 feet high and 60 feet wide, and for its plant house 23 feet wide, 18 feet high and upwards of l00 feet long which stood without a single rafter or standard.

All this excitement was the result of a series of great expeditions, mostly French, to South America. One of the first was that of Charles-Marie de La Condamine. The basic quest was to to measure the diameter of the globe, but Joseph de Jussieu went out as the expedition botanist. They sailed from La Rochelle on May 16th 1735. The whole trip was a drama; when on land they were caught up in riots and war, while at sea, seem continually to have been wrapped in storms, or long calms when men got sick and died. Botanically, it was, though, vastly influential. Jussieu sent home the first Cinchona trees, the first coca plants, and La Condamine noticed indians using a strange resin that could be moulded and which bounced. The rubber tree, *Hevea brasiliensis,* thereby reached the West. Joseph sent back the first heliotropes, the first cinnamon, sumptuous magnolias, and more. It was all carried out under terrible difficulties; several members of the expedition went mad, some were slain, some died of disease. La Condamine lasted it out for ten years, returning in 1744. Joseph seems to have become deeply, even morbidly, mesmerised by the jungles and couldn't tear himself away. He stayed on in Peru, earning a living as a doctor. His brothers entreated him to return, and once they even managed to get him to the dockside. He vanished back into the wilderness just as the ship was to sail, and ended up ministering to the miners of Bolivia, especially in the notorious Potosi mines. At last, a few years later, his surviving brother sent friends to fetch him home. His notes were lost at sea or mouldered, and in Paris, crushed, he sat mute in a darkened room until death released him.

However, such of his collections that had reached home made it abundantly clear that South America was packed tight with economically important plants, and ones of the greatest beauty. The French Government, and the ageing Bernard de Jussieu thought that another expedition should be mounted to replace Joseph's missing material. Bernard suggested a pupil of his, Joseph Dombey. He had a personality very different to Bernard's brother, being gay, charming, extravagant, and quite deeply in debt. He loved gambling. He loved women. He was also quite a good botanist, and a good doctor. Perhaps he would hold up better. However, he needed the consent of the Spanish government, if he was to visit Spanish South America. Though his expedition increased the glasshouse flora with many cactus, including the fascinating white-haired *Cephalocereus*, with many new begonias, many new orchids, and the ineffable bedding plant *Salvia splendens*, he should never have set off. The Spanish authorities, having consented to the project, imposed ridiculous conditions. The best of his material was to go to Madrid, not Paris. He had to travel with two Spanish pharmacists who would oversee his work. Draughtsmen were to be included in the personel too, but their drawings were not to be available to Dombey. He was made to wait for two years in Madrid before the expedition even set off.

They sailed at last about the end of October 1777, and arrived at Callao on 8 April 1778, proceeding to Lima the following day; this was to be their base for nearly four years. There was a curious unreality about the whole affair. Though paid much less than the Spaniards, Dombey seemed to have inexhaustible funds. He himself travelled with several servants, bought Inca antiquities, including an Inca robe which had cost him nearly seven months' salary, and which he wanted to give to Louis XVI. He loaned money to his companions, spent much of his time treating the sick for free, and dispensing free medicines, even setting up, at his own expence, hospitals for the needy. One of the Spaniards, Hipolito Ruiz Lopez (1754-1816) travelled over mountain ranges, and through virgin jungles, with a full wardrobe that contained five suits (one of silk), three pairs of velvet breeches and seven of plain white; two dressing-gowns, sixteen pairs of stockings, fourteen shirts, twelve pairs of shoes, three cloaks, hair-nets and sleeping-caps; his camping equipment included four table-cloths, many pieces of plate, a chintz bedspread and a silver chamberpot. He later lost them all in 1785, during a brush fire at a camp in the jungle at the hacienda of Macora. He and Pavon lost tents, equipment, collections, three years' journals, and even the garden where they had been growing plants for despatch to Spain.

In 1778 Dombey sent his first duplicate collections to France and Spain. Next year, he sent of an even larger amount of material, both plants, seeds and bulbs, and Peruvian antiquities. Spain, France and the American colonies were now at war with England, and his consignment had the misfortune to be captured by the British. His collections were ransomed by Spain, who then claimed the whole contents as its own. The war ended in 1783, making it possible for the botanists to return home. Now it was Dombey's turn to become obsessed with the strange pyramidal jungle ruins. He was equally absorbed even by their Jesuit replacements, like the cathedral that they built on the ruins of the Temple of the Serpent. He, who had once been lighthearted and frivolous, was now absorbed by the sense of death that they emanated. But he was getting ill with scurvy. He had dizzy spells. With permission received, and a free passage home, at which he never ceased to marvel, he sailed for Cadiz on 4 April 1784. He had with him his French share of the collections: seventy three cases of minerals, manuscripts, dried plants, antiquities, wood and bark samples, fish, birds, insects, reptiles and shells. The Spanish share he handed over to Ruiz and Pavon, who despatched it with their own collection by the 'San Pedro de Alacantara'. There were fifty-five cases and thirty-one tubs of living plants, together with bulbs and seeds. But the 'San Pedro' was lost at sea, and the Spanish government insisted on holding on to all of Dombey's material when it reached Cadiz. He reached Cadiz on 22 February 1785. There, ignorant and obstructive officials ensured that plants died, specimens and manuscripts mouldered away. Spain acquired thirty-seven boxes out of his seventy-three; an exact copy was taken of all descriptions and field-notes. His property was not released, nor his departure allowed, until he had promised not to publish anything before Ruiz and Pavon's return. He reached Paris at last with the scant remnants of what he had hoped would bring him fame on 13 October 1785. It is hardly surprising that the once happy and confident Dombey became a misanthrope and a recluse.

What happened next is still a matter of of accusation between French and Spanish botanical historians. It was undoubtedly Dombey's botanical knowledge that made the expedition possible. It was undoubtedly carried out on what was then Spanish soil. There was a race to publish. Once Dombey had got back to Paris, the 'Journal Géneral de France' published, on 14th January 1786, the news that the Chevalier L'Heritier would take charge of studying and describing the plants. The celebrated naturalist Buffon himself presented the Domby Collection to Ch. L'Heritier and arranged the publication of the work. Cheekily, it was to be done on English printing presses to circumvent the condition set by the Spanish Court. It almost became a diplomatic incident. However, the first volume of the 'Flora Peruviana et Chilensis' by Ruiz and Pavon appeared in 1798. Eight volumes and an appendix were planned, but only three were published. The book was largely based on Dombey's work; his name appeared in the preface, but there was no further reference to him. Though he had in fact got back to Paris with 60 new genera, discovering that the Spaniards published first, and with no acknowledgement of his huge work, he burnt his manuscripts in disgust. Though the Revolution hailed him, he couldn't bear to see its upheaval and violence. He obtained a permit to go to back to America to buy corn and other commodities for a needy France. When he landed at Guadelupe in the West Indies, he found that revolution had spread there too. He was imprisoned. He was released. On further mischance, he fell into a river, thereafter had acute fever, and was told to leave the island. He did, but his ship was attacked by two corsairs, and he was detected disguised as a Spanish sailor. He was eventually imprisoned by the British on Montserrat. He died there in 1796. His herbarium material, which had been taken to England, was collected by l'Heritier, who was himself assassinated on his return to France.

Ruiz afterwards wrote that he had suffered 'heat, fatigue, hunger, thirst, nakedness, want, storms, earthquakes, plagues of mosquitoes and other insects, continuous danger of being devoured by jaguars, bears and other wild beasts, traps of thieves and disloyal Indians, treason of slaves, falls from precipices and the branches of towering trees, fording of rivers and torrents, the fire at Macora... the separation from Dombey, the death of the artist Brunete, and the most touching of all, the loss of manuscripts'.

Ruiz and Pavon got back in 1788; it was January 1793 before suitable accommodation was found for them, and where their cases could at last be unpacked. Their material is now at the Botanical Garden of Madrid, or the Office of Natural History. It contained one hundred and fifty new genera and around fiive hundred new species. Ruiz died in 1816, and Pavon, impoverished, was reduced to hawking round his spare herbarium specimens. He died in Madrid in 1840.

Whatever human wreckage there was, nothing could stop the rise of the glasshouse mania in the garden. After the opening scene at Chatsworth, three years later the royal couple heard of even more astonishing things that the duke's gardeners were nurturing. There were some extremely precious seedlings, and it took several seasons before these young plants flowered in their extraordinary ducal foothold. Even so, they had already become a legend, and had spawned, at least amongst the very rich, large numbers of the new glasshouses built especially for them. They didn't flower at Chatsworth until 1848. Nevertheless, the duke was the first owner in Europe to see his ones in flower. The blooms were soft pink, many petalled, pineapple scented, and over forty five centimetres across. They rose above leaves that were often two metres in diameter. The plant was a waterlily.

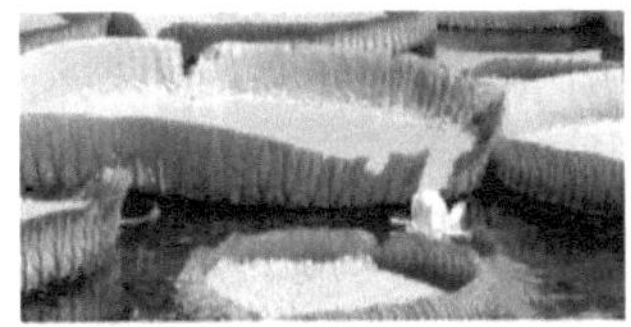

Then named *Victoria regia* after the queen herself, what is now called *Victoria amazonica* is still one of the world's most extraordinary plants. It was first discovered growing in that river on January 1st. 1837 by Sir Robert Schomburgk. Though he collected and sent home orchids and other exotics, he didn't manage to collect seed of the waterlily. His stories of it, though, created a sensation in Europe. Rich gardeners had to have it, even though it was obviously going to need huge pools and warm water in which to flourish. If the hugely wealthy dreamt of growing it, collectors worldwide dreamed of harvesting seed. The first to do so was Aimee Bonpland, but that he was still alive at all was a miracle.

On a day in 1821, the skies above an old Jesuit college in northern Argentina, recently converted to a botanic garden, were thick with smoke. The newly restored buildings and the surrounding village were in flames. Its fields were burning. Badly wounded and wrapped in chains, the garden's director, Aimee Bonpland was dragged away, past the bleeding corpses of his beloved Indian workers. He must have thought his own last day had come. He had already contributed hugely to gardens worldwide, and to European glasshouses in particular. Yet, his most extraordinary contribution was yet to come.

Aimée Jacques Goujaud Bonpland was born 28 August 1773, in a house on one of the lovely arcaded streets in the ancient seaport of La Rochelle, France. His father was a prosperous surgeon who was also a fanatical gardener, and whose private conversation was filled with plant names. The young Aimee took on his both his father's interests, and studied to be a physician, though all the while being more fascinated by plants than humans. Studying in Paris under Lamark, Jussieu, and Desfontaines, he gravitated towards the more scientifically orientated 'salons' of that exciting city. In particular, he was drawn to the circle that surrounded the rakish, handsome and immensely civilised Louis-Antoine Bougainville (1729-1811). Bougainville plays a central role in another fascinating relationship later in this chapter, but for Bonpland he was to play a vastly important role too. One evening in Bougainville's company, Bonpland met a man who was to completely alter his life, who was to remain a constant and involved friend until death parted them, and with whom he would travel on an epoch making journey to tropical South America. Their names will be linked for as long as mankind likes plants. The man was Alexander von Humboldt. Humboldt has always been seen as the brightest star in the partnership. He was an aristocrat. He was, when he met Bonpland, rich. He was voluble and sociable, and found it easy to make influential connections. Yet, it was Bonpland who was to make the largest contribution to the garden, and whose own personal journey became a quite extraordinary story.

Friedrich Wilhelm Heinrich Alexander von Humboldt had been born in Berlin on Sept. 14, 1769. His father, a minor aristocrat, was an officer in the army of Frederick the Great. His mother, a French Hugenot, a cold and bigoted woman, raised her two sons in a rigorous way that would fit them both for high public positions. Alexander didn't thrive under her regime, and spent fruitless years trying to study economics at Frankfurt and Berlin. Then, apparently out of the blue, he became passionately interested in botany. He began to collect plant specimens and to classify them. Brandenburg's flora is not rich, and he was soon dreaming of travel to the jungles. He began to develop a career in mining, but also began to develop and odd theory that the rich flora of the world's jungles was due to magnetism of the area in which they grew.

On his mother's death, he was left substantial means. Resigning his mining job in 1797, he moved to Paris, a city then in intellectual and political ferment. He was 29. Believing that all the sciences were interdependent, he most passionately wanted to go to South America, thinking that the luxuriant and primitive jungle there would bear out his theories. It was immediately apparent once he and Bonpland met, that a very strong friendship would develop. Like Dombey, he too needed Spanish permission to visit South America. Unlike Dombey, he was well connected. Through Baron Forell, Ambassador of Saxony, Humboldt and Bonpland were introduced to King Carlos IV and received direct permission from him to explore Mexico and South America, though at their own expense. Bonpland had no private means, and the French state was similarly embarassed. Humboldt decided to finance the whole expedition himself, paying all of his friend's expenses too. In the early summer of 1799 they set sail from Marseille, and landed near Caracas on July 15 1799.

The impact on them of the tropics was immediate. They were both completely overwhelmed by the sheer size and exuberance of the vegetation, and realised that no European could conceive, from the literature, what it was really like. The very European Humboldt was equally astonished to find that man was not in the least central to all this raw nature, but just one of a myriad of peripheral animal. He found that 'this animated nature, where man is nothing, is both strange and sad' He should have rejoiced.

The journey that the two men made was astonishing. They spent five years, from 1799 to 1804, in Central and South America, covering more than 6,000 miles (9,650 kilometres) on foot, on horseback, and in canoes. It was a life of great physical exertion and serious deprivation. They proved that the Casiquiare River formed a connection between the vast river systems of the Amazon and the Orinoco. In the dense tropical forests, tormented by clouds of mosquitoes and stifled by the humid heat, they became exhausted. Their provisions were destroyed by strange insects and incessant rain. They subsisted on ground-up wild cacao beans and river water, never ceasing to be amazed by the marvellous plants and the exotic animals, even though on one trip they lost seven horses, electrocuted by electric eels. After all that, the two men and their party arrived at San Carlos de Rio Negro near Brazil/Colombian border, and on the Brazilian side, Humboldt was at once arrested by the Portuguese on suspicion of being a Spanish border survey, but he managed to convince them that that was not the case, and after some harassment, they were all released. In spite of the privations, both travellers, buoyed up by the excitement of their collections, remained healthy and in the best of spirits. Only once they reached civilisation, at places like Cuidad

Bolivar, did they immediately succumbed to a severe bout of fever. Bonpland became seriously ill. Once he had recovered, he sent yet more plants back to France, and as Humboldt had agreed, to Spain. They already included around fifty new species of passion flower, endless fuchsias, cinerarias, zinnias and new genera of orchids. He had also become entranced by the hundreds of sorts of palms, and the roles that they played in the lives of the jungle indians. Some of the palms found new roles in the drawing rooms and glasshouses of Europe. Some found their way to Chatsworth.

Humboldt was very anxious to visit a correspondent who had become a serious collector, but also an expert on the cinchona tree, source of quinine. José Celestino Mutis, whom Linneus had grandly named 'phytologorum americanorum princeps', had an estate near Bogota. They decided to make the journey by land and a long fifty-five day river journey up the Rio Magdalena, where they were welcomed by Mutis with great cordiality, and lodged in a house adjacent to his own. Mutis had studied medicine at Seville and Madrid and, from 1757, practised as a physician at Madrid, where he became fascinated by plants. Soon afterwards he went to South America as physician-in-ordinary to the newly-appointed Viceroy of New Granada. He rapidly tried to develop the scientific world in Spanish South America. He taught mathematics. He became an astronomer and set up an observatory. He became a priest too, even whilst planning to write a flora of New Granada. He settled in Mariquita, near Bogota. It was there that Humbolt and Bonpland stayed, fascinated by his collections and his plantation.

The travellers stayed three months in the capital, partly to allow Bonpland to recuperate after another bout of fever, contracted on the journey. They set off once more on 8th September 1801. At times they hacked through virgin jungle. At other, they rested in towns like Popayan, where the botanizing was good and the climate delightful. They climbed volcanos like Purace and Chimborazo, where they both suffered from mountain sickness, which Humboldt correctly attributed to lack of oxygen. They survived the rainy season in the paramos where the gales were bitterly cold and, far above the treeline, there was no shelter. Finally, in the spring of 1803, the two travellers sailed from Guayaquil to Acapulco, Mexico, where they spent the last year of their expedition. After a short stay in the United States, at President Jefferson's invitation, they arrived back in France in August 1804.

As Humboldt had sent back accounts of their travels and discoveries throughout the journey, they were both now famous. They had enriched the known flora of the world by an astonishing five percent. There was a huge demand for not only their scientific results, but also for their travellers tales. The scientific material eventually took up 26 volumes of notes and stories. Once the travellers tales were published, and which were a huge success from 1810 onwards, Bonpland still needed a job. While Humboldt settled back naturally enough, though with a much reduced income, into the sophisticated society of Paris, Bonpland somehow hadn't returned from Amazonia. However, the Empress Josphine, with her 5000 acres at Malmaison, and her huge plant collections, including most of Masson's cape heaths, the newly imported dahlias, cactuses, orchids, roses, Bonpland's passionflowers, needed a botanist. Bonpland went to work for her. He compiled, with the artist Redoute, the 'Plantes de la Malmaison'. He was consulted by every grand gardener in Europe, and was in touch with great nurserymen like Vilmorin, Perregaux, Noisette, and Cels. It wasn't enough. He was also at the mercy of othe people's lives. When Napoleon at last rejected the extravagant Josephine, Bonpland lost his job. Bonpland was once more depressed, and had also married unhappily.

He began travelling. In England he met Joseph Banks at Kew. That seems to have made him realise, in 1816, that he had to get back to South America. By chance, one evening at Humboldt's modest attic appartment in the Latin Quarter, he met Simon Bolivar. Bolivar was fascinated to meet someone who knew so much about South American crop plants and their local uses. Bolivar also knew that the botanist's personal life was miserable and unsettled, and that he had detested the sometimes shoddy glitter of Josephine's entourage. When Bolivar then suggested that they both travel back to the wilds of Argentina, Bonpland's dream of escape was answered. Leaving his wife behind, he set off back to South America in 1816. Bolivar had found a former Jesuit college in north of Argentina, near the Paraguayan border. It had a large estate, and Bonpland at once started its restoration. It was soon magnificently productive.

Bolivar wanted him to create a botanic garden and experimental farm. Argentina being poor, Bonpland was financing the new institute by growing and selling mate plants, an important and profitable tea crop. It was a great success. That made it dangerous. Across the Parana river, Jose Gaspar Rodriguez Francia, the despotic 'el supremo' of adjacent Paraguay, wanted to set up a monopoly of mate for himself. Argentinian growers had to be destroyed, amongst them, Aimee Bonpland. He organised the raid, at whose end we first met the hapless Bonpland.

Though the Indians were murdered, Bonpland was too famous throughout Europe and the Americas to be killed. Nevertheless, despite an almost immediate flood of threats and pleas from more law abiding states, including the United States, Francia kept Bonpland in chains for several months. Surviving this treatment, the botanist was then placed in detention in a remote Paraguayan village. He remained there for ten years. With no financial support, but an extensive knowledge of local medicinal plants, he turned doctor in order to eat. Ironically, with his simple life and his care for the indians, Bonpland became universally loved throughout Paraguay, and gradually became a political, rather than an economic, challenge to the dictator. To his immense surprise, Bonpland was banished back to Argentina.

Aged 58, he once again started to form a botanical institute, this time near Corrientes, a trading town on the banks of the River Parana across which he'd once been dragged. He began, once more, to send plant material back to France. He even tried marriage again, this time to an indian woman. The new institute, and the new marriage, was a success, and while he was most especially absorbed by the study of indian food crops and medicinal plants, astonishingly, he went off to collect seeds of the gorgeous but useless Victoria amazonica growing in the Parana river system. Once found, he sent seed back to the famous Parisian firm of Vilmorin. French grandees, as well as the English Duke of Devonshire, were soon busily redesigning their conservatories to enclose suitably large pools.

Bonpland and Humboldt never forgot one another. Every so often, Humboldt would beg his friend to return to Europe. But Bonpland had now a great mission of his own. However, nothing for Bonpland was easy. Accepted by neither indians nor their rulers, his children turned out to be uninterested in what he was trying to accomplish. Money was always a difficulty, but he struggled on. On the death of his wife, he finally lost heart. He retired to a two-room shack on the estate, and without his leadership to guide it, the weeds, however desirable some were in European glasshouses, began to encroach on the fields and plant beds. Humboldt begged him once more to return to his care, and getting no reply, sent a Dr Lallemand to see how Bonpland was doing. The doctor found a radiant but frail old man, muddling dates and endlessly returning to thoughts of his terrible captivity in Paraguay.

There was one final strange touch. Bonpland died in hospital on May 11 1858. His fame was so great that his body was to be embalmed, awaiting a great state funeral. As it lay on its bed, awaiting the process, a passing indian, a close acquaintance of Bonpland's in life, drunk, passed the time of day. Recieving no reply, he stabbed the corpse in a frenzy. It had to be buried immediately. Humboldt himself died the following year. He was ninety, and had just finished his great work, based on his and Bonpland's travels of all those years ago: Kosmos.

By now, in Europe, exotic flowers from the jungles of the world had become the rage. The great waterlily flowered in 1849. The duke's gardener, Paxton, designed the immense glasshouse of the Crystal Palace for London's Great Exhibition of 1851.

But there was a third, tremendous, French expedition. Philibert Commerson was late. In his hectic life, this wasn't unusual. This time he was liable to miss a boat, one on which he very much wanted to sail. It was the Etoile, docked at Rochefort, an ungainly four hundred and eighty ton storeship, 33.8 metres long, and with a complement of 8 officers and 108 men. The captain was the kindly Francois Chenard de la Giraudais. The companion ship to the Etoile, the Boudeuse, was docked at Nantes, and together they were to embark on on one of the first great global scientific expeditions. The expedition's prime mover was the young Louis-Antoine

Bougainville, whom we have already met. Commerson, a botanist, was taken on as the ship's naturalist and doctor. He was also a man escaping private unhappiness.

He pressed the postillion to drive faster. He later wrote, 'I had to traverse the dangerous part of the Luberon... to find that no postillion would agree to go, because four or five days before this a chaise had been robbed on this road. I exhibited the King's order, for I was travelling on his service, and so forced the postmaster to obey me. Yet, in spite of this, the only person willing to ride the posthorse was a young rascal of eleven or twelve years old, who indeed was both skilful and courageous, for his beggarly comrades did all they could to discourage himg crying 'Go and get yourself killed.' He replied quite cheerfully 'Oh no, I'm too young. The gentlemen will pay for the two of us.' All this commotion was foolish, for we met nothing more alarming than a hat lying by the roadside. Seeing the hat the young imp had stopped and was preparing to dismount, I asked what was the matter. He answered, 'A hat, Sir. I must pick it up.' 'Go on, leave it, and I will give you a crown.' 'Oh, no, sir,' he replied, 'I would lose by that, for it has gold embroidery'. And so the young rascal mounted and rode on with the hat on his crupper.'

Commerson travelled as fast as he could manage, clattering through both night and day, travelling more than eight hundred miles in less than three days. He didn't even give himself time to take off his boots. He just reached Rochefort just in time for the right tide, but after all his haste, the boat was delayed. It remained in the harbour for another couple of weeks, though the 'Boudeuse' had set sail on 5th November. The two ships were to rendezvous at the Falkland Islands, where Bougainville, to his great chagrin, was to hand over the colony which he had founded there to the Spanish.

Commerson's enforced wait at Rochefort gave him time to collect himself. He carried out administrative chores, like reconsidering his will. Much of it was concerned with his infant son, left in the care of relatives. Commerson also took care of his servants, especially the housekeeper he had engaged. He left her the furnishings of his Paris flat at M. Le Gendre's, Fauxbourg St Victoire, Rue des Boulangers. He left her all its contents, and allowed her a year's tenancy, during which time she was to administer his natural history collections before giving them to the state.

He was a strange man with a strange childhood. He was born, a second son, on November 18, 1727, at Chatillon-les-Dombes (now Chatillon-sur-

Chalaronne), Ain, France. His grandfather had been a Michel de Commerson, Chatelain of the Seigneurie de Romans. It was an ancient family, and the stump of their ancient castle still stands. However, he was so poor that he dropped any pretence of grandeur, sold what was left of the estate, and became a lawyer in Macon. Philibert's father followed the same profession, though perhaps nursed regrets for the family's loss of status. He seems to have been very hard on his many children. Our Commerson wrote to his own son's guardians, 'I wish you to draw the conclusion that children must be brought up hardly. That was the system of my poor father, and I owe him many obligations for having put it in practice in my own case. He made me go about in winter without special winter clothing, and also in summer without takings my clothes off. So, in spite of the tender affection which I bear to my child, and of the kindness which I have asked you to show in his moral education, my intentions are that you subject him to hard gymnastics and the greatest sobriety. Let him never wear hat or bonnet, gloves or mittens; keep him in winter as far away from the fire as is possible without his suffering too severely. Let him become strong by chopping wood, carrying successively heavier burdens, jumping hedges and ditches, and using both left and right hand. The value of this last accomplishment is not sufficiently understood...'

Such an upbringing seems to have produced in Philibert a sense of insufficiency rather than self-sufficiency. Philibert's father was successful enough as a lawyer to provide all his children with small incomes. He saw Philibert's obsession with botany, and sent him to Montpellier University. There, the young Commerson was quickly recognized as brilliant. It was equally clear that he was a compulsive, indeed maniac, collector of plants, herbarium specimens, botanical treatises, books and catalogs. His local expeditions were filled with hair-raising exploits, and were often undertaken with no thought for his preservation. He travelled with neither money or provisions. He would return home ill, scarred by accidents, worn out by the intensity of his enthusiasm. He was completely dominated by the need to collect, and accepted the fact when his friends called him a botanomaniac. Nothing stopped him, not even morality; he sometimes stole plants from other collectors, and got into considerable trouble. After one trip, he returned home shaking with fever, and wondered if he could find a cure at the baths of Bourbon-Laney. Even when there, he couldn't stop plant hunting, and began visiting the cure of a nearby village. Perhaps the cure knew something about plants. Certainly, he had a pretty sister. She and Philibert were soon married. His new wife brought him fortune, but her influence seems to have calmed the fires that burnt within him. She also bore him a greatly loved son whom they christened Archambault. Two years later she died. Grief set Philibert once more ablaze.

In Paris, he had already come to the attention of Bougainville. Soon, young Archambault was consigned to the care of an uncle, and Commerson set off to travel the world. At Rochefort, and at long last, the 'Etoile' was ready to sail. Amidst the muddle of departure, just as the gangway was about to be pulled aboard, a young man pressed forward, begging to be taken on the voyage. M. Commerson had need of a valet. In the rush and haste, he was waved up the gangway with no questions asked, no answers given. The Fates must have smiled behind their hands. The 'Etoile' finally sailed from Rochefort on 2 January 1767.

Philibert seems to have been a trifle cocksure. He wrote, soon after the French coast vanished below the horizon, 'Once on board, the slight experience I have so far had of the sea has not been particularly trying. I believe that I shall soon get my sea-legs, and I have not yet suffered from sea-sickness...' In a later letter, he writes 'What repentance everywhere. A ship is like a mousetrap wherein each perceives his piece of cheese. Once the sails are spread, the trap falls.' He was later almost mortally seasick, and never became a good sailor. He did, though, recover quickly at each landfall, and his usual obsessive pattern started up. He collected whatever he could find. He wrote, 'Often I do not know where to begin. Often I forget to eat and drink. Indeed, the captain, an excellent friend of mine, has gone so far as to forbid me any light after midnight, because he perceived that I was injuring my health in thus robbing myself of sleep – for I need the whole night to examine properly all that comes before me.'

Meanwhile, Bougainville had reached Montevideo, now capital of Uruguay, then the only good harbour in the whole of the Spanish colonies in South America. He had to meet up with the future governor of the Malvinas islands, or Falklands, then sail back to those islands for their official exchange. But he had accomplished all that, yet still the 'Etoile' had not appeared. Not giving it up for lost, on 21 June 1767, Bougainville anchored in the harbour of Rio de Janeiro. The 'Etoile' was waiting for him. The ship had been there for six days, and already its chaplain had been murdered ashore. For gardeners, something more important had happened. Commerson had been collecting. At their first anchorage of Montevideo, he saw why the Spanish explorers of 1513 had called the river the Rio de la Plata, not from its silver, but because its banks grew endless millions of white zephyr lilies (*Zephyranthes candida*). It's a lovely thing to grow.

He was enchanted, and indeed, the whole exquisite beauty of Brazil delighted him. Of the area around Rio de Janeiro, he said,'This country is the Loveliest in the world; in the very middle of winter oranges, bananas, pineapples continually succeed one another. The trees never lose their greenery. The interior, rich in every sort of game as well as in sugar in rice, in manioc, etc., offers, without any labour of cultivation, a delicious subsistence to its inhabitants, as well as to thousands of slaves who have but the trouble of gathering its fruits... You know my mania for observing everything: in the midst of all these troubles, in spite of a formal prohibition to go outside the town, and even notwithstanding a Fearful sore on my leg which had appeared at sea. I ventured to go out twenty times with my servant in a canoe, which was paddled by two blacks, and visited, one after another, the different shores and islands of the bay.'

He found another species of Zephyr lily, and also a rather showy violet-flowered scrambling climber. Perhaps he thought it would make an ironic tribute to the expedition's leader. Without telling him, Commerson wrote home, describing it scientifically as *'Bougainvillea'*. Once the plant reached Europe, it went suddenly onwards from its erstwhile habitat in the margins of South American forests to get an almost planet-wide distribution. Unaware that there was now a plants that would make his name live forever, and more scuffles having broken out between his crews and the Portugese settlers, Bougainville thought it prudent to leave straight away.

Bougainville's plan was to circumnavigate the globe whilst carrying out scientific investigations. A pattern developed whereby whenever possible the ships would find safe harbour, and let the scientists get on with their observations. Commerson was indefatigable. However, his exertions were vastly helped by his faithful servant, Jean, whom he often mentions in his letters, and who carried all the equipment that was necessary. Commerson took to calling the boy his 'faithful beast of burden', and was very obviously grateful for his fortitude, for his ingenious attempts to make both their lives more comfortable, and for his endless willingness to carry firearms and all the substantial amount of collecting equipment.

In April 1768, the ships anchored in a coral-ringed bay on the shore of one of a group of beautiful islands. Bougainville, as he had been doing throughout the expedition, at once claimed them for France, naming the island Nouvelle-Cythere, and the whole group of islands, Archipel de Bourbon. The local name for the island was Tahiti. On 7th April, Bougainville met the local chieftain and somehow managed to establish permission to set up a camp near the beach. The ships' sick were brought ashore, and fresh water was given them from the nearby stream. They found rest in a land of plenty. For iron, earrings, and other baubles, they bought pigs, chickens, pigeons, bananas, shells, strange cloths, and native weapons and fishing gear. The French entertained the Tahitians with music and a fireworks display.

Commerson was, of course, soon furiously busy, describing and dissecting new and rare fishes, or gathering the many new plants. His valet accompanied him. The local chief, Ereti, took a strong interest in the young man, and, with a group of followers, made off with him. French sailors set up a pursuit. In the following scuffle, the young man's clothes were ripped apart. He turned out to be a young woman. She was, in fact, Jeanne Baret, Commerson's Paris housekeeper. She was hurried back to the 'Etoile' and interrogated by Bougainville.

Bougainville's cool account is as follows: 'There had been a rumour that M. de Commerson's servant (Bare by name) was a woman. His features, the tone of his voice, his beardless chin, the scrupulous care which he took never to change his linens etc., before anybody, as well as other indications, seemed to confirm this suspicion... When I was on board the 'Etoile', Bare confessed to me, her eyes streaming with tears, that she was a woman. She told me that at Rochefort she had deceived her master by presenting herself before him in men's clothes at the very moment when he was about to embark. She said she had already been a lackey in the service of a Genoese in Paris, she was an orphan born in Burgundy and had been rendered utterly destitute by the loss of a lawsuit, so that she has chosen to disguise her sex. Moreover, she knew that it was a case of Voyaging round the world, and this had aroused her curiosity for she would be the first of her sex to do this. I must, in justice, say that on board she had always conducted herself with the utmost propriety. She is neither ugly nor pretty and is not more than twenty-six or twenty-seven years of age.'

Commerson's will suggests that he had no idea that she would follow him. Yet, fiercely observant, he can't have failed to notice his new servant's features. Was she in the carriage clattering through the Luberon? Commerson did name a genus of plants after her. Alas, unlike Bougainvillea, it has become submerged as a synonym for another genus. She was faithful to her master until his end. Commerson was not well.

The 'Etoile' sailed out of the Tahiti anchorage on the 14th. The 'Boudeus'e managed to raise its anchors and leave the next day. Though, later, many of the sailors began to show signs of siphilis, the French, who had only been on the island for nine days began, in their writings and memoires, to create a picture of an earthly paradise. In spite of the thieving, the constant quarrels, the episode of abduction, the Tahitian people were depicted as proof that Rousseau's 'noble savage' really did exist, and that with the right climate, the abundant crops and game, the irrelevance of work, Utopia was possible. But Utopia had its dangers. Commerson had not got a sexual disease but, like many of the crew, was wrecked with dysentery.

The expedition continued onwards, Jeanne in her usual 'valet' role, until it eventually arrived on the shores of Mauritius in December 1768. The island was then a French possession and known as the Ile de Bourbon. The 'Etoile' anchored on the 8th December. Several of the crew were ill, among them Commerson, who was still suffering agonies of seasickness on top of dysentery. Jeanne Baret went ashore with him. He couldn't go on. He decided, together with the expedition's astronomer, to leave the expedition, recuperate, and return to France by a separate route. Before they parted, Commerson told Bougainville about the climber he had discovered in Brazil, and the name he would give it.

Commerson gradually seemed to get better, and made a trip to Madagascar between October 1770 and January of 1771. Whilst leaving it, he was seriously injured and though desperate to return to France, had to remain on the Ile de Bourbon. He didn't even get back to Mauritius for a whole year. France had become a mirage. He wanted to see his son. He wanted to describe scientifically some of the huge number of plants he had collected, and to receive some of the recognition he felt was his due. After all, he knew around twenty five thousand plants, and had found around three thousand species, and perhaps sixty genera that were new to science. That is a truly astonishing haul.

Fame waited, and waited. There were endless delays and disappointments. Finally, he was forced to buy a house in Port Louis in which to store his baggage, especially the forty cases of plant and animal specimens. Jeanne made him comfortable, but his health was failing. He wrote to his old friend Lalande on the 19th October 1772, that he had 'scarcely strength to write to you, and it is an equal wager that I shall succumb, owing to my excessive night-watchings and severe labours. After an attack of rheumatic gout which kept me in bed for nearly three months, I thought I was convalescent, when, in addition, dysentery attacked me; up to the present it has been incurable – and it has brought me to the very edge of the grave. My strength is almost utterly exhausted and I am already more than half worn out. If country air and a diet of rice and fish do not cure me of this attack, you may as well, as you once said (prophetically, no doubt), begin to work on the history of my martyrology.'

However, at last, he had permisson to return, and a comfortable berth assured to make his seasickness less dreadful. He became just too ill to travel. The ship sailed without him. He rallied slightly, and had enough strength to reach the cooler windward side of the island, sixteen miles from Port Louis, at Flacq, in a house called La Retraite. Jeanne stayed behind to look after their collections. On the 13th March 1773, her master died. He was buried in an unmarked grave. Eight days later, in Paris, he was elected a member of the Academy of France by a unanimous vote in a full assembly. It was an unprecedented honour, for no other man had ever been elected while absent from France. He was also give the Cordon of the Order of St. Michael.

Jeanne Baret eventually guided many of the cases of material still on Mauritius back to France. She had, by then, married a soldier, but seems to have returned to France alone. She settled down near her master's family at Chatillon-en-Dombes. When she herself died, in 1816, and without children of her own, she left all she owned to Commerson's son, Archambault. She was, as she had hoped, the first woman to circumnavigate the globe.

Many of Commerson and Baret's herbarium specimens still exsist. The Linnaean Society of London possesses about fifteen hundred specimens. The Delessert herbarium in Paris has three thousand. Far more are scattered through museum collection in France and elsewhere. Archambault followed family tradition and became a prominent local notary. Bougainville went on to have an extraordinary career, survive the Revolution, find a perfect wife, and die in August 1811 of the dysentery he had once caught in Tahiti. He was given a state funeral on 7 September and his ashes were buried in the Pantheon. His heart, though, was removed and placed next to his wife in the cemetery of St. Pierre at Montmartre. The symbol of his friendship with Commerson grows in at least half of the glasshouses and gardens across the entire globe.

But the new glasshouses could have a huge flora, and that was one of their vast appeals. Their owners could share in the excitement of the great expeditions, could have a tiny piece or orchids or fern-filled jungle, could marvel at carnivorous plants, or the strange succulents from the Cape, or the even stranger opuntias, Cereus, echinopsis, epiphyllums, selenicereus, melocactus, from the deserts of the Americas. Perhaps it is still the orchids that tease and seduce gardeners most. Certainly, in the later half of the nineteenth century, they spawned some tremendous plant nurseries in every capital in the Western world, and the nurseries employed some tremendous collectors, several hunting some species of orchid to extinction.

It had started with a sensation in 1818. William Swainson, a visitor to Brazil, sent off a consignment of tropical treasures to Mr William Cattley of Barnet, packing them round with some dull plants which had an orchid's 'pseudobulbs' but no flowers. Cattley got them to flower: they had blooms five inches across with mauve petals and a trumpet-like lip with frilled edges, a purple base and a yellow throat. It was by far the most beautiful orchid then known and no more of its kind were found for the next 70 years. Hugh Culling, another unknown, was in the Philippines in the 1830's and managed to send back live orchids. They were gorgeous too. There was then almost a gold rush of orchid prospectors. Karl Theodor Hartweg spent nearly seven years in Mexico collecting for the Horticultural Society. One of his most valuable finds came after he had noticed an unusually fine bloom in the hat of a Quichole Indian. He found the original plant and half a dozen other new species. The Duke of Devonshire started his Chatsworth collection in the early 1830's when he saw *Oncidium papilio* at an orchid show. Collecting became so competitive that some collectors like the strange, silent, Thomas Lobb, who signed a three-year contract in 1843 with the Veitch nursery to collect orchids in Malaysia and the islands, became quite paranoid. He sent sent home marvels like *Phalaenopsis amabilis,* the Moth Orchid with its broad white petals (and now so popular as a houseplant that there are now excellent plastic copies), and *Vanda tricolor*, the cowslip-scented orchid with cream or pale mauve petals spotted with brown, and with a rosy pink lip. He also sent home misleading telegrams to his employers, disguising where he was so that fellow collectors couldn't duplicate his travels.

There was the extraordinary Benedict Roezl, who had an iron hook for a left hand, and collected orchids all the way from California to Patagonia. He was born in 1824, worked as a nurseryman in Vienna, then emigrated to Mexico in 1854. At first, he sold Mexican conifers. In 1861 he introduced the cultivation of a Mexican textile plant called ramie (*Boehmeria tenacissima*), which he hoped to develop as a fibre for the European market. He then began to send orchids to the nursery of Henry Sander of St. Albans in England. He almost pillaged Central America; he sent home 10,000 orchids from Panama and Colombia in 1869. He went across the Isthmus of Panama to Guayra and Caracas and sent eight tons of orchids and ten tons of other plants back to London. In Mexico, in the vicinity of the volcano of Colima, the Indians learned that Roezl would pay for orchids and they brought him 100,000 plants. They were all rare masdevallias or miltonias. There were sometimes huge losses. Of 27,000 plants once dispatched by Roezl in a consignment from New Granada (present day Colombia), just two plants survived the long and disastrous journey to England.

Nurserymen started hybridising orchids in the 1850's, when John Dominy, working for the Veitch nursery, crossed two species of Calanthe. That was just the start. It was soon found that wide crosses between different genera were also fertile, giving rise to some of the most popular of today's orchids, given strange generic names that relate to nothing ever found in a real wild environment.

And what about *Victoria amazonica*? Though hardly a plant suited for a backyard glasshouse, astonishingly it has developed a backyard following. There turn out to be two species, *V. amazonica* in quiet parts of that river, and *V. cruziana* from rivers in cooler Argentina, Bolivia and Paraguay. This last species is hardier and has white flowers. Recently, gardeners have

discovered that they can be crossed, producing hardier plants than *V. amazonica*, with pink or red flowers, and a heavier perfume of pineapples. Once the plant of plutocrats, or the showiest botanic gardens, they are now grown by ordinary enthusiasts in the southern parts of the United States from Oregon southwards. While some gardeners swear by two hundred gallon tanks, some have flowered their victorias in forty gallon plastic buckets. Clearly, one of the most astonishing plants in the world, having been known for less than two hundred years is, at the hands of gardeners, set to increase its range further still.
    END

Chapter 7

Of the Wilderness and the Shrubbery

David Stuart

The Wilderness and Shrubbery

The remarkable way in which an ancient element of the garden called 'the wilderness' both survived and developed into modern times has been driven, since the 18th century at least, by some marvellous plants introduced by brave men. That it is now, in one form or another, one of the most vigorous and exciting areas of the garden is due to two quite extraordinarily brilliant and tenacious individuals, and a whole dynasty of rather duller ones who owned and ran an immensely important nursery. Its stock brought to the 'wildernesses' of Europe and America some of the most thrilling plants of the East.

It is early summer, 1835. On tables piled with books, crisp paper sheets bearing pressed flowers, ebony handled lenses, ink pots and quills, space is cleared for a large, flat, package. At other tables in Russia, America, France, and England, tables of rough planks, or tables of marquetry and ormulu, the packages have been tossed aside, the contents eagerly scanned, and a new desire kindled.

At the same moment, in a sunlit garden on the Rapenburg, one of the smartest streets in Leiden, the ancient and picturesque university town in Holland, Philipp Franz Bathasar von Siebold strolls past bushes of moutan paeonies bearing their last flowers, Chinese roses just starting to unfurl, and huge clumps of chrysanthemums yet to produce their flowers. When these flower, they will prove to be far more splendid than anything any European gardener had yet seen. He wears a splendid kimono, has sandals, and is sipping tea from a rough eathenware cup.

The packages, some still travelling rough roads in creaking waggons, others already lying empty on Persian rugs, contain or contained the first batch of engravings of his long projected 'Flora Japonica'. This is to become a vastly influential work, and describes some of the most beautiful trees, shrubs and herbaceous plants that von Siebold collected and grew in that exotic country. Similar packages will leave Leiden for the next nine years, though the entire project will never be completed in his lifetime. He himself will continue to publish major works on the culture and history of Japan, and will briefly return to his beloved garden there. Though he will be loaded with honours for his contributions to science, the most intense years of his life are over. He is thirty nine years old.

The herbarium material upon which much of the botanical work for the flora has been based will eventually be given to the university herbarium at Leiden, where the sheets of dried specimens still remain. The fabulous quantity of illustrations, some two thousand in all, on which the engravings have been based, mostly drawn and painted by Japanese artists in Japan, will eventually reach what is now the Komarov Institute in Russia. Some of the plants illustrated will eventually grow in gardens worldwide, and some will have enormous influence on garden design.

However, on this summer morning, some of the plants themselves are only just beginning to flourish. Enchanting small trees, like *Malus floribunda*, in a Japanese spring a billowing mass of palest pink flowers, are as yet little more than single branches. These horticultural riches, on which he is starting to build a business, are but a fraction of the ones that von Siebold loaded on the ship at Deshima. Almost all of them reached Europe alive, in spite of the enormous sea journey from Japan to Europe. It wasn't the immense variations of climate of the voyage, or the hazards of being at sea, that decimated them. It was a strange fate met during a strange war.

Philipp Franz Bathasar von Siebold, was an extraordinary and energetic man, arrogant, callous, perceptive, foolhardy, but with a quite perfect eye for a good plant, or piece of porcelain, when he saw it. He was born on February 16th, 1796, in the Bavarian town of Wurzburg, and into a family of strong minded, indeed often distinguished, men and women. His father and his grandfather were well known doctors, and an aunt, trained in obstetrics, attended the Duchess of Kent at the birth of the little girl who was to become Queen Victoria. Philipp's future must have seemed mapped, and he did indeed enter medical school at Wurzburg. Once qualified, he set up a small practice. It provided him with enough money, but not enough excitement, in order to live. As a student, he'd become interested in natural history and fascinated by the extraordinary plants and animals that the planet supported. Wanderlust gripped him. He set out for Rotterdam, intent on launching a new career as a scientific explorer. An attractive, well qualified and persuasive young man, he soon found a post as surgeon major in the Dutch East Indies Army, and was, by September 1822, aboard a ship setting sail for the Dutch outpost in Java. However, Fate took hold of him, and he was hardly in Java before he was swiftly moved on towards Japan and his destiny.

The Dutch had first reached Japan much earlier. In 1600, a ship called the 'Liefde' drifted ashore in Usuki Bay in Bungo Province (now Oita-ken). It was the only survivor from a fleet of five sailing ships that set out from Rotterdam in 1598. Most of the men on the expedition had suffered cruelly, freezing to death in the Strait of Magellan, starving, being killed in fights with the Spanish and Portuguese on the Pacific, or sinking in terrible storms. The 'Leifde' suffered too, with only twenty four of the original one hundred and ten crew living to see Japan. Six of those died within two days of landing, and only six could walk unassisted to shore. Two of the survivors went on to earn important places in Japanese history: William Adams and Jan Joosten. Adams became an advisor on diplomacy and trade, Joosten on military matters. Both were to prove so important, that the Dutch trading company was granted extensive trading rights.

That priviledge was gradually reduced, and by the time of Siebold's arrival, only the tiny coastal settlement of Deshima remained to them. The company's employees were virtually prisoners there, allowed to trade, but in few commodities. Holland, knowing how profitable trading with Japan could be, was anxious to re-establish secure trading as soon as possible. They were even keener to outflank other European trading nations who had their eyes on Japan. A special embassy to Tokyo was planned, to ask for better conditions. A skilled physician was an asset, and von Siebold was especially suitable. He had graduated as an eye-specialist, and could operate for cataracts. His ability to make the blind see soon gave him immense prestige almost as soon as he began to work at Deshima. His Dutch employers must have been very pleased. It may be that they asked him to take on subtler duties.

With his almost demonic energy, he took every opportunity to learn as much about Japan and the Japanese as possible. He plainly wanted to become the leading European authority on every aspect of the culture. It turned out to be easier for him than any previous foreigner; the cataract operations, for which he refused money payments, brought him not only gifts as an alternative, but also disciples. The gifts he treasured, and the disciples he taught, and, at his bidding, they began to act as explorers and researchers into the countryside that was forbidden to him. Japanese artists were trained to make illustrations plants and animals. Von Siebold even asked the governor general in Java for additional help in this task, and a highly skilled draftsman and artist was soon sent to his aid.

However much it seems as if von Siebold was intent on exploiting Japan and its inhabitants for his own ends, and those of the Dutch, he was himself captivated. Like many other collectors in this book, he 'went native'. He fell totally in love with Japan's culture and history. He also fell in love with a beautiful eighteen-year-old girl whom he met at the house of a client. After much difficulty, they were allowed to marry, though to do this, his new wife had, uncomfortably, to register as a prostitute for the use of all the Dutchmen in Deshima. She must have loved him. Certainly, she went to live with him on Deshima, and in 1827 a daughter, Ine, was born.

Deshima already had an overgrown botanic garden, set up by his

Swedish predecessor. Carl Peter Thunberg (1743-1828, and who contributes much toa previous chapter. Von Siebold refurbished it, and soon filled it with more Japanese plants, both wildlings from the hills, but also with plants from the huge numbers of Japanese gardens and nurseries in and around Nagasaki and the capital. It soon expanded. He rapidly became such a favoured foreigner that he was allowed to move his base of operations to the mainland and occupy a house on a hillside above Nagasaki. The surrounding grounds were transformed into another botanical garden and arboretum.

His world must have seemed glorious. A wife. A child. A teaching school filled with pupils eager to learn whatever they could about Western medicine. An obviously immensely important collection of plants which he knew would fascinate Western gardeners. A house filling with lacquer, porcelain, and bronzes. But he overreached himself. He knew perfectly well that the Japanese state was paranoid about its military weakness in the face of western technology. He knew that certain things it was forbidden for him to own. Yet in the autumn of 1828, he met, and charmed, the Court Astronomer at the capital. This man, presumably knowing the immense danger of the act, gave von Siebold secret maps not only of Japan itself, but of important adjacent regions such as the province of Amur, the island of Saghalien, and the Liu Kiu islands that lie between Japan and Formosa.

Von Siebold had been amassing huge numbers of plants from the nurseries of Tokyo, and the collections were already packed on the vessel that was to take them from the capital back to his base at Deshima. Alas, the ship was beached in a storm, and before she could be refloated, the forbidden maps were discovered. When the news reached Tokyo, the astronomer killed himself. Several of von Siebold's Tokyo pupils and friends were imprisoned and brutally tortured. Even still, von Siebold fought hard to retain the maps, only giving them up once he'd made hasty copies by torchlight, and hidden them among his zoological collections.

Fate had turned against him. He was imprisoned from 18th December 1828 to 28th December 1829. His Dutch employers were too wary of the scandal to give him any great support, though they presumably got hold of the copied maps. When he was at last released, it was only to discover that he was sentenced to permanent banishment from Japan. On January 2nd, 1830, after six years and three months spent in the country which had so enchanted him, he left, driven from Eden. Unlike Adam, he left wife and daughter behind and set sail for Holland.

He took with him a collection of five hundred or so new garden plants, which he hoped to unite with a shipment he had already sent to Europe the previous year. That seems to have happened, but Fate dealt him another blow. The whole collection fell foul of war. After the defeat of Napoleon, an event which had a number of effects on the evolution of the garden wilderness, Holland and Belgium had been uneasily united. However, history proved strong, and neither could forget language or religion. Belgium wished to regain her independence, and war broke out between the two states in the summer of 1830. It isn't clear what exactly happened, but von Siebold's plants seem to have been growing in a garden either at Antwerp or Ghent. War engulfed the collection in August, and he tells the story that the garden was used to house a cavalry regiment. The collection was already subject to the intense envy of local horticulturalists, and they siezed the opportunity for pillage. Eager gardeners began to scuttle, doubled up, between the milling horses and shouting riders, gathering up what they could of von Siebold's Japanese flowers from amongst the noise, stench and glitter of war.

Amongst the plants that changed ownership so dramatically were many brilliantly coloured azaleas from the nurseries of Japan. In later years, von Siebold claimed, and the nurserymen of Ghent acknowledged, that the whole prosperity of that city became based on the prodigious popularity of what became called 'Ghent' azaleas. However, once the fighting died down, von Siebold fled to Holland. When he tried to reclaim his property, the local inhabitants, sensibly claiming that they'd saved his collection, did make some attempt at recompense. They gave him back at least one plant of everything they had managed to propagate. However, that only amounted to about eighty or so of the many hundred species that had set out from Deshima. Even with that reduced number, von Siebold soon established a 'Jardin d' Acclimatisation' at a new home in Leiden.

He seems to have had most of his earnings and his zoological and ethnographic collections intact. He also had his Japanese household goods.

He bought a fine house on the Rapenburg, one of the town's most fashionable thoroughfares, and with it a large garden. It must have been the first house in Europe to be furnished in the Japanese style, though forty years later, almost every household in Europe showed off at least a Japanese fan, or an Art Nouveau vase that relied on Japanese inspiration. But that was in the future. By the early 1830's, he was soon selling plants created from his introductions. He himself was also a sight of some considerable interest for the town's conventionally minded inhabitants. Not only did he wear Japanese costume while out in the town, take of his shoes when entering houses, use chopsticks to eat his food, and sleep on tatami mats; there was also the shocked whisper of his abandoned wife and child.

His 'Japonism' was perhaps a marketing tool for his business' promotion, and for his many other books about the customs, animals, and history of Japan. For all this, he became much honoured and rewarded. Eventually he liked being painted in European costume, clothes almost completely obscured by some of the many medals he had from William II of Holland. More usefully, he was also awarded an official post in the Dutch East India Company, and a patent of nobility, with the title of 'Jongheer'. Payment for the map, perhaps.

But the old garden 'wilderness' was in a state of change. This was true of the whole gardening, indeed botanical, world into which the 'Flora Japonica' found its way. Part of the difference was, of course, due to the colossal number of new plants pouring into Europe. They not only made new sorts of gardening possible, but their immense diversity was beginning to alter how people thought of Nature itself, of how some plants were identical even when found growing on continents separated by vast oceans, indeed, and more radically, of how species and varieties were created. The 'Flora Japonica' was part of this. Of large format, the new work was sumptuously illustrated with elegant, hand-coloured engravings showing marvellously drawn Japanese plants, often life-sized, on folio-sized plates. The engravings alone made the Flora worth purchasing by middle ranking gardeners, and gave a wide range of horticulturists, nurserymen, and gardeners their first exciting view of an array of the decorative plants of Japan. Better still, many of the engravings retained the Japanese feel for plant form, and placing on the page, and that alone must have intrigued the subscribers. Plates range from very double pinks forms of *Anemone hupehensis* var. *japonica* (Robert Fortune was only to bring back the single white form in 1847), arisaemas in quantity, gorgeous paeonies, an edible tulip (*T. edulis*), Lycoris, and more. His plate of *Iris ensata* shows a flat flowered variant that every gardener must have instantly desired.

But it is amongst the small trees and shrubs that gardeners found plates that made them throw the Flora's wrappings impatiently to the floor, and carry the engraving to the window, the more thoroughly to scan them. Several of the shrubs have entirely new properties: they have perfumed flowers in winter. *Chimonanthus praecox* with yellow bells on bare branches; the astonishing *Mahonia japonica*,with its spiky and glittering foliage, and arching sprays of yellow flowers that have one of the most bewitching perfumes in the whole garden, viburnums (*Viburnum carlesii* with a ravishing smell in early summer), and more. He illustrated the strange flowers of clerodendrons (whose foliage has one of the nastier garden smells), camellias, hydrangeas, the lovely *Styrax obassia*, the first *Forsythia* to be illustrated in Europe, and on and on, even including roses that will go on to become vastly influential in the garden, like Rosa rugosa, *R. multiflora*, and *R. Banksiae*.

There are marvels amongst the trees too; new maples with exquisitely shaped leaves and blazing autumn colours, new magnolias to offer relief from the American species already long familiar, new oaks, new cherries, including a fine soft pink form of *Prunus pendula* var. *ascendens*. None of these plants are suitable for the 'American garden', now filled and shady with big trees. None can mar the crisp and colourful beds of annual flowers now being copied all over Europe and gardened America, using Lady Grenville's ideas as a base. The only place for the maples and viburnums, the hydranges and paeonies is the 'wilderness'.

The 'wilderness' is an ancient aspect of the garden. The gardens of ancient Rome often had, beyond the elaborate schemes of topiary, a few areas of supposedly naturalistic 'wilderness'. There, plants were allowed to grow as they pleased, the emphasis was on the natural and the native, and wild Pan and his ilk were supposed to take refuge therein, though statuary of gods like Terminus and Bacchus were acceptable. With their shade and murmuring springs, European gardeners never quite forgot them, and whenever the ancient world was remembered, and space permitted, artificial wildernesses formed an important part of the garden.

Many grand Renaissance gardens, especially in Italy, developed a system of design that was supposed to be Roman, whereby the formal, high maintenance and highly artificial, gardens were close to the main building, and the wilderness began beyond the reach of formality. Wildernesses were still unashamedly artificial, containing statuary, fountains, pavilions and seating. Villa Lante and the Sacro Bosco at Bomarzo are well known examples. Wildernesses were sometimes hopefully paganised, and called, as at Bomarzo, the 'sacro bosco', but even if the ancient gods didn't return, at least the trees were allowed their head, and formed shady walks and rides which weren't possible nearer the house.

By the 17th century, when the passion for building gardens engaged the owners of vast and flat estates in France, the wildernesses were penetrated by formal rides which stretched, if the owner could afford it, to the horizon. The rides naturally radiated outward from the house and it's flower filled parterres, whilst lesser rides joined features of interest, whether hunting pavilion, pool or statue of Diana the Huntress. To make the division between formal axis and wilderness suitably clear, the rides were given substantial hedges. The contrast between clipped greenery, and wild, makes for great visual excitement. In large estates used for hunting, the division may also have helped steer both quarry and hunt into open country. Neither had time to observe the plant species used.

The English tried to catch up on French developments. At Hampton Court, the great Tudor palace on the banks of the Thames, William of Orange began to garden again after the death of his wife, Queen Mary, in the 1690's. Old medieval garden features like the mount were swept away, and although a wilderness was planted, it merely re-used shrubs from the old privy garden. A few decades later, a visitor to the Duke of Devonshire's vast house at Chatsworth in Derbyshire could write : ' When we had satisfied our curiosityes within doores .... we walk't out into the Gardens, which fill'd our

Eyes with fresh Objects of delight and admiration... There is a large Grotto... and a Willow tree in the Centre of a Wildnerness which spouts out of every branch and leafe, there are also severall basins with Jet d'eaux.... the whole Wilderness guarded with Satyrs.... also a charming long arbour... and a Firr Wilderness... from thence we entered a walk with Statues on each side...' Clearly, the plants were rather dull.

Another garden visitor of the age, Celia Fiennes, was not an especially botanically educated gardener, but she was a snob. Had there been something rare and valuable to see, she would have at least noted the cost. She did sometimes notice the difference between 'firrs' and broad leaf trees, and sometimes even how they were pruned. She visited Tixall Hall in Derbyshire late in the 17th century, and found '... just by the Bowling-green is a very fine wilderness with many large walkes of a great length, full of all sorts of trees... and so shorn smooth to the top which is left as a tuft or crown, they are very lofty in growth which makes the length of the walke look very nobly....'

Like Tixall and Chatsworth, most wildernesses seem to have been botanically unexciting. It is hard not to feel that they were merely the unloved and untrodden interstices between the walks and rides. Contemporary garden writers and designers threw up their hands. Stephen Switzer's marvellous book 'Ichnographica Rustica' of 1718, suggests that "We must cashier that mathematical stiffness in our gardens, and imitate Nature more.... ", largely by growing a diversity of plants. In the next decade, Batty Langley's 'New Principles of Gardening' of 1728, was aimed at gentle rather than aristocratic gardeners. For them, he suggested that a wilderness should be of "shady walks and groves, planted with sweet briar, white jessamine and honeysuckle, environed at the bottom with a small circle of dwarf stock, candytuft and pinks". Such a wilderness would have been very pretty, but early-eighteenth-century plantings often included the smaller types of fruit and nut trees, but only because these were often decorative in leaf, flower and fruit. They were grown in orchards for produce.

The plant-dunce Sir William Chambers, whatever his other sophistications, described a Chinoiserie wilderness cum shrubbery in his 'A Dissertation on Oriental Gardening' published in May, 1772. This consisted "of rose, raspberry, bramble, currant, lavender, vine and gooseberry bushes; with barberry, alder, peach, nectarine and almond trees..." He seems unaware of the new trees and shrubs fast appearing from the Americas at then hands of collectors like Andre Michaux and John Bartram (who appear elsewhere in this book), let alone new ones actually from China itself.

Even by 1754, when landscapers were busy sweeping them away, there is a long section on how to design, plant and manage the wilderness in that year's edition of Philip Miller's 'The Gardeners Dictionary'. He says, in his rather garden-worthy manner, 'if rightly situated, artfully contrived, and judiciously planted, [wildernesses] are very great Ornaments to a fine Garden', and then, equally garden-worthily, goes on both to complain about how bad most are, and how they ought to be when well done. Not surprisingly for the curator of the Apothecaries Garden at Chelsea, he gives generous planting lists. He writes: 'In the Distribution of these Plantations, in those Parts which are planted with deciduous Trees may be planted next the Walks and Openings, Roses, Honeysuckles, Spirea Frutex, and other Kinds or low flowering Shrubs, which may be always kept very dwarf, and may be planted pretty close together ; and at the Foot of them, near the Sides of the Walks, may be planted Primroses, Violets, Daffodils, and many other Sorts of Wood flowers; not in a strait Line, but rather to appear accidental, as in a Natural Wood. Behind the first Row of Shrubs should be planted Syringas, Cytisus, Althea Frutex, Mezereons, and other flowering Shrubs of a middle Growth; which may be back'd with Laburnum, Lilacs, Gelder-roses, and other flowering Shrubs of large Growth: there may be back'd with many other Sorts of Trees, rising gradually to the Middle of the Quarters, from whence they should always slope down every Way to the Walks. By this Distribution you will have the Pleasure of the flowering Shrubs near the Sight, whereby you will be regaled with their Scent, as you pass through the Walks;...' Lovely.

Most of these plants were perfectly familiar to gardeners since the late 16th century, but elsewhere he suggests some more adventurous shrubs, though almost all American in origin, and often introduced in the previous century. They include fine things like the snowdrop tree (*Halesia* species from North America in the 1750's), the beautifully flowered indigo trees (*Indigofera* species), various sumachs (*Rhus glabra and R. typhina,* both from the US in the 17th century), coluteas, the spicily scented benzoin tree with its fine autumn colours (*Lindera benzoin,* also from America in the 17th century), as well as the azederach (*Melia azedarach,* from either India or China in the 17th century). Of middling-sized trees, there were many acacias (*Gleditsia* and *Robinia)* and numerous maples. There was also the American

Styrax, now rare in spite of the lovely flowers, five species of *Celtis*, as well as many hollies, bays, laurels and the three then-known types of lilac, including the too rarely seen (and smelled) Persian lilac.

A richer wilderness flora than ever before, but the scene was getting set for much faster change still. Pierre Nicholas le Cheron D'Incarville (1706-1757), an abbe trained in botany by Bernard de Jussieu, the famous French botanist, was in Beijing for 16 years after joining the Chinese mission of Jesuits in 1740. It was direct to M. de Jussieu that he sent his herbarium collections. His seeds had a much more complex route. He sent seeds of the pagoda tree (*Sophora japonica*) to friends in Moscow. From there, seeds were fowarded to Paris, and some seedlings finally reached Miller in 1753. It took another fifty eight years for plants to reach New York. It was also d'Incarville who introduced *Ailanthus altissima*, the 'Tree of Heaven', to Europe, and which began to colonise America soon after. He also sent out the Golden Rain Tree (*Koelreuteria paniculata*), from the traditional plantings around the graves of high officials. This little wave of new introductions was the merest taste of what was to come.

With all these small trees and large bushes, the wilderness was fast becoming a suitable garden element for a small garden, perhaps one around the new and unpretentious villas beginning to appear in prosperous regions. The owners of such gardens had been disenfranchised from 'garden taste' for much of the previous century. High French style needed vast spaces. They were also excluded from the English landscape style that developed from the 1720's, for it was hardly suited to a few acres. Both styles, both aristocratic, paid no attention whatsoever to the diversity of plants.

Philip Miller was watching developments. Here he is on small gardens: 'Where there is not room for these magnificent Wildernesses, there may be some rising Clumps of Ever-greens, so designed as to make the Ground appear much larger than it is in Reality; and if in these there are some

Serpentine walks well contriv'd, it will greatly improve the Place, and deceive those who are unacquainted with the Ground, as to its Size.... but if there is a distant Prospect of the adjacent Country from the House, then this should not be obstructed, but rather a larger Opening should be allowed for the View... and on the back part from the Sight, may be planted the several kinds of flowering Shrubs, according to their different Growths, which will still add to the Variety.'

Variety was aplenty, and as wildernesses were seen as being adaptable to small gardens, they were soon very popular. They were even espoused by the public tea gardens in the major cities, often places that set the very latest styles of gardening. One at Enderby, near Leicester, had a strawberry garden, a plant nursery and a wilderness with serpentine walks, all being advertised for sale in 1849.

Even in the settled states of North America, and where there was a terrifying amount of real wilderness, some grander gardens followed European tastes, and built themselves artificial ones. Blithewood, with its manicured lawns, was also admired for its wild and picturesque ravines; Montgomery Place had a wilderness with rustic seats, as well as lake and flower gardens. So the area of the garden suited to Seibold's new plants was beginning to appeal to a wide range of gardeners, wealthy and middling, European and American. Perhaps they waited for a signal, and the 'Flora Japonica' provided it.

Von Siebold's nursery was a success, but he couldn't forget the plants he had lost of left behind. After much negotiation, he managed to get back to Japan in August of 1859. By the time he reached his old haunts in Nagasaki, including the school he had set up, he found that things were very different. Six years earlier, a rather threatening array of American ships had entered Edo Bay, and the Japanese authorities decided to open their country to foreign trade. Japan could never be the same again.

Even on this return, his happiness was short. This time he had moved with great caution, collecting plants as fast as he deemed wise, but this time he fell foul of intrigue between the various foreign powers that had established themselves in Japan following Perry's success. The Dutch were, perhaps understandably, anxious that he would create more problems than his presence might solve. However, he was much more eminent now than in his previous sojourn, and so, rather shoddily, they tricked him into leaving Japan in 1862. They promised him that he would soon return as the main Dutch advisor in Japan. It isn't clear if he believed them.

The deck of the vessel on which he sailed, again without his Japanese family, was a veritable nursery. He returned to Leiden with yet more marvels, and this time no war stopped their introduction. His garden soon sported things which are now garden centre stalwarts, and his catalogue for 1863 listed an astounding 838 species and varieties of Japanese plants. These ran from *Forsythia suspensa* var. *sieboldii*, making it the first of the genus to be introduced into European gardens, the fabulous Japanese wisteria (*Wisteria floribunda*), with masses of lavender or white pea flowers in the familiar long racemes, to the popular climbing hydrangea (*Hydrangea anomala* subsp. *petiolaris*) and the now widely grown *Hydrangea paniculata* 'Grandiflora', with its immense late-summer flowerhead, cream at first and later ageing to weird shades of bronze-greens. There were some marvellous small trees too, including more forms of the most beautiful of all ornamental crab apples, the Japanese flowering crab (*Malus floribunda*), and the handsome Sorbus known as the Korean mountain ash *(Sorbus alnifolia)*,though it has a range that encompasses Japan as well as central China.

Curiously, though he'd written a substantial report on Japanese flowering cherries, and had clearly seen the hundreds of types being grown in Japanese gardens in the 1820s, when they were at the peak of popularity in Japan, he'd brought none back. Most of the double flowered ones he saw he called the 'temple cherries", as they had become popular gifts to monks and their gardens. None of this seems to have influenced him, for in the first shipment of his plants to reach Europe, there were no cherries. It seems, with hindsight, an odd lapse. Perhaps the market wasn't ready; a double pink cherry had been received and described by a French nurseryman called A. Jacques in the autumn of 1832, but it did not create a sensation. Even by 1877, von Siebold's nursery only showed one at the international horticultural exhibition held in Amsterdam, and yet by then almost everything Japanese was in fashion. The cherries had to wait.

The sudden, glorious, discovery of all these new small trees enriched the mid 19th century wilderness, but also enriched the possible look of the suburban garden, freeing them, if their owners wanted, from annual and half-hardy bedding schemes and the constant work and expense that they entailed. All of a sudden, small gardens could have trees that didn't overwhelm them, and which could provide abundant colour for the hungriest of eyes.

When Philipp von Siebold returned to Japan for his second trip, he was no longer the only collector. Wonderful things were pouring into Europe and North America from many other hands; glorious things like the katsura tree, *Cercidiphyllum*. Now one of the delights of Western summers, with its oval jade green leaves, and one of the wonders of autumn when those leaves turn butter yellow, in Japan, where it grow to a size hardly ever achieved in the West, it is used for cabinet making and panelling. It was first collected by Thomas Hogg, an American citizen, but one with a famous name in British floristry. His father was a well-known Scots-born London nurseryman cum florist who had given his name to some successful auriculas and pinks. However, he seems to have found London not to his taste, and set our for New York in 1822. Finding few nurseries in that city, he set up his own. He may still have had an interest in the London one, for the breeding material material of carnations, picotees, pinks and auriculas were auctioned off on December 12th, 1842, by Protheroe & Morris at Paddington Green.

Thomas Hogg's New York nursery was a success. Our Hogg, one of his two sons, seems to have made some interesting friends, for he was sent out to Japan by Abraham Lincoln, and was in Tokyo from August, 1862. Like von Siebold, he became fascinated by Japan, and when his American work finished, he remained in Tokyo to work for the Japanese customs service. While there, his brother was looking after the family nursery on 23rd St and Broadway, and it soon grew some handsome Japanese plants. While *Cercidiphyllum, Stewartia pseudocamellia, Styrax japonica*, the now widely grown *Symplococcos paniculata*, described by von Siebold but introduced by Hogg, were Hogg junior's triumphs, he also sent home some disasters like the kudzu vine (*Pueraria lobata*), now a vicious American weed.

Though at least his shrubs are lovely inhabitants of the northern garden, as far as the wilderness is concerned, his perfectly splendid achievement is overshadowed by that of Joseph Dalton Hooker, (1817 1911), yet another of the plant collectors who started his professional career as a doctor. He became one of the most influential botanists and travellers of his age, director of Kew gardens, publisher of a mountain of scientific works, but also of fascinating travelogues illustrated with his own lively drawings.

He was born at the family estate of Halesworth, Suffolk, on 30th June 1817, and was born into almost the centre of the botanical world. His father was William Jackson Hooker (1785-1865), at that time teaching botany at the ancient university of Glasgow, and to become, in 1820, its Professor. From there, he was to move south to become Director of the Royal Botanic Garden at Kew.

Joseph was immersed in botany throughout his childhood. Even as a small boy he had found some rare mosses surviving in the smokes of industrial Glasgow. While some sons rebel against their father's enthusiasm, plants and exploring became part of him; as a teenager, his bedtime books were travel adventures like those of Mungo Park and Captain Cook. He was later an avid reader of Darwin's 'Voyage of the Beagle', and a decade later still, a chance meeting with the great man led to a lifelong and very productive friendship. Joseph nourished dreams of being a great collector-explorer, of having hair-raising tales to tell. Fate decided to fulfil his fantasies. Nature, too, took a useful hand. He proved to have quite astonishing powers of physical endurance, as well as formidable energies. He also seemed to have a tremendous luck in the face of frightening odds that many other collectors might have envied.

He graduated as M.D. in 1839. Unlike von Siebold, he didn't even try building a private practise, but was at once appointed as Assistant-Surgeon aboard the HMS 'Erebus', for a proposed expedition to the Antartic, under

the command of Sir James Clark Ross. It was to be an extraordinary journey.
It's most spectacular aim was to find the South Magnetic Pole, and later to
call at the Falkland Islands, New Zealand and Tasmania. Even before Hooker
could begin collecting in southernmost Argentina and the Falklands, there
were adventures. After Sir James had indeed found the South Magnetic Pole,
in what was later to be called George the Fifth Land, the 'Erebus' and
'Terror' sailed north to avoid the Antarctic winter. The weather worsened
instead of improved. Gales were so extreme that eight and ten-inch hawsers
snapped like threads, causing the whole ship to shudder. Sails were shredded
by storms. Both ships nearly capsized. They got embroiled in dangerous floes
of ice, and sailed dizzyingly between icebergs that lay so close together that
they themselves often collided. The cold was so intense that the very foam on
the wave crests froze, and the ships' decks, spars and ropes were top-heavily
weighted with ice. One night, the two ships, normally in constant sight of one
another, found that they were alone in the storm. It was days, amongst the
ice, before they found one another. Another night on the 'Terror', a swaying
lantern started a fire below decks which blazed for two hours until finally
extinguished. Later, a wild blast of wind sweeping down between cliffs of ice
caused the 'Terror' and the 'Erebus' to crash together with such force that the
masts and frozen rigging of each boat became enmeshed. Spars and rigging
had to be sawn free, leaving the 'Erebus' almost totally disabled.

Sir James was a superb seaman, and he managed to manoeuvre the
'Erebus' away from the nearest ice, and the ship was repaired sufficiently to
make it to the quieter waters of Berkeley Sound in the Falkland Islands on
April 6. Joseph's dreams of excitement were being amply fulfilled. He
dreams of collecting fine plants were fulfilled too, for over the next arduous
few months, he found *Lapageria rosea*, the beautiful, waxy leafed climber,
with drooping bells of that look as if they've been cast from the drippings of
a pink candle. Though fairly hardy, it rapidly became a favourite in Victorian
conservatories. Another famous plant from that trip is the strong holly-like
Desfontainea spinosa, with coral red flowers, and an exotic-looking
inhabitant of the more sheltered shrubbery. But he also found the flame-
flower, *Tropaeolum speciosum*, now entwined through every yew hedge in
northern Europe. He also brought back a new berberis, *Berberis darwinii*,
which now hangs over every suburban fence, and has brash orange flowers.
Most spectacular of all, and unsurpassed in cool countries as a tree with the
most brilliant flower colour, was *Embothrium coccineum*. It, too, was a huge

hit. One Scottish landowner, the Earl of Stair, was so enraptured that he at once replanted his magnificent 17th avenues with alternate trees of this plant, and the dark green, dulled, leaves of *Quercus ilex*. The effect is still quite remarkable.

It was Joseph's next big collecting trip to the then unknown parts Sikkhim and Nepal, a journey that lasted from 1848 to 1851, that had most effect on the European garden: new rhododendron species. Even while travelling, he managed, characteristically, to organise their illustration, publishing his magnificent 'Rhododendrons of the Sikkim Himalaya' , most of which he himself soon introduced into England. He returned, together with his co-collector Dr. T. Thomson of the Bengal Army, to Kew with specimens of around six and a half thousand species. They included twenty-eight entirely new rhododendrons, many new orchids, balsams, ferns and mosses, and over three hundred specimens of different timbers for his father's Museum of Economic Botany at Kew. Gardeners will either horrified or grateful that, amongst the many plants he introduced, bergenias must now be amongst the most widely grown.

Books appeared too; he published two volumes of his 'Himalayan Journals' in 1854, 'Illustrations of Himalayan Plants' the next year, which also saw the beginning of the colossal 'Flora Indica'. His appetite for work was clearly prodigious. He himself was appointed Assistant Director of Kew Gardens in1855 and, on his father's death, Director in 1865. He held that august and influential post for twenty years, still travelling extensively, and publishing ever larger projects. His father had edited the 'Botanical Magazine', founded in 1786. It was, and remains, a widely read periodical that illustrates a number of new plants in each issue, together with a page of notes on the plant's history and botanical relationships. For over thirty years, all the plants introduced into Kew from China were described by him, and illustrated with his own coloured drawings. Parallel with that magazine, he also took over from his father the "Icones Plantarum, or Figures with short descriptions of new and rare plants'. While none of these were quite as glamorous to look at as von Siebold's 'Flora Japonica', they were very much cheaper, and reached a much wider audience.

Nothing could stop the flood of plants from the east. Max Ernst Wichura, a German collector, found in Japan the rose that has given rose fanciers so many gorgeous climbers. The Russian Emil Bretschneider scoured the Western Hills or China, sending seed to Charles Sprague Sargent at the Arnold Arboretum in Boston, to Kew, the Jardin des Plantes in Paris, and the botanical gardens in Berlin and St. Petersburg. One tattered tin reached Sargent which contained the first seeds of a widespread northern Asian rhododendron, (*Rhododendron mucronulatum*), whose purple flowers are now the bane of early spring gardens throughout the temperate world, and look particularly dreadful amongst daffodils. The Russian Carl Maximowicz arrived in 1860 and stayed for three and a half years. His Japanese assistant, Tchonoski, is immortalised in that perfect wilderness tree, *Malus tschonskii.* The American collector George Rogers Hall even met von Seibold in Japan, and sent some of that great man's plants directly back to the United States.

By now, the wilderness was becoming a popular garden element in new American gardens too. The idea was being promoted by several writers, most notably by George H. Ellwanger, who wrote the enchanting book 'The Gardens Story' in 1896, and was partner, with Patrick Barry, in a business called Mount Hope Nurseries. To grow the new tree flora, the Arnold Arboretum, set up by outside Boston by Charles Sprague Sargent, was swiftly becoming a gardeners' paradise. Sargent was publicising its development, and thereby promoting the new garden flora in a newsletter called the 'Illustrated Weekly Journal of Horticulture, Landscape Art and Forestry'. One of the genera he championed in its pages was one which had been present in European wildernesses since the sixteenth century, and in Middle Eastern gardens for probably a thousand years before that. These ancient lilacs must have travelled the ancient trade routes from China. The new lilacs travelled new trade routes from China, where many had been collected by Emil Bretschneider. Of these, the issue of June 26, 1889, reported: *Syringa villosa* has, now that the plants are thoroughly established, and of large size, flowered here more abundantly than it ever has before. It is certainly an ornamental plant of the first-class and one of the most important introductions of late years among flowering shrubs.' *Syringa pubescens* was another species which Sargent tipped for future garden grandeur: 'this species is one of the most beautiful Lilacs in cultivation. The individual flowers are not large, and the clusters are smaller than those of other species; they are produced, however, in the greatest profusion, and quite cover the branches. The flowers are at first a delicate rose-color, but, before fading, become almost white; they are deliciously fragrant'. Both are still producing marvellous hybrids at the hands of American breeders.

The final triumph of Japan, and the huge development of the wilderness into the average suburban garden, was due to the vastly influential London nursery of Veitch and Co, run by a long dynasty of Veitch's, most of whom were gardeners, two of whom did some collecting. Overall, the Veitch Nurseries were instrumental in bringing in endless astilbes, birches, Clematis species, Corydalis, many cotoneasters, the fabulous handkerchief tree (*Davidia involucrata*, and one of Wilson's most prized introductions), deutzias, *Dipelta*, endless gentians, *Kolkwitzia amabilis* (now a staple shrub in temperate American suburban shrubberies), dozens of lilies and honeysuckles, magnolias aplenty, *Malus* species, moutan and herbaceous paeonies, hundreds of primulas and rhododenrons, the new *Rodgersia*, many lilacs and viburnums. It is an astonishing list.

Perhaps in response to the plethora of plants, the Veitch family seemed to like a limited number of Christian names, and the relationship between the various James and Johns takes some working out. However, one John collected abroad, and one James. James had the most influence on this chapter, being instrumental in introducing to Europe and America some of the most sumptuous forms of Japanese cherry.

John Gould Veitch was eldest son of a James, and born at Exeter, where the first Veitch nursery was set up in 1839. He was a devoted horticulturist,

but the business' prosperity gave him wider horizons, and he became an
intrepid voyager. In April 1860 he set off for Japan and China. He stayed
briefly at von Siebold's old haunt of Nagasaki, but soon moved on. He was
amongst the first party of Europeans ever to climb the sacred Mount Fuji, and
he cheered wildly when the party's leader had the temerity to implant that
sacred mountain with a Union Jack. Later, in Tokyo, he met Robert Fortune,
and did some collecting in nearby nurseries. Aspects of his trips made heavily
edited copy for the 'Gardeners Gardeners Chronicle and Agricultural
Gazette', a weekly newspaper that makes a fascinating document of
nineteenth century gardening. The clamber up Fuji is described in the issue
for December 22nd 1862, amongst adverts for 'Surplus Stock of Imported
Dutch Bulbs', others for 'Scarlet Rhododendrons, Kalmias (and other plants
for the American Garden)', 'seedling *Cedrus deodara*', and entrancing
articles on topics as diverse as 'Peach Trees and Weevils', 'Holly Tea', and
'The Show of Dogs at Birmingham'.

The first of John Gould Veitch's letters is dated Dec 15th, and he's
visiting gardens in Nagasaki and finds *Cryptomeria japonica*, *Aralia
sieboldii*, viburnums, camellias, and is getting Wardian cases built by local
carpenters, who are amazed by his needs. He ships home ferns like
Gleichenia dichotoma, and collects many acers, variegated aucubas, azaleas,
variegated bamboos, a buddleia of which the Japanese use the bark to make
paper *(Buddleia davidii)*, *Cephalotaxus*, *deutzias*, *Euonymus japonica*, the
first variegated hosta, *Hydrangea japonica*, *H. bracteata*, *H. hirta*, new
gardenias, new spireas, wiegelas, pernettya, pines, podocarpus, oaks... It was
an amazing list.

The viburnums were a Veitch speciality, and absolutely perfect for the
Victorian wilderness. He found some good ones. However, one of the most
famous species, Viburnum farreri (first introduced as, and sometimes still
called, *V. fragrans*) had to wait until 1911, when William Purdom sent seed
to Messrs Veitch. This seed came from plants in the Temple Gardens in
Gansu, where Purdom actually found two forms, one white flowered, the
other pink. The seedlings didn't flower until 1920, which was, sadly, six
years after the nursery itself had closed. Here's Reginald Farrer, writing of its
discovery in 'On the Eaves of the World' of 1917: "Shallow scrub and
coppice descended here to the track-side, and here we came on the
Viburnum, at first isolated and suspicious, but soon in such quantity and such
situations that one could no longer doubt that here this most glorious of

flowering shrubs is genuinely indigenous. Its place of origin had long been in doubt, though all over North China it is probably the best-beloved and most universal of garden plants; so that there was real satisfaction in thus having traced it to its home, in the wild hills immediately to the south of Shi-hor (Xi he) and probably elsewhere in this narrow belt, though after this day we never set eyes on it again in nature'. Later he refers to its "gracious arching masses, ten feet high and more across, whose naked boughs in spring. before the foliage, become one blaze of soft pink lilac-spikelets, breathing an intense fragrance of heliotrope. The white form, indeed, is pure and lovely as the best of forced white lilac, but my own heart goes out yet more specially perhaps to the commoner pink type, whose blushing stars glisten as if built of crystals. after the pleasant fashion of so many spring flowers...'.

James Harry Veitch, eldest son of John Gould Veitch, was also responsible for some marvellous things, especially the beautiful Rhododenron Schlippenbachii, first discovered forty years earlier on the coast of Korea. In Japan between 1891 and 1893 (together with India and Australia) he shipped home the Japanese lantern vine *(Physalis franchetti)*, for the delight of children, gardeners and endless numbers of flower arrangers. To his regret, though, he missed the flowering of Japan's fabled cherry orchards. Presciently, he arranged for local nurserymen to send young plants to his nursery at Chelsea. From the early 1890's the business began to receive some of the huge numbers of Japanese Prunus species and cultivars. Almost all of the one hundred and fifty sorts introduced were an instant success, and it is no wonder that 1930's suburban gardens still full of them. Rows of red brick houses have them as street trees, sometimes alternating pink and white, all over Europe. Design conscious gardeners pride themselves on growing only 'Tai haku'. The parks of great American cities grow them with a sense of scale that is entirely Japanese in inspiration.

These cherries have an immense and august history, and have long been a favourite in noblemens' gardens in Japan. In 'The Tale of Prince Genji', a romance written around 1000 A.D, the garden of a prince has 'a very pleasant arrangement of lakes and hills. The hills were high in the southeast quarter, where cherry trees were planted in large numbers. The pond was most attractively designed. Among the plantings in the forward parts of the garden were cinquefoil pines, red plums, cherries, wisteria, Kerria, and rock azalea…., and far away in the private gardens a willow trailed its branches in a deepening green, and cherry blossoms were rich and sensuous'.

A scholar called Rassho Naba (1595-1648) was the first to write a book devoted entirely to cherries, and covered Chinese and Korean types, as well as those of his own hillsides. After it appeared, a knowledge of cherry varieties was as much part of intellectual culture as was an appreciation of painting, music and poetry. His garden contained well over two hundred varieties of flowering cherry, and even in 1822, an illustrated catalogue, romantically entitled 'A paragon of bowers' shows many of them. Rather as in nineteenth century roses, their names alone are rich and poetic, making the gardener want to plant them almost for the name itself. Certainly, Western gardeners, taking up Japanese ideas in a way that even von Siebold can hardly have dreamed, fell instantly in love with them. Planted in their milliards, with the introduction of the Japanese cherries, the ancient European 'wilderness' finally dissolves into the way we garden today.

Around mid-point in the nineteenth century, the old wilderness begins to show very clearly how garden elements evolve in response to incoming plants. The sort of phylogenetic diagrams that illustrate how the the variously branched tree of reptiles budded off, milliards of years ago, a branch of tiny, warm-blooded and befurred proto-mammals, and elsewhere a branch of animals with feathers which, by flapping their forelegs, could take to the air, is an example. Botanists have endless fun and feuds doing similar things for the plant world. Gardeners can easily copy zoologists and botanists.

The wilderness sprouted one amazingly vigourous branch, and one which now, like the mammals and birds, has a powerful and independent life of its own. When discussing the wilderness in the mid-eighteenth century, Philip Miller's list suggest that the wilderness walks be bordered with roses. Of Europe's wild species, only the eglantine rose (*Rosa eglanteria*), with its deliciously apple-scented leaves was much grown in the garden. Most of the rest were ancient garden plants, often so old and of such complex parentage, that they had lost complete contact with any known wild species. All these old garden roses are doubles, sometimes with so many petals that they have been called 'centifolias'. In double flowers like these, the pollen-bearing anthers have been transformed into petals, and therefore the plant is male-sterile. In spite of this, there seems to have been some breeding going on in Holland in the early 17th century, though quite what plants were involved, and how it was done, isn't clear. In any case, the total number of roses in cultivation was still only around fifty or so.

In Britain, the 'Society of London Gardeners' published a catalogue in 1730, in which only forty three roses are listed as being 'available to the public and recommended for being intermixed with flowering trees and shrubs in small wilderness quarters...' The 1754 list of William Joyce, who had a nursery at Gateshead, near Newcastle contains thirty two roses, including the ancient Rosa Mundi and various 'cabbage' and centifolia roses, as well as a double yellow and a musk.

Things were soon to change. Andre Michaux (who plays a bigger role elsewhere in this book) was collecting roses from Persian gardens in the early

1780's. Plants were coming in from China too. These were to be vastly important. In China, with its warm south, species had evolved that, like many sub-tropic plants, bloomed throughout the entire season of growth. All European and Middle Eastern roses had but a single, evanescent, flowering. This had engaged the sympathy of the poetically minded since Western literature began, but always irritated gardeners. The Chinese admired roses too, and that rich and ancient garden culture had gradually selected a number of roses that were almost perpetual flowering, were reasonably double, but were rather scrawny shrubs, or rampant climbers. Screen paintings around 1000AD show the delicate, slightly nodding flower and distinctive foliage of what became known in the West as the 'China Rose'.

There is a slight possibility that it had been grown in Europe in the sixteenth century, for something appears in a painting by the Florentine artiste Angelo Bronzino, dated 1529, that could perhaps be one of this group of plants. It may have reached Venice as an item of trade, but its owners probably didn't realise that it would die out in a cold winter. The first European herbarium specimen in existence is dated 1733. Linnaeus doesn't seem to have known of that sheet when he described the species, using a specimen probably from Peter Osbeck's garden, a pupil of his, who was collecting in Canton in 1751. Living plants reached the West soon after, and a China rose was grown at the Chelsea Physic Garden in 1759. From there, cuttings being easy to root, it was soon at the Princess Augusta's garden at Kew, and, following social precedence, in the garden of the redoubtable Dr Fothergill soon after that. With the name Rosa semperflorens, it reached the pages of the 'Botanical Magazine' in December, 1794. It was described thus: 'We are induced to consider the rose here represented as one of the most desirable plants in point of ornament ever introduced … its flowers, large in proportion to the plants are semidouble, and with great fragrance; they blossom during the whole of the year, more sparingly indeed in the winter months; the shoot itself is more hardy than most greenhouse plants…'

Unlike European doubles, it soon proved to be highly fertile, and enthusiasts like M. Thory and M. Redoute were raising seedlings in their Paris gardens from 1798. Soon, all gardeners realised that if they could combine the long season the the new China roses with the robust habit and heavily petalled flowers of the current European ones, they would achieve an extraordinary horticultural and commercial 'coup'. French nurserymen seem to have been the first to notice that the old European roses, if grown in very starved conditions, produced fewer petals, but the occasional fertile anther. Rose breeding was possible; nurseries were soon springing up. One in London was specialising in roses from the 1780s, and one in New York soon followed. But the French gardeners began rose breeding in considerable earnest. M. Dupont sold the best of his seedlings to the first major rose collector, the Empress Josephine. M. Descemet did the same. Soon there were so many marvellous new sorts that it was clear the old wilderness couldn't do them justice. Gardeners had to create a brand new part of the garden to hold them all - the rosarium.

As something to occupy her mind during Napoleon's Egyptian campaign, Josephine bought the Chateau de Malmaison, near Choisy, in 1799. She began her collection of roses in 1804, and by 1814 it contained all the species and varieties then known. With her English gardener, Howatson, she began to ransack British and French nurseries. One British nurseryman, John Kennedy, even had a special passport to enable him to cross with plants from the one warring country to the other. Josephine's gardens at Malmaison were famed for roses several years before the English garden designer Humphry Repton made his designs for a rose garden at the Earl of Bridgewater's estate at Ashridge in Hertfordshire in 1814.

The garden at Malmaison proved an enormous stimulus to large-scale hybridizing, encouraging the French nursery industry which produced Descemet, Cochet, and Laffay. In 1815, and for the second time in this chapter, the chaos of war played a part in the garden. The Napoleonic Wars ended with the British troops over-running Paris, and a whole regiment chose Descemet's nursery as a place to bivouac. His plants were mostly ruined, and as neither the French or the British government would recompense him for the losses, he went bankrupt. The owner of a nearby hardware store, Jean-Pierre Vibert, had survived commercially. Interested in roses, he bought out what remained of Descemet's premises and properties, including remnants of his breeding-notes, and his roses. A man of great energy and acumen, he soon became one of the most influential rose breeders of the 19th century, fuelling the demand for rose gardens, with many of his productions being so beautiful that they are still in our gardens.

Vibert was born on January 31, 1777. With more business sense than Descemet, he nursed his venture into considerable prosperity. He bred with, and offered, roses of all sorts, especially the new Chinas and Teas. He imported the first yellow Tea, 'Parks' Yellow Tea-Scented China'. He developed the new Noisette roses. He also used traditional sorts like the Albas, Gallicas, Centifolias, Mosses, and Damasks, and so loved them that he kept breeding them even after his public had moved on to Portlands, Bourbons and the rest.

At length, in 1851, at the age of 74, he sold his business to his nursery foreman, who kept it going into the 1890's. He is supposed to have said, towards the end of his life, "Like the rest of the world, I have thought that I adored and detested many men and many things. In reality, I have loved only Napoléon and roses.'. His close family must have been chilled by this. It is perhaps fitting that his most famous climbing rose, named after a daughter, the pale 'Aimée Vibert', became a favourite flower to wind through the railings of cemetery plots. It mixes the American 'Champney's Pink Cluster' with a double form of R. sempervirens. The firm still exists.

'Champney's Pink Cluster' shows how close the links between French and American rose fanciers had become. Brothers Louis and Philippe Noisette were nurserymen respectively in Paris, France and Charleston, South Carolina. Roses moved swiftly between the two. John Champney, a wealthy farmer in Charleston, crossed some plants he'd bought from Louis: Rosa moschata and a China monthly. He called the best of his seedlings 'Champney's Pink Cluster'. This was soon sent to France. Philippe himself used either Mr. Champney's rose, or similar crosses, to produce a charming double lilac pink climber, low on perfume, but flowering well into November. Excited, he sent plants to France, where it was marketed as

'Blush Noisette', and became part of a whole new group of roses called the noisettes. Blush Noisette is still a marvel. American gardeners, too, were soon making their own collections. Francis Parkman assembled a collection of a thousand sorts of rose assembled in a sumptuous rose garden at his summer home on the shores of Jamaica Pond, near Boston, in the 1850s. The same garden also held a vast number of new Japanese introductions.

Soon these endless sorts of new rose were exported to India, and China. In China, they causes a furore, and even Chinese gardeners competed to grow 'Madame Hardy', 'Robert le Diable' and the rest. Humphry Repton, John Caie, and Mrs Lawrence may have been famous rose garden designers, but they became that only once the flood of new cultivars had begun. And with the Empress Josephine as a collector and their publicist, the new roses could hardly fail; the rose garden, an offshoot of the wilderness, soon became almost a synonym for the whole garden itself.

Chapter 8

The Rock Garden

David Stuart

THE ROCK GARDEN

'...on the higher alpine meadows, from the summits of the cliffs to the verge of the snows, is an indescribable wealth of bloom, the colour-scheme changing from month to month as the seasons advance. Most of the species being gregarious, absolute sheets and carpets of colour are the result. *Trollius, Anemones, Primula, Gentiana, Cremanthodium, Cyananthus*, blue and yellow, *Corydalis, Meconopsis, Pedicularis, Phlomis, Parnassia, Saxifraga, Orchis, Roscoea, Delphinium, Oxytropis, Plectranthus, Salvia, Cerastium, Incarvillea, Morina* – these are only a few of the many genera represented, as well as *Ericaceae* and many peculiar species of *Rhododendron*. Two of the finest, seeds of which were secured in 1913 are the magnificent *Dracocephalum isabellae* and the equally beautiful *Anemone lancifolia*... *Saxifragae* are rampant on every hill, scree, and stony Meadow, brightening the dullest spots with their orange and golden blooms. One splendid new species, a cushion plant named *S. pulchra,* has rose-coloured petals and silvery grey-foliage. Many other new species were found on the range. *Campanulaceae* is well represented by several new *Codonopsis* and many new *Adenophora.Campanula crenulata*, with its deep black-indigo bells is on every ledge and humus-covered boulder…'

This is George Forrest, writing about his exploration of China looking for plants for a new part of the garden: the rockery. His books, and articles for the 'Gardeners Chronicle', must have launched ten thousand new rockeries per page, especially when he wrote passages that describe the hills: 'But the scenery of the upper Ealwin can never be forgotten by anyone who has wondered at it in the rich sunshine which prevails after the autumn rains have given way to the first touch of winter. The great variety of rock formation, the abundant forests and vegetation, and the diversity of light effects between the summits of the ranges (at 10,000 to 13,000') and the abyss in which the river flows produce a vast panorama of ever-changing beauty. In the morning, the sun, as it touches the top of the Mekong divider sends wide shafts of turquoise light down the side gullies to the rivers which seems to be transformed into silver. The pines along the top of the ridges stand out as if limned by the hand of a Japanese artist. In the evening all the wide slopes of the Mekong side are flooded with red and orange lights, which defy photography and would be the despair of a Turner. The traveller whose fortune it has been to explore the great rivers of this, our north-east Indian frontier will admit that the Salwin, while it is inhospitable, difficult and barbarous, far exceeds in natural beauty all the valleys of the sister rivers, the Yang-tru, the Mekong or the Irawadi .' Of course, no gardener could do anything like that, but a yard or two of saxifrages or codonopsis, and a few pieces of stone, would at least have the right association.

Since the late eighteenth century, gardening has become, more and more, a way of classifying plants. The system doesn't look at their possible evolutionary relationships. It is entirely plant centred, looking at what a plant needs to grow. It started with the American garden, where plants that were assumed to like wet, peaty conditions were grouped together. As the gardeners' access to a wildly increasing range of lovely plants grew easier and simpler, new plant groupings emerged that demanded a part of the garden to themselves. The rockery, that still fast-evolving form of gardening, or part of the garden, is one of them.

Rockeries were, at first, pure theatre. From the middle of the eighteenth century, artificial grottos and mock ruins became fashionable adjuncts in any garden large enough to pretend to 'landscape'. To make these theatrical and often gimcrack elements look more ancient and authentic, they were sometimes draped with ivy, or even planted with plants known to like growing in rocky crevices. Wallflowers and the European saxifrages from the Alps were the most decorative plants used, almost until Joseph Pitton de Tournefort returned from his travels bearing lovely plants like the marjoram *Origanum tournefortii* and the violently violet *Aubretia deltoides*.

No gardener, then, wanted anything in the least reminiscent of rocky or mountainous terrain. Most eighteenth century travellers found mountain landscapes frightening, passing through them as quickly as possible, eyes tight shut in terror. The mountains and their plants were associated with chaos; climatic, geological, and social. Brigands and outlaws lived, in the popular imagination, amongst peaks and ravines. Perhaps Tournefort's aubretia was the turning point. Gardeners began to wonder what other showy plants might decorate their polite rockwork. Some began to explore. Miller's 'Gardeners Dictionary' of 1731 lists a few species now thought of as 'alpines': *Androsace lactea, Aster alpinus, Geranium argenteum, Gentiana acaulis* amongst a few other from Europe. From America, where the real rocky Rockies were as yet unexplored, he lists eastern woodlanders, now commonly found in shaded parts of rock gardens: *Sanguinaria, Trillium erectum, Uvularia*, but not much else.

William Forsyth, who succeeded Philip Miller as Curator of the Chelsea Physic Garden, began to assemble one of the first proper rock gardens in I 774. Unfortunately he also set a strange precedent, probably never himself having looked carefully at a rocky landscape. He seemed to think that a rock garden could be made out of virtually any material remotely hard. This early garden contained forty tons of assorted stone rescued from the roadside outside the Tower of London, as well as substantial quantities of flints and chalk from the nearby 'downs'. But it also had some lumps of lava brought back from Iceland two years earlier by Sir Joseph Banks. This heterogenous mix was heaped in a pile, but was rather short of plants.

In 1775, Dr John Fothergill and his friend Dr Pitcairn of Warwick Lane, London, sent the Scots gardener Thomas Blaikie to Switzerland to hunt the Alps for plants. Blaikie travelled into the Jura as well, sending back over four hundred parcels of plants to Chelsea. His bag included *Ranunculus glacialis, Campanula cenisia, Trifolium alpinum, Veronica bellidioides, Hutchinsia alpina, Pyrola uniflora, Androsace villosa, Polygala chamaebuxus,* and the enchanting *Rhododendron ferrugineum.* It was an immense augmentation of the mountain flora, and gardeners must have wondered quite how to integrate these new things amongst the ivies draping their mock-frightening grottos or 'gothic' castles.

In any case, many gardeners didn't have room or means to make fake caverns and castles, but they still wanted to grow these exciting new 'alpines'. They took up the Physic Garden's mode of rockery-making with enthusiasm.   Then as now, whatever its size a rockery allowed the gardener to grow large numbers of small species in a small space. It also appealed to something in human nature that likes small-scale models of something much larger and less controllable. Unfortunately, the new rock gardeners also copied Chelsea's other lead, incorporating all sorts of rubbish amongst the saxifrages and aubretias and all the new plants being illustrated in 'Curtis' Botanical Magazine'. These were all immensely desirable. Between 1787 and 1804, now also under Forsyth's control, the magazine illustrated exquisite European plants like *Cyclamen coum, Gentiana acaulis, Ranunculus graminifolius, Ramonda myconii, Daphne cneorum,* and some exciting Americans like the new phloxes, especially *Phlox divaricata, P. subulata, and P. setacea.* Gardeners had to have them, but didn't know how best to show them off.

It started first in America. John Bartram had already sent over things like *Epigea repens,* powerfully perfumed but difficult to grow, as well as small irises, creeping phloxes and even *Dicentra eximea.* But as the 'white' colonisation of North America continued, and the continent's exploitation began, it became clear that the western lands needed to be mapped and explored, and an easy way found through the great Rocky Mountain ranges to get to the Pacific coast. Some of the old indian tracks went through Montana, and the homelands of the bitterroot (*Lewisia rediviva*). No-one then had any idea that it would go on to become one of the great rock garden genera, one which has fuelled many gardeners love of alpines, and one which is still developing fast.

In 1803, President Thomas Jefferson won approval from Congress for a project that became one of North America's first great adventure stories. He wanted to know if there was a route to the Pacific Ocean following two rivers: the Missouri to get to the as yet uncharted Rockies from the West, and the Columbia, which flows down from them to the east. He hoped that if the sources of the two great rivers turned out to be reasonably close, then perhaps American traders would have an easy route from west coast to east. This would help them compete with British fur companies and their associated traders expanding southward from Canada. He also wanted to reach the western Indian tribes, largely to tell them that American, rather than Canadian, traders would soon come to buy their furs. But he also wanted access to the East.

Jefferson selected as leader for the expedition Meriwether Lewis, a twenty-eight year old Army captain, a family friend, and by now Jefferson's private secretary. Lewis was already a keen naturalist, having spent long hours as a boy tramping and hunting in the woods of Virginia. He chose a former army friend, 32-year-old William Clark, to be his co-leader of the expedition.

Lewis and Clark reached their first staging point at the junctions of the Mississippi and Missouri rivers near St. Louis in December 1803. They spent the whole of the first winter camped at the mouth of Wood River, on the Illinois side of the Mississippi, opposite the entrance to the Missouri River. During that season, they recruited young woodsmen and enlisted soldiers who volunteered from nearby army outposts. The mixed bag of men included ex-trappers, hopeful explorers, and men who could speak Indian languages. They even found a Frenchman with a bought Indian wife who spoke several tribal languages. She proved of enormous worth throughout the entire period of the expedition.

The troupe broke camp on May 14, 1804. Clark wrote in his journal: "I set out at 4 oClock P.M and proceeded on under a jentle brease up the Missouri." The river journey was hard and long, and progress, either by boat, or on the shore, was slow and exhausting. When winter began to close in again, in early November, they were near present-day Washburn, North Dakota. They were 164 days and approximately 1,510 miles distant from their last winter camp at Wood River. Even by next summer, it wasn't easy. Lewis's journal records 'July 20, 1804

For a month past the party have been troubled with boils, and occasionally with the dysentery. These boils were large tomours which broke out under the arms, on the legs, and, generally, in the parts most exposed to action, which sometimes became to painful to permit the men to work.

This disorder….has not affected the general health of the party, which is quite as good, if not better, than that of the same number of men in any other situation.' Later that summer, Clark wrote: 'August 30, 1804 … a Council under an Oak Tree near where we had a flag flying on a high flagstaff … The Souex is a Stout bold looking people, & well made, the greater part of make use of Bows & arrows. Some few fusees I observe among them, notwith standing they live by the Bow and arrow, they do not Shoot So Well as the Northern Indians the Warriers are Verry much deckerated with Paint Porcupine quils & feathers, large leagins and mockersons, all with buffalow roabs of Different Colours. the Squars wore Peticoats & a White Buffalow roabe with the black hare turned back over their necks and Shoulders.'

A whole year later, on August 21, 1805, interpreter and hunter George Drouilliard was hunting along the shore of the Beaverhead River. He met a group of Shoshoni indians. At first friendly, things turned sour when one the Shoshoni snatched his gun, and they all raced off. Drouilliard, bravely, gave chase, and overtook one of the tiring Indian horses. Fortunately the gun wasn't loaded, and instead of being shot, he managed to retrieve his weapon. In the fracas, the Indians had left behind their scant belongings. Drouilliard took them back to his camp. Amongst the haul, Captain Lewis found 'a couple of bags wove with the fingers of the bark of the silk-grass containing each about a bushel of dryed service burries some ch[ok]echerry cakes and about a bushel of roots of three different kinds dryed and prepared for uce which were foalded in as many parchment hides of buffaloe.' One lot of roots 'were brittle, hard, of the size of a small quill, cilindric and as white as

snow throughout, except some small parts of the hard black rind which they
had not seperated in the preperation. This the Indians with me informed were
always boiled for use. I made the exp[e]riment, found that they became
perfectly soft by boiling, but had a very bitter taste, which was naucious to
my pallate, and I transfered them to the Indians who had eat them heartily."
The plant was called by Indians and French trappers alike 'bitter root.' It was
to become called *Lewisia rediviva.*

    It was an important Indian winter food crop, heavy with legend. One
described how an old Flathead Indian woman sat weeping on the bank of the
In-schu-te-schu, or Red Willow River, in the shadow of the Chi-quil-quil-
kane, or Red Mountains, singing a death song for her starving sons. The
rising sun heard her plaint, and sent a red spirit-bird to comfort her. The bird
promised that from each of her falling tears a new flower would grow, tinted
with the rose of his feathers and the white of her hair, and springing from a
root as bitter as her sorrow but as nourishing as her love. The prophecy came
true, and her people called the plant spatlum, meaning 'bitterroot'.
    Lewis later collected whole plants at a place now called Bitterroot
Valley in July of 1806, and took them back to Philadelphia, where they were
formally described by the botanist Frederick Pursh (1774-1820). The ancient
meadows where it once grew in such abundance, and which were so
important to several local tribes, particularly Flatheads, Kutenais, Shoshonis,
and Nez Perces, are now destroyed by development.
    Lewisias, which ironically became the state flower of Montana, turned
out to hybridise easily. Long thought fussy, some of the new hybrids have
set out from the rockery and are due to colonise other parts of the garden.
They have already become easy pot plants, but vigorous new plants like one
called 'Little Plum' may turn out to be easy border plants too. It's a genus

that has come a long way since those shrivelled roots were found in an Indian's bag.

In September 23, 1806, the tattered Lewis and Clark's Corps of Discovery arrived at last at St. Louis and "received a harty welcom from it's inhabitants." The men had covered 8,000 miles of territory over a period of 2 years, 4 months, and 9 days. There had been only one fatality, though many terrible times. Lewis and Clark remained firm friends. Congress rewarded the officers and men of the military enterprise with extensive grants of land. The Indian woman Sacagawea, an essential ambassadress and translator for the expedtion, received nothing.

However beautiful the new Americans like lewisias, carpeting penstemons, dwarf rhododendrons were, and however arduous their collection had been, there seemed no limit to the vulgarity of the garden in which they were planted. Wealth simply increased the awfulness of the taste. Things got worse before they got, generally, better. By 1838, rockeries were beginning to look dreadful. As always, in a new and quickly developing field, all sorts of people adopted the role of 'the expert'. A writer in Sir Joseph Paxton's 'Magazine of Botany' suggested some pretty little rockwork thus: 'the turf on which the pedestals stand is to be inclined at an angle of 45", and the pedestals [for vases] are enclosed in small circular borders, on which may be placed fragments of rock, or shells, and by the introduction of a little soil amongst them, alpine plants may be successfully grown'. After suggesting adding a parterre, grass pyramids in the corners to hold statuary, the writer continues: 'The introduction of fountains, of chaste and unique structure, and ornamented with every variety of rock and shell, into the central compartments, with jets of water issuing from every crevice, and propelled with diverse and ever-varying degrees of force, would form most delightful and refreshing spectacles during the summer months'.

In the 1840's, the rockery could be composed of broken porcelain plates, broken bricks, flints, and tattered statuary. By 1853, the 'Book of the Garden' suggested 'stones, the fused masses of brick procured from brick kilns, or indeed, any coarse material most convenient to be got. These are built up in the most rugged and mis-shapen forms imaginable and afterward covered over with Roman cement, and formed into recesses, projections, and overhanging crags, according to the taste of the artist. Sufficient apertures are left for receiving soil, in which rock plants are planted. When the whole is perfectly dry and set, it is painted with oil paint to represent veined or

stratified granite, or any other kind of natural rockwork that may be desired'.
It's difficult to know how any plant at all survived that.

The most unnatural rockery was at the Duke of Marlborough's private
garden at Blenheim. Though this was actually formed on a scar of natural
rock, it had been hewn into zig-zag paths with numerous hand-cut niches on
each side to receive plants. However, most of the niches were lined with
spar, a richly coloured, expensive and glittery natural rock. The final result
was a rich and sparkling effect, which can have done little to make the plants
it contained look at home. Slightly quieter in effect was the rockery at Syon
Park, London, where a pile of only moderately large granite stones had been
shipped from Scotland. Assembled and planted, they were compared by most
London journalists "to the scenery of a Highland glen". Only Jane Loudon
was brave enough to "confess there does not appear to me the slightest
resemblance. In fact, the Syon rockwork is so overpowered by the
magnificent conservatory in front... that it becomes quite a secondary
object... It consists of masses of granite, intermixed with broken capitals
planted with ornamental flowering plants, principally exotic...'. Even she
approved of some rock gardens which must, in their hey-day, have appeared
equally odd. One she especially liked was Lady Broughton, at the Hoole,
Cheshire. Mrs Loudon wrote that one 'stands quite alone, the only one of its
kind. The design for this rockwork was taken from a small model,
representing the mountains of Savoy, with the valley of Chamouni... The
plants are all strictly alpine – the only liberty taken being the mingling of the
alpine plants of hot and cold countries, or rather of different elevations,
together, and this is contrived very ingeniously, by placing fragments of dark
stone to absorb the heat, round those that require most warmth, and fragments
of white stone to reflect the heat, round those that require to be kept cool'.
Thomas says that at Hoole House, efforts made to grow pyrolas, *Coptis
trifolia* from Japan, *Calceolaria fothergillii* from Patagonia, *Jeffersonia* from
North America, and *Cortusa,* soldanellas and so on from Europe.

That all sounds a bit better, but even much later in the century, Sir Frank
Crisp's rockery was a model of the Matterhorn, replete with scale models of
chamois goats made of tin. He took it very seriously, and when someone
made fun of the whole thing, there were court cases and poison pen letters.
Another made in 1847 under the close direction of Sir Charles Isham, at his
seat of Lamport Hall, Northamptonshire, was a huge rockey wall decorated
with miniature caverns designed to show off his collection of German garden

gnomes. The mountain's slopes were planted with dwarf conifers.

The 1850's were notable for the development of the pocket rock garden system developed by James McNab at the Royal Botanic Garden, Edinburgh. In these, small rectangular containers were made of pieces of stone, all joined together like a piece of dishevelled honeycomb. The idea was to give each contained plant it's own special receipe of soil. The whole thing looked horrible, and didn't really suit the plants either.

At last, William Robinson wrote a book on alpines, suggesting that their rockery should look like an outcrop of natural stone, with mossy rocks showing through a sward of sedums, saxifrages, pinks, and so on. Unusually for Robinson, it wasn't a freshly minted idea. The first rock garden to use a natural outcrop seems to h ave been made at Redleaf, at Penshurst in Kent, in 1839. The great Greek Revival house of Belsay in Northumberland had been constructed with stone from a quarry only a hundred yards away from its foundation. By 1939 too, this had been turned into a splendidly romantic rock and ravine garden. In America, naturalism took a bit longer. It seems to have been General Stephen Minot Weld who made the first naturalistic rock garden near Boston in the early 1880's. Best of all, he planted it up with a vast collection of American native plants. Back in Britain, the nursery trade slowly caught on to the new ideas, and companies like Backhouse of York, with a thriving 'alpine' trade by the 1850's, soon began creating huge exhibits constructed with huge rocks a few decades later.

But the real impetus for change originated at least partly with a strange Englishman called Reginald Farrrer. Farrer was born in 1880 to a well-to-do family with a pleasant estate at Ingleborough, high on the limestone fells of western Yorkshire, England. The child had a slightly deformed palate, and as such a defect would have been outrageously mocked at the private schools of

the day (though children are as cruel today), his parents decided to educate
him at home. He was highly gifted, and seems to have been born with a love
of flowers. When only three years old he was, he later wrote, overwhelmed
when he saw his first fields of narcissus at Cap d'Antibes. He was soon after
in the South again, later claiming to have been thrilled at his first discovery of
a Lady Tulip (*Tulipa clusiana*, and indeed very beautiful)). At ten, he knew
the flora of his local Ingleborough hills, and at fourteen, had made his first
rock garden in an abandoned quarry on the estate. He entered Oxford
University at 17 years of age and graduated in 1902.

He already knew a lot about gardening when he went to Japan for eight
months, also managing to visit China and Korea. Already entirely confident,
he immediately wrote 'The Garden of Asia' in 1904. Once back in England,
he tried turning novelist too, but soon realised that he could more easily make
lively copy out of his gardens, not out of his limited personal life. Many
associates had already noted his extreme egotism. He became influential in
the garden when he published 'My Rock Garden' in 1907. It was a best
seller, catching the mood of the moment and continuously in print for the
next forty years. Following books met with less success: 'Alpines and Bog
Plants' (1908), 'In a Yorkshire Garden' (1909) and 'Among the Hills' (1910),
and a book about the alpine plants of the Dolomites. With the rather
grandiose title of 'The Dolomites: King Laurin's Garden', it appeared in
1913, just before the Dolomites became firmly out of bounds for most British
gardeners. Through successes and failures, he extols naturalism of planting,
not so much in copying the plaster Matterhorn and the rest, but handling
rocks in as naturalistic a way as possible, and making them look like natural
outcrops even in a small suburban garden of solid London clay. He seems
not to have been aware of how much easier it all was amongst his native fells
at Ingleborough. At least he certainly caused the end of McNab's awful
'pocket system', though he didn't manage to kill off what he called 'Dogs
Grave' or 'Almond Pudding' sort of rockeries still so common.

In his own plantings of his own collections, he took great trouble over plant associations. He wanted to make them look as authentic as he could, making sure too that the plants had ideal conditions for growth. In his books, he had a way of making the plants very much larger than life, and he was sometimes accused of over-promoting plants which, once in the rock garden, failed to live up to their new owners hopes. Sometimes the plants do indeed disappear beneath the superstructure of words. Here he is on eretrichums… 'No eye of faith is quite keen enough to gulp the whole glory of …. those irresistible wads of silky silver nestling into the highest darkest ridges of the granites and almost hidden from view by the mass of rounded yellow-eyed little faces of a blue so pure and clear and placidly celestial that the richest Forget-me-not by their side takes on a shrill and vulgar note. The blue of *Eretrichium* is absolute … it has a quality of bland and assured perfection impossible to describe as to imagine. And still more impossible to believe by those who have only seen the comparatively rare and squalid stars of faded turquoise which are all that *Eretrichium* usually condescends to show in cultivation – if it ever condescends to reach that pitch of ostentatiousness at all. *Eretrichium* is the typical high-alpine, only to be seen with climbing and effort; it is the motto of the Mountaineers and the crown of achievement for the walker in the Alps, who will have trudged over leagues of Flannel-flower before once he catches sight of the King of the Alps, set in blobs of sky across the face of some dark cliff or in some sunny slope of the highest ridges making blots of fallen heaven among the scant herbage of the hill'.

Though many gardeners no doubt resisted the lure of the *Eretrichium*, he made it very hard for readers not to want to rush out at once in search of a meconopsis or an androsace of their own, perhaps from Farrer's own nursery in Yorkshire. Known as the Craven Nursery, it was where he built his first moraine, or 'scree' as he named its successors. They proved a wonderful way of growing alpines. His own enthusiasm carried him further and further afield. He bored quickly, and needed greater and greater doses of horticultural and botanical beauty to keep his senses alive. The mountains of western China called.

His great Chinese trips, first with Purdom and then with Euan Cox lasted between 1914 and 1919. He and his companions brought back wonders like *Allium cyaneum, Anemone narcissiflora* var. *villosa, Daphne tangutica* surely one of the most memorable small evergreen shrubs in the garden, and overwhelming in flower (it was first found, but not brought home, by Antwerp Pratt in 1888), *Gentiana farreri, Semi-aquilegia ecalcarata*, the marvellous shrub *Viburnum fragrans* and many more. One of the most sensational alpines was *Meconopsis punicea*. He wrote: 'At all times and in all places the Blood Poppy calculates successfully on taking your breath away, but never does it do so more triumphantly than when you see its huge poppy flags of vermilion hovering in the sunlit patches of a copse ... of all its race it is perhaps the most overwhelming... Never among all its millions could I discover the least inconstancy of colour, though needless to say I quested long and far in search of the pure albinos which must assuredly be one of the loveliest flowers on earth.' It is certainly dramatic, but in cultivation the colour of the elegantly hanging petals is a sombre rust-rose.

Cox later wrote of him: 'Even after the lapse of eleven years I have a vivid memory of Farrer in the hills, his stocky figure clad in khaki shorts and shirt, tieless and collarless, a faded topee on his head, old boots and stockings that gradually slipped down and clung about his ankles as the day wore on. The bustle of the early start; the constant use of the field-glasses which always hung around his neck; the discussions very one-sided owing to my ignorance about the value and relationship of the various plants; his intense satisfaction when a plant was once in the collecting tin and was found worthy; his grunt of disapproval when it was worthless... the Luncheon interval with its attendant cold goat rissole and slab chocolate; his enjoyment of our evening tot of rum, a necessity in the rains; and above all his indomitable energy that never spared a frame which was hardly built for long days of searching and climbing, All these I say are as fresh to me as if they had happened yesterday.'

He died on a 'one-man and his servants' expedition in Upper Burma. His head servant wrote to Cox that from October 1st, Farrer had suffered

from a cough and serious chests pain.'On the l4th', he went on, 'he
discontinued to take his food except soda water and whisky and medicines
for his benefit . ... And without giving any pain and trouble to us he breathed
his last on the morning of the l9th October 1920, at about 11-30 a.m.' The
servants carried his body down to the nearest out-post of Empire. His grave is
marked by a memorial plaque paid for by his beloved mother.

Though Farrer's end was sad, other collectors searching for alpine
beauties in the mountains of western China and its neighbouring states had
some terrible experiences that Farrer managed to avoid. The region was
always turbulent and lawless, but the British invasion of Tibet, and the first
Chinese attempts at its settlement, made it even more dangerous.

It is worthwhile, when looking at some charming and innocent saxifrage
or androsace nestling on its scree, to remember that its collecting quite
probably cost some blood-spattered collector dear. One wrote, in the
'Gardeners Chronicle' of his appalling trials: 'The narrow valleys, broken by
cross ridges and great spurs, are cut off from each other by difficult and
dangerous passes, closed for half the year by snow. The great rivers' which
flow through funnel-like gorges are quite unnavigable; the upper Mekong can
only be crossed by bridges consisting of a single rope composed of split
bamboos, across which passengers are slung, trussed up with leather thongs
like chickens ready for the spit.

Here and there in the folds of the mountains the Lamas of the yellow
sect have established huge gombas, or lamaseries, and, by a combination of
force and fraud, have become the real masters of the country... they terrorise
the poverty-stricken superstitious peasantry and pay little or no regard to the
nominal sovereignty of the Celestial mandarins.

In the summer of 1905, I found myself in [their territories] .... quarters
being with the hospitable and venerable chief of the Tzekou mission, Pere
Dubernard. He first settled at Tzekou when Napoleon III.was at the height of
his power, and he had never left the country since....

It soon became clear that Lamas meant business, and were determined
to pay off old scores of jealousy against the missionaries, who had
endeavored for so many years, not without success, to deliver the people
from the moral and material chains of Lamaism. Soon our friends among the
Tibetans fell away from us or proved false. The mission house was
indefensible, and, if defensible, had no one to defend it save two aged French
priests and myself....

The rising moon that night saw us making our way [to safety] by a narrow and dangerous track Along the right bank of the Mekong, the two Fathers on their mules, and myself and the little band of native Christians on foot; on our left roared the Mekong in furious flood; on our right rose the great Mekong-Salwin dividing range ... in the dark we passed the lamaserie of Patong...'

All seemd to be going well until some in the writer's party slipped and made a noise. A lookout on the lamaserie walls noticed them and sent out a shrill signal whistle to warn the countryside of their escape. The party fled awkwardly down the steep valley, but having a desperate rest, the writer clambered up a bank to look back and see if they were still pursued. He goes on: 'To the north I had a clear view of the crest of the ridge we had descended, and had not long to wait ere my expectations were realised. Suddenly, there appeared a large number of armed men running at full speed in Indian file along the path we had just traversed. I gave the alarm at once and immediately all was confusion, our followers scattering in every direction. Pere Bourdonnec became completely panic-stricken... and made his way across the stream by a fallen tree, and, despite my attempts to slop him rushed blindly through the dense forest which clothed the southern face of the valley. However, escape in that direction I was sure would be impossible, as our delay had given the enemy time to mature their plans and close in on us. The Pere had not covered a couple of hundred yards ere he was riddled with poisoned arrows and fell, the Tibetans immediately rushing up and finishing him off with their huge double-handed swords....

Our little band, numbering abort 80, were picked off one by one, or captured, only 14 escaping. Ten wives and daughters of some of our followers committed suicide by throwing themselves into the stream to escape the slavery, and worse, which they knew awaited them if captured. Of my own 17 collectors and servants, only one escaped.

When I saw all was lost I fled east down a breakneck path, in places formed along the faces of beetling cliffs by rude brackets of wood and slippery logs. I went down towards the main rivers only to find myself, at one of the sharpest turns, suddenly confronted by a band of hostile and well-armed Tibetans, who had been stationed there to block the passage.

I fell into dense jungle, through which I rolled down a steep slope... tearing my clothing to ribbons, and bruising myself most horribly in the process. I then got behind a convenient boulder and made every preparation for a stand should they succeed in discovering my ruse, which I never doubted but they should…'

The writer was George Forrest. He hid for the next eight days and nights, trying to work his way south during the night. He had no food but a few scraps he found in his pocket. Hunted by dogs, he discarded his boots, and waded along whatever watercourses he could find. At one point his pursuers were so close that two poisoned arrows passed through his hat. Finally, with his feet and hands swollen and torn, and half dead with hunger and exhaustion, he didn't care whether he lived or died. At last, desperate, he stumbled into a village detemined to ransack it for food. Fortunately, he didn't need to. The villagers were friendly. They were soon making arrangements to smuggle him out of the valley.

Alas the other elderly missionary, Pere Dubernard, fared far worse. He was eventually run to earth, trapped in a cave farther up the valley. Forrest writes: 'His captors broke both arms above and below the elbow, tied his hands behind his back, ind in this condition forced him to walk back to the blackened site of Tzekou. There they fastened him to a post and subjected him to most brutal mutilation; amongst the least of his injuries being the extraction of his tongue and eyes, and the cutting off of his ears and nose. In this horrible condition he remained alive for the space of three days, in the course of wbich his torturers cut a joint off his fingers and toes each day. When on the point of death, he was treated in the same manner as Pere Bourdonnec, portions of the bodies being distributed amongst the various lamaseries in the region.'

The terrifying ordeal deprived Forrest of all of his plant material, and he was too unwell after it to collect more. However, he had already sent home a few seed pods, amongst them a new species of meconopsis, now called *Meconopsis speciosa*, and a tiny creeping *Rhododendron* with large crimson flowers. It seems not to have long survived, or been given a name.

The readers of the 'Gardeners Chronicle' were able to follow his further journeys in issue after issue, even if some tender stomachs were churned by his stories. Yet, they had to read, they had to desire the gorgeous plants he described, indeed, was building the market for. The plants were really astonishing. He was responsible for introducing some of the most desirable plants of scree and rock garden: plants like many species of speckle-flowered *Nomocharis* (now mostly in Lilium), endless species of *Primula*, the now ubiquitous but glorious *Gentiana sino-ornata*, three species of *Adenophora*, alliums, androsaces, a good handful of anemones. irises, omphalogrammas, roscoeas, saussureas, trollius. Some of his most gorgeous introductions include: *Primula bulleyana, P. beesiana, Rhododendron forrestii, R. radicans, Arisaema candidissimum, Roscoea cautleoides, R. humeana, Allium beesianum, Codonopsis meleagris* (once *C. ovata*). Any or all are enough to make sheets of sumptuous colour, though perhaps less exciting if reached by a short trip over the lawn, rather that by the swinging bamboo rope bridges Forrest used to cross the Mekong. At least suburban gardeners didn't often risk a brush with the Yellow lamas. Few, too, risked contact with Forrest's luxuriantly described insect life. 'On the other hand, the river banks at a low altitude, and where wholly sheltered from the north winds, have an almost tropical climate, and vegetable and insect life is both vigorous and troublesome. Creatures with inconveniently long legs plunge suddenly into one's soup; great caterpillars in splendid but poisonous uniforms of long and gaily coloured hairs arrive in one's blankets with the business-like air of a guest who means to stay. Ladybirds and other specimens of *Coleoptera* drop off the jungle down one's neck, whilst other undesirables insert themselves under one's nether garments. The light in the tent attracts a perfect army of creatures which creep, buzz, fly, crawl and sting. Scissor insects make the day hideous with their strident call, and the proximity of Lissoo coolies introduces other strangers, of which *Pulex irritans* [the flea] is by far the least noxious.'

Not all of his lovely introductions were especially keen to grow away from their native hills, bringing into being the sort of gardener who finds this a challenge to his or her nurturing skills. It has, at base, little to do with aesthetic concerns, though some impossible-to-grow plants can indeed be lovely to look at. Nevertheless, groups of connoisseurs grew up, devoted the the plants of the high hills, and calling themselves Alpine Garden Societies or Rock Garden Clubs.

It seems, so often, to be a largely Sino-British story. Great collectors like William Purdom (1880-1921), or Frank Ludlow (1885-1972) and George Sherriff (1898-1967) all collected in the steep valleys of China and Tibet. Botanist from Kew and Edinburgh still go, and still find new species. Yet other continents have immense mountain chains, but we less often to have plants from them. Other mountain systems can be almost as rich in species as the Himalayas. They can be every bit as romantic. Here is Ira Gabrielson, writing in 'Western American Alpines' of 1932: 'The outstanding range in our territory is the Steens Mountains, whose summit is slightly under 10,000 ft, and whose easterly face is a sheer basaltic cliff of 4,000 ft. Less known, but equally picturesque is Fiart Mountain, sixty miles to the west, with its sheer face to the westward. [on the slopes are]...phlox in abundant variety, Erigerons of the usual types but also including strange lithic gray-leaved shrubs which hold much garden promise, Eriogonums in bewildering profusion, penstemons, oenotheras, lewisias, linums, and many others furnish the floral display which at times for a few brief days is spectacular....

...Near the corner of the three states where the Snake splits this range with its gigantic canyon and where every tributary has a canyon, unnoticed only because of its proximity to its greater neighbor, is some of the most spectacular scenery to be found in the United Status. Towering ridges, snow-capped peaks, mile deep canyons, and mighty precipices mingle in such wild confusion as to benumb the imagination of the beholder. ..... Entire cliffs are covered with the pale green rosettes of *Lewisia katawbiana*; whole slopes glow with the soft pink of *Phlox hispida.* One entire talus slope stands out vividly in my memory, blue enough to match the sky above with the flowers of *Penstemon venustus*, a tiny meadow by a lake, high in the Wallowas, glowing with the velvety blues of *Gentiana calycosa*, a bog-back ridge whose entire summit carried a soft blue tone from the nodding croziers of *Mertensia pulchella...*' There are still far more plants to come in to our gardens from the mountains than Lewis and Clark, or any rock gardener of the past, can ever have imagined.

Chapter 9

The Water Garden

David Stuart

The Water Garden

Water means life. Without it there can be no gardens. It is no wonder that from the very beginnings of gardening, and civilisation itself, water has been prized. Prehistoric gardens of ancient Mesopotamia were filled with its noise as it splashed into containing pools, swirled down runnels, or spouted out of cooling springs. In Middle Eastern gardens too, astonishing feats of engineering brought water from the wet mountainsides to the dry gardens of the plains. Springs and wells were sacred. Where water entered the city or local neighbourhood was a special place, a place for meeting, and for show. Wealthy communities gave their fountains grand sculptural surrounds, often depicting the gods and goddesses of water, even of the sea itself. In historical times, in the gardens of the West, and much of the Middle East, little changed. Water was part of the display of the garden, meant to glitter, to spurt and splash, sometimes to cool. Pools, tanks, canals, runnels, were all edged with stone margins, or, in the north, crisply cut grass. Even the 'landscape' gardens of 18th century England, the expensively excavated lakes were kept clear of any plants, however eager they were to colonise, that might obscure the reflective surface.

In the Orient, particularly in China and Japan, gardening had taken a slightly different route. Water was just as important as it was in the West, and quite as enveloped in magic and in the spiritual, yet it was never divorced from the plants and soil of the garden in the way that characterised western tradition. It was immensely admired. Some gardens were entirely based on water and rocks. Yet, there were never fountains or chadars to play with water's formal possibilities. Water was certainly for reflection, and a surface in which to borrow the sky, but it was a place for fish and for plants too. Two plants were especially important; the sacred lotus (*Nelumbo nucifera)*, and the iris (Iris ensata).

In the West, change in the old attitude to water in the garden began slowly. The second of these beautiful plants was sent to Europe in the 1690's by Dr. Engelbert Kaempfer. He was the first of the three major botanist-doctors working for the Dutch East India office out of Deshima, Japan. The third of the botanist doctors, von Siebold, whom we have already met, called it *Iris kaempferi.* It can still be found under that name. It isn't though, correct. The second botanist-doctor at Deshima, Dr Carl Thumberg, whom we have also met, had previously named the same plant *Iris ensata,* but von Siebold hadn't realised this. Just to add to the confusion, some Japanese gardeners use the name *Iris laevigata.* Western botanists see this as a separate species, though it may have been used in the breeding of the garden forms of *I. ensata.*

Whatever the taxonomic status of the flower, its intense violet-blue flowers, perfectly shaped, held just above the broad green leaves, have been admired in Japan at least since the eight century. They appear in poems found in 'Manyoshu', an anthology compiled in about 760AD, made up of traditional poems written between 300AD and 750AD. While some them use the iris as a metaphor for a beautiful woman, more prosaic ones suggest that the flowers were used for dyeing fabric. An eleventh century writer said that all violet things, whether flowers or fabrics, were the most beautiful and *I. ensata* was the most beautiful flower of all. The flowers also appeared in carvings and architectural decoration from the twelfth century. They also appear, gloriously formalised, in the elegant heraldic devices of Japanese nobles. Those whose badge it was decorated their clothes and armour, even their ox-drawn carriages, with the real flower. Many 'iris' clans still exist.

Japanese artists loved painting them. One of the most extraordinary pictures of all, indeed one of the most wonderful paintings of any plant anywhere, is a folding screen painted by Ogata Korin towards the end of the seventeenth century. Drifts of indigo blue irises are thrown carelessly across a blank background of gold leaf. In several versions, the one at the Metropolitan Museurn of Art, New York, also shows the eight wooden bridges from The Tales of Ise. 'Ise' is now one of the names of a group of iris cultivars that existed when Korin was working, and which can still be grown.

Kaempfer's irises caught European gardeners fancy. Almost anything from that mysterious country captivated the west, for in 1633, the Tokugawa shogunate adopted a policy of national isolation that continued until the signing of the Kanagawa Treaty 221 years later in 1854. Between those years, Japan maintained contact with only three countries: China, Korea, and the Netherlands. From China and Korea, little information reached Europe. From the Netherlands, there was a trickle. The Dutch were restricted to an artificial island called Deshima (Dejima) that was built by the shogunate in Nagasaki Harbor so that they could keep the barbarians at arms length, and under constant supervision. Generation after generation of Dutchmen and a scattering of other Europeans signed on with the Dutch East India Company and were assigned two-year stints at Nagasaki, but they were completely forbidden to look at the country or converse with its inhabitants. The inquisitive found that an overwhelming lure. Kaempfer was overwhelmingly inquisitive. He was also brilliant, but had too an amusing and warm personality. He easily made friends with the Japanese guards and the numerous translators. He helped them through illnesses, and taught them about western medicine. Better still, he could easily drink his Japanese contacts under the table, and before they became insensible, his new friends talked about their fascinating country. He recorded everything they told him in meticulous detail. Unlike von Siebold's friends, none got into trouble, even though they had sworn terrifying oaths in ink and blood not to fraternize with the Europeans. He even got some of them to bring him plants from the nearby gardens and hills, saying that he needed herbs for his medicines.

He'd had an extraordinarily peripatetic childhood. He was born Engelbert Kemper, the second son of Johannes Kemper was in Lemgo, Germany, on 16th September 1651. At four years old, he attented the "Lateinschule" (grammar school) in Lemgo, but moved at the age of six to the one at Hameln. Soon after he was at high school in Lüneburg, and from 1670 at the one in Lübeck. Soon he was studying at the University of Cracow, then at the University of Königsberg, and by 1681, he was in Sweden, studying medicine at Uppsala university. By now he was polished in the ways of the world, and began attending the court of Charles XI in Stockholm. Desperate for more travel still, he got himself appointed secretary of the Swedish legation to the Persian court in Isfahan. In that capacity, he set off in 1683. The eighteenth century English translator of Kaempfer's subsequent book wrote 'After a dangerous passage over the Caspian Sea, where they were like to have been lost, through the violence of an unexpected storm, and the unskilfulness of their Pilots, (the ship having two Rudders, and consequently two Pilots, who did not understand each other's language) they got safe to the Coasts of Persia, and landed at Nisabad, where they staid for some time, living under tents after the manner of the natives.'

He was in Isfahan for a year and a half, partly beecause Shah Suleyman's astrologers kept the Shah terrified of a malignant constellation, and it was only on 30th of July 1684, that the stars moved into a better position. He then threw a lavish party for his Court, and for the foreign ambassadors waiting to see him. There were dozens. They came from the kings of Sweden, France, Poland and Siam, from the Czars of Muscovy, from the Emperor of Germany, from several Arabian and Tartarian princes, even an ambassador from the Pope in Rome. Dr. Kaempfer attended too. The Europeans had deep motives. Although some, like the Swedes, wanted to establish trade with Persia, as well as routes through it to the further Orient, some were trying to detach Isfahan from the influence of Constantinople. The diplomacy was all in vain, and Suleyman was not minded to be helpful to Sweden, or willing to break with the Sultan of Turkey. The Swedish embassy was recalled. Kaempfer should have gone back too. He'd been offered a very lucrative post as chief doctor to a Georgian Prince, but he wanted to go further east, not to Georgia or north-west back to Sweden. By chance the fleet of the Dutch East-India Company was cruising in the Persian Gulf, and he got himself appointed instead as chief 'Surgeon to the Fleet'. On the 30th June 1688, he set sail for India via Muscat on the Horn of Arabia. After many adventures, he arrived in Deshima two years later.

His two years in the European enclave were enlivened by the annual trip to Edo (now Tokyo) to be displayed at the imperial court. He was there first in March 1691, and again in spring 1692. Each trip was something of a festival, for native princes, lords and vassals of the emperor were at Edo too. The Dutch party consisted of three or four inhabitants of Deshima, surrounded by an escort of nearly two hundred Japanese. The Europeans travelled in palanquins carried by up to twelve bearers, though Kaempfer tried to travel on horseback as much as possible, so that he could see more of the surrounding countryside. The whole expedition, with twenty or thirty days in the capital, took about twelve weeks. When on a horse, Kaempfer carried on his saddle 'a very large Javan box', which he filled with 'plants, flowers, and branches of trees, which I figured and described'. He had a compass concealed inside so that he could map the journey. He wrote that his escort 'were extreamely forward to communicate to me, what uncommon plants they met with, together with their true names, characters and uses, which they diligently enquired into among the natives.' Perhaps he travelled with a large stock of alcohol too.

On the journey to Edo, the Dutch were treated like performing animals, for they were closely guarded during the day, were locked in at night, and put through tricks on arrival. Kaempfer and his superiors were obliged to dance, sing, jump and mime. Their party tricks had to be shown not only in front of the Emperor, but also at the houses of the Edo nobility.

Kaempfer left Japan in 1692, stayed a while in Java, then set out for home aboard the 'Maelstrom', with the humble job of office clerk. He arrived in Amsterdam on the 6th October 1693. He resumed his busy life, and it was not until 1712 that a Lemgo printer brought out his 'Amoenitates

Exoticae'. Only around a fifth of that books is devoted to plants, but it included the first descriptions and illustrations of shrubs and flowers totally new to western gardeners: aucuba, skimmia, hydrangea, chimonanthus and ginkgo, *Lilium speciosum, L. lanceolatum* (still often grown as *L. tigrinum*), two magnolias, various prunus, azaleas and tree-paeonies, and nearly thirty varieties of camellia. The book was a sensation. He had, though, a much larger work in preparation. However, as doctor to the count of Lippe and his family, he was kept extremely busy, and found working on his next book extremely difficult.

His English translator wrote of Kaempfer's end: 'The long course of his Travels, the fatigues of his profession, and some private misfortunes in his family, had very much impair'd his constitution, and in the latter part of his life he was often troubled with the Colick, of which he had two very severe attacks, one in November 1715, and another at the beginning of 1716. This last fit laid him up for three weeks, however he recover'd it so far, that he was able to attend the Count de Lippe and his Family, as their Physician, at Pyrmont, and return'd, in July, to his Country Seat at Steinhof near Lemgow in pretty good health. On the 5th of September following he was suddenly seized with fainting fits, and a vomiting of blood, which continued upon him all night reduced him very low. From that time he continued in a lingring condition, though not altogether without hopes of recovery, having gather'd strength so far, as to be able to walk about his room: But on the 24th of October, having been ever since this last attack troubled with a nausea and loss of appetite, his vomiting of blood return'd upon him with great violence, and a fever, which lasted till the second of November, on which day he died, at five in the evening, 65 years and six weeks old. He was buried in the Cathedral Church of S. Nicolas at Lemgow.'

When he died, he'd been working on his 'History of Japan', the manuscript and its materials scattered around him. They might all have been lost had not Sir Hans Sloane purchased the whole lot from Kaempfer's nephew, between 1723 and 1725. Sloane got his librarian Scheuchzer to translate the work, which appeared with notes by Scheuchzer, in 1727. It proclaimed itself

The History of Japan

Together with a Description of the Kingdom of Siam 1690 – 92

BY

Engelbert Kaempfer, M.D.

Physician to the Dutch Embassy to the Emperor's Court

and translated by

J.G. Scheuchzer, F.R.S

Unfortunately, Scheuchzer was a devout Christian, and some of Kaempfer's material outraged him. It was omitted or distorted. Modern translations are currently underway. Whatever modifications Scheuchzer made, the book was a huge success. It was translated into French and Dutch by 1729, back into German by 1756, into Russian by 1773, and into Japanese by 1782. In 1791, Sir Joseph Banks published a small selection of the botanical drawings made by Engelbert Kaempfer as "Icones selectae plantarum quas in Japonia collegit et delineavit Engelbertus Kaempfer".

The irises that Kaempfer had so admired didn't make a lasting impact in Europe. They needed additional forces to make a conquest. However, in their native country, they didn't stand still either. Japan had florists societies in quite as much abundance, and with as much enthusiasm, as did Britain, Holland and France. *Iris ensata*, already long moved away from its wild form when collected by Kaempfer, was taken up by Japanese florists and vastly developed from the 1840's onwards. One famous breeder, Sho-od (or Showo) Matsudaira, produced around two hundred named varieties. Though most of these are now thought of as Edo Irises, some of the most flamboyant were bred in the Higo district. In these, the flowers' styles are so broad and colourful as to be almost indistinguishable from petals. The petals themselves are flared and overlapping. Not surprisingly, they created a sensation in Japan. When they got to Europe in the 1860's they created yet another. Every Western gardener had to have some. Every gardener, even if not yet in thrall to the waterlily, therefore had to have a pool. Many were disappointed. The original Higos were bred for pot culture, and were to be admired indoors, where the sumptuous petals were at no risk from rough weather. Indoors, too, the flowers changed after opening: by the second day they often nearly doubled in size. Japanese conoisseurs claimed that flowers were at their best at midnight on the second day. Some were, and are, double, even treble, and under perfect conditions can sometimes reach twelve inches (30cm.) across. Gardeners in the West began instead to collect the 'Ise' strain of *Iris ensata*, more suitable for the garden, with single flowers in pink, pale blue, and the ancient indigo, and with narrower and longer leaves. Modern forms also have strong and weather-resistant petals.

Japanese irises are hardy. Few western gardens could support the subtropical lotus (Nelumbo nucifera), however important a garden plant it was in India and southern China. Few western gardeners could afford to grow the astonishing *Victoria amazonica,* yet the idea of waterlilies, rather than lotuses, stuck in many minds. Surely there must be good things to grow other than the rather dull European representatives of the genus *Nyphaea*? Gardeners began to look enviously at the smaller waterlilies of the tropics and subtropics. The southern states of the USA had lovely things like *Nymphaea texensis.* Central and South America had endless exciting species. Africa had *N. zanzibarensis* or the enticing yellow-flowered N. burttii from Tanganyika. Australia had the wonderful *Nymphaea gigantea,* with huge flowers varying from violet blue to white or even pink. Breeders began to wonder if some of these could be crossed into hardy species, to give hybrids hardy in Europe, but with large, even perfumed, flowers. They could have all the romance of the East, without the expense of providing warm water. After all, in Egypt and the Orient, the true waterlily was an ancient garden plant. Petals of *Nymphaea lotus* and *N. coerulea* were used in the funeral wreaths of Rameses II (1580 BC) and Amenhotep I. The same species were portrayed in the decoration, pottery and furniture of their tombs. Amenhotep IV and Rameses III grew them in ponds of their palace gardens.

In China, waterlilies, especially the white and perfumed *Nyphaea tetragona*, had been grown at least since the eleventh century, when Chou Tun-I wrote 'it has been fashionable to admire the paeony; but my favourite is the water-lily. How stainless it rises from its slimy bed. How modestly it reposes on the clear pool, an emblem of purity and truth. Symmetrically perfect, its subtle perfume is wafted far and wide; while there it rests in spotless state, something to be regarded reverently from a distance, and not to be profaned by familiar approach.'

In western Europe, the earliest gardening reference to the waterlily is in Phillip Miller's Gardeners' Dictionary (1731). He writes, 'in some gardens I have seen plants cultivated in large troughs of water, where they flourish very well and annually produce great quantities of flowers.' One hundred years later, things were about to change in an amazing way. In a garden at Temple-sur-Lot in the Department of Lot et Garonne in western France, a gardener had an important revelation. His garden, below the ancient castle of Marliac, contained a series of warm-water springs. He'd never thought much about them, but suddenly the owner, Joseph Bory Latour-Marliac, realised that he could use them to feed pools that would be warm enough to grow tropical water plants. In 1858, he'd read an article by the botanist Leveque, who bemoaned the fact that the bright colours and large flowers of tropical nymphaeas weren't found in the hardy species.

Marliac's imagination was fired, and he started to collect different species from all over the world. Almost paranoid about being copied, he didn't reveal his sources of material. However, the plants grew in their new surroundings. He tried to cross them, and seems to have worked for several years without much happening. Suddenly, in 1879, he bred *Nymphaea* 'marliacea rosea'. Nothing could then stop him. Other breeders tried to copy his success, but he was always very vague about what species he was using, and of techniques he used for crossing them. He seems to have used the hardy N. alba and its Swedish variety 'rubra', crossing them into the exotic *N. odorata, N. mexicana, N. tuberosa* and *N. tetragona* (pygmaea). He then produced more than seventy new varieties. Many were extraordinarily beautiful, some were perfumed, and only three were commercial failures. Everyone, including the artist Monet, just had to have them. Some of the Marliac waterlilies were immense sprawling plants. Others were small and neat. Suddenly, there was a point in having a pool, in whatever size of garden. There was a waterlily variety that was suitable.

Other breeders, like Amos Perry in Britain, tried to repeat his crosses, but have either been unable to get seed, or have produced only worthless seedlings. Alas, Latour-Marliac went to his grave in 1911, taking most of his secrets with him. His garden still exists, and is devoted, of course, to showing a colossal collection of waterlilies, including some of the glorious Australian *Nymphaea gigantea* group of waterlilies haven't yet been much used in breeding, though they do grow well in hot-summer regions like Texas. Great things are expected from them, generally accepted as the largest and most beautiful of all the species in the genus *Nymphaea*.

The 17th and 18th century gardener, as well as a passion for the glitter and reflectivity of open water, also had a passion for drainage. With everyone's hatred and fear of bogs and marshes, the garden, unless it was the 'American' section of a large estate, was dried out to make it suitable for both feet and flowers. Flower borders had, at least since medieval times, been raised above the general soil level, using board or stone margins. Even in modest cottage gardens, and where possible, this was undertaken late into the 18th century, and my own garden still has the stone kerbs used for this purpose. However, once iris and waterlily made the pond an essential garden element in the nineteenth century, gardeners soon saw the advantage of moist, even soggy, ground. They discovered the huge flora that grows in precisely those conditions, and plant collectors were busily bringing them back to Europe at just the right time. Plants like primulas, rodgersias, meconopsis, ferns, hostas, astilbes, podophyllums, ligularias, all combined to make up the great 'marginal' flora.

Primulas first. The genus included some ancient garden plants, from the double white primroses to the more modern laced polyanthus. All were short. No gardener was prepared to imagine a primula four or five feet high. Yet, in Nang Dzong, in the furthest reaches of the Brahmaputra river, where it descended from the Tibet plateau, a plant collector found one in huge quantities in 1925. Here's its collector describing it: ' It was most happy in the woodland brooks, which in summer overflow and flood the thorn brakes. Here it manned the banks in thousands and, wading into the stream, held up the current. It choked up ditches and roofed the steepest mud slides with its great marsh-marigold leaves; then in July came a forest of masts, which spilled out a shower of golden drops, till the tide of scent spread and filled the woodland and flowed into the meadow to mingle with that of the 'Moonlight' primula. And all through August it kept on unfurling flowers and still more flowers, till the rains began to slacken and the brooks crept back to their beds, and the waters under the thorn brake subsided; but the seeds were not ripe till late October....' Not surprisingly, after such a write up, every gardener wanted it. It was a huge success, flowering well into August, and even becoming an aggressive weed in some Scottish gardens. Few gardeners would care.

It is indeed a massive plant, the largest of all the primulas. It grows throughout south-east Tibet, and the Tsangpo Basin from Tsari to the Pachakshiri, often amongst drifts of the fine *Primula alpicola*, also one of Frank Kingdon Ward's magnificent discoveries. The species cross cheerfully, and will also include P. sikkimensis in the relationship. The progeny often contains plants with splendid chestnut to orange flowers. All are strongly perfumed, and alone make a 'marginal' garden an object of desire.

Kingon Ward called the giant plant *Primula florindae*, named after his then wife, Florinda. It was, like her, large, stately and with a taste for show. They didn't have an easy relationship. He wasn't an easy man. Born in 1885, the son of a Professor of Botany at Cambridge University, Frank Kingdon Ward might have been expected to hate plants. In fact, he loved them, but did hate anything approaching a settled, comfortable or conventional life. He left for Cambridgeshire for Shanghai as soon as he could, and after a brief spell teaching, headed off into the wilds. He swiftly became a garden-orientated travel writer, eventually publishing hundreds of articles and twenty five books about his remarkable journeys. When he couldn't live by the pen, he financed his travels by collecting for seed firms and syndicates of gardeners. Not that he seems to have needed much money; like many explorer-collectors, he was a loner, and like many modern ones, liked travelling light. He got by on a number of trips by taking little sustenance but milk, and living off the land. Sometimes he travelled with a companion. The Primula florindae trip was made with Lord Cawdor, a Scottish aristocrat's with a

handsome Scottish castle. Cawdor's own journals suggest that he found
Frank's company a trial by silence. Kingdon Ward wrote at times chillingly
of the earl. Many found Frank austere, even bitter, and on his travels he was
often consumed with intense loneliness that sometimes turned into bouts of
suicidal despair.

His real love were the great river valleys of China, Tibet and Burma. On
one of his first trips he wrote 'For two entire days the trail over the mountains
led through a gorge of exquisite beauty, the cliffs, covered with pine and
bamboo, rising abruptly two or three thousand feet above the ice-choked
stream, making a grand play of colours in the winter sunshine. At one time
alongside the frothing torrent, at another giving precarious foothold amongst
the bush-clad precipices which yet towered far above, the trail wheeled
sharply round bend after bend as it followed the sinuous curves of the river,
affording endless views of matchless beauty … a tiny white temple nestling
amongst the dark pines which clothed a tongue of land; a glowing ochre
scarp, several hundred feet high, crowned by waves of feathery bamboo…'
He loved the life of those countries too, whether watching a band of
brigands winding through the passes, or the excitement of shooting two
hundred miles of rapids halfway down the Yangtse river: 'on 7th September
we reached Kweichow-fu on the borders of Szechwan and Hupei, and saw
before us the cliffs of Bellows Gorge towering to the sky, and the dark slit
into which the river plunged. Suddenly the sun was hidden behind the
mountain peaks, a blast of cool air whistled out of the ragged rent in front of
us, and we sped between vast cliffs rising over three thousand feet on either
hand; we seemed to be speeding to some frightful destruction in the bowels
of the earth. There were no rapids now. The confined water boiled and
writhed around us; huge whirls sprang into existence everywhere with the

crash of the avalanche, and we were at the mercy of the river, broadside on, stem first, flying round and round, while the lon-pan stood at the tiller yelling at the four oarsmen who stood on the forward deck, rowing like men demented to keep the boat's head straight on...'

The brigands were less frightening, for 'They formed nonetheless a striking picture, winding in single file up the narrow ravine, rather more than two hundred of them. There were Lissus and Minchias, sturdy little tribesmen with muscular chests and swarthy complexions, often ferocious of aspect, carrying rifles, most of them muzzle-loaders; men with extraordinary-looking guns of abbreviated length and immense calibre, after the pattern of a blunderbuss; others carrying scarlet banners and long trumpets; and half a dozen men, including my friend Captain Li, riding ponies. Occasionally the trumpeters put the long trumpets to their lips and throwing back their heads, made the welkin ring; and on they hurried, banners fluttering; till they wound out of sight on the narrow gorge...'

On another occasion, described in one of his best books, 'In The Land of the Blue Poppy', he writes of an impromptu entertainment he was given when lying comfortably in a mountain hut, writing up his diary for the day: . .. in stalked three Tibetans, all of them over six feet high. Their coarse gowns were tied above their knees, the right shoulder thrust jauntily out exposing the deep muscular chest, and they were bootless. One of them carried a fiddle, consisting of a piece of snakeskin stretched over a bamboo tube with strings of yak hair, upon which he scraped vigorously with a yak-hair bow. There was little enough room, but my visitors soon lined up, stuck out their tongues at me in greeting, and began to dance, to and fro, up and down, twirling round, swaying rhythmically to the squeaky notes of the violin (there were only two notes on which to ring the changes), and singing in high-pitched raucous voices... I can still picture the scene in that dim little smoke-blackened room, the rain lashing down outside, and the roar of the river below us, while I lay back on my bed enjoying it hugely, all cares forgotten. Those great giants of men looked strangely weird in the flickering light of the blazing torches...'

Ironically, whilst collecting plants that altered European gardening forever, he came across evidence of the universality of plant collecting, and the way in which plants cheerfully disseminate themselves across the globe. Once he and Lord Cawdor, stopping off at Napo Dzong, stayed in the local governor's house. It was splendidly set up, and even had glass in the windows. He writes: 'The paved yard was a regular flower-show, gay with Hollyhocks, Asters, Sunflowers, Dahlias, Pansies, Geraniums, Roses, Poppies, Brompton Stocks, Tropaeolums and other favourites. Clearly the dzong-pen (the local governor) was a man of taste, and advanced thinker, and a traveller. He had been to Calcutta and had brought back with him a tin Sutton's Seed; hence the Mammoth Show. Later in the same journey Kingdon Ward received a letter from the Tibetan government asking him to send them some of the seeds he collected, 'as the Dalai Lama is very fond of flowers, and at his private residence on the outskirts of Lhasa grows a great many, which he tends with loving care'.

During his long collecting career, he found glorious plants like the incomparable yellow-flowered *Rhododendron wardii*, and *R. maccabeanum*. He found gentians too, as well as cotoneasters, berberis and prunuses. He found splendid bulbs like the exquisite lily *Lilium macklinae*, named after his second wife, whom he married, and loved, when he was 65. But perhaps the most astonishing discovery was yet another good 'marginal'; the glorious blue poppy (*Meconopsis betonicifolia*). It had first been seen by the Abbe Delavay, then Bailey and George Forrest, but it had not been successfully introduced. Kingdon Ward's huge seed collection from Tumbatse that established it safely in cultivation. It was a sensation. There were mass plantings of it in Hyde Park in London, and at Ibrox Park, Glasgow. The beds were constantly surrounded by admiring crowds. At the 1927 Chelsea Flower Show, seedlings were sold at a guinea apiece. A few years later it had become so widespread that packets of seed were advertised at a shilling.

Good marginal plantings were adding plants apace. The gorgeously textured foliage of the rodgersias were a huge addition. The six species, all emanating from the Himalayas, China, Japan and Korea, are named after Commodore Rodgers of the United States Navy, who discovered *Rodgersia podophylla* in Hakodate, Japan, in 1855. He sent material back to America, and Asa Gray described it in 1857. The two Chinese species, *R. aesculifolia* and *R. pinnata* are now common garden plants. The first was described by A. Batalin from specimens collected by Potanin in Gansu and Sichuan in 1885, and by Augustine Henry from Hupeh (Hubei) in 1887 and Sichuan in 1889. Writing of it in The Gardeners Chronicle in 1902, Henry said "It is a plant of the mountains of Central China, occurring in shady places, numerous plants growing together.... The rhizome is used as a drug". Henry must have sent some to the Veitch nursery, for they had it in commercial quantities by 1914.

The other species was also introduced by Augustine Henry, who sent seed to Kew in 1898, the plants raised from it flowering in 1902.

Henry, who also added other 'marginal' genera to the fringes of our pools, was a fascinating man. Unusually for this book, he almost totally avoided the destiny of so many plant collectors. He seems never to have been completely consumed by the collecting mania that destroyed so many others. Indeed, halfway through his life, he changed career, and turned his back on the plants of China and the Yangtse gorges forever. However, his time as an exceedingly successful plant collector began on the banks of the frightening rapids down which Frank Kingdon Ward later plunged with such excitement. They were far more than just a visually breathtaking if dangerous impediment to the traveller. They were of considerable economic importance to the Chinese state. The lands around the upper part of the river produced rich crops of drug plants and food crops which were all consumed in the lands around the river's lower stretches. The rapids acted as a customs barrier, for the boats that risked them were either frequently unloaded, or at least much slowed down, during their passage downriver. This gave customs officials a chance to inspect and tax the cargoes.

The Chinese government had, by 1880's, set up a customs service staffed by Europeans, believing that native Chinese officials were too immersed in the ways of China to maximise the collection of duties. The Imperial Chinese Maritime Customs Service recruited a young Irishman called Augustine Henry. Though born in Dundee, Scotland in 1857, his parents moved immediately to Ireland, where he was brought up and educated. With a masters degree from Queen's College, Belfast, and a smattering of Chinese, the young man soon had enough medical training to land a post as Assistant Medical Officer in China. First based at Shanghai, in 1882 he was soon posted to the town of Ichang, in Hupeh province. It, and its treaty port of Shasi, was a thousand miles away up the great river. His customs duties took up only a few hours a day and, almost as a hobby, he began to look first at the drug plants that passed through his hands, then at the more general flora around Ichang. In search of advice, he wrote to the director of Kew Gardens, his first letters to Sir Joseph Hooker, and subsequent ones to Hooker's son-in-law Director, William Thistelton-Dyer. He received very encouraging letters, the first enclosing a leaflet of routine collecting instructions. Kew got, and still gets, hundreds of similar letters from bored would-be botanists, and used, at least until recently, to send out leaflets and advice without expecting much in return. A few months later, in November 1885, Henry sent them his first collections. Botanists at Kew were quite unprepared for the results. They received a thousand perfect herbarium specimens, amongst which Kew's stunned botanists found ten new genera.

William Thiselton-Dyer was so enthusiastic that he immediately wrote to Sir Robert Hart, the Inspector General of Chinese Customs, to request that Henry be given leave from the service in order to collect more widely in the mountains west of Ichang. Once that was granted, Kew financed the next of Henry's botanical expeditions. The mountains of Hupeh turned out to be even richer than expected. Henry found many new conifers, ten new maples, many roses and viburnums, new lilies, rhododendrons, prunuses, pyruses, and loniceras. He began to accumulate names. *Lilium henryi* was one, soon followed by *Clematis henryi,Parthenocissus henryana, Rhododendron augustinii*, and evergreen climber *Lonicera henryi.*

On one trip back to Europe he married. His new wife, Caroline, seemed to acclimatise well to the strange conditions at Ichang, but then fell ill. 1893 was a terrible year for them both. Henry's letters to Thiselton-Dyer contain worried passages on her health. In May she was desperately unwell. In June the weather was dry and she seemed better. In July it was clear that China wouldn't do for her, and she must have a better climate. Henry arranged for her to go to Denver in Colorado, in company with his favourite sister, Mary. The two women set out on the huge journey in January 1894.

Curiously, in America, and in that same year, something was afoot that would affect Henry's life, and crystallise his feelings about plant collecting. The same events would completely enthrall another man, who would take over Henry's work, and carry it on to the most astonishing conclusion. Charles Sprague Sargent (1841-1927), a Bostonian, patrician, wealthy, comfort-loving yet immensely energetic, was trying to involve London's Veitch nursery firm in a joint venture with his own organisation, the Arnold Arboretum of Harvard. He wanted James Herbert Veitch, with whom he had already travelled in Japan, to go on an intensive collecting trip to central and eastern China. Veitch's owner and James Herbert's uncle, Sir Harry Veitch, was not happy. In a letter to Sargent, dated January 10, 1893, he played the Victorian autocrat, and refused to allow his nephew, and heir, to remain away from the businsess for so long. Sargent was gainsayed, but was still hearing stories from London about the marvels emerging from the region of the upper

Yangtse.

The following year, Augustine Henry was getting alarmed. The Japanese were at war with China. It seemed a good time to get out. He dreamed of getting some sort of job in Colorado, where his wife seemed to be recovering. He knew his reputation as a botanist was spreading. He wrote hopefully to Professor Sargent in May 1894, hinting that he needed a job, and offering to sell Sargent his own marvellous herbarium. Sargent wanted the material, but Henry was only of use to him in China. Sargent wrote back encouragingly, but was vague. Henry thought he would take a gamble and go to America anyway. As he was packing up his books and collections, a telegram arrived. It was from his sister Mary. His wife had died. It was a colossal blow. It took him several years to come to terms with it. He wrote to a friend: 'I think I might have saved her had I fought more strenuously, if I had taken the decision to leave China sooner.'

Time passed. Henry remained in China and had several other postings. By 1898, Sargent was still searching for a man to collect there for the Arnold Arboretum. Finally, after many attempts to lure Augustine Henry into his grasp, he asked Henry, point blank, if he would collect for him alone. Henry gave Sargent all sorts of advice about what needed doing. He suggested the routes that a collector should travel. He even offered to help anyone that Sargent appointed. But he was tired; he wanted to get back home. He refused.

In October 1899, shortly before leaving China for the last time, Augustine Henry welcomed a visitor in the remote village of Szemao (now Simao) in Yunnan Province. At this meeting, Henry handed on the collector's mantle, and also the collector's destiny. In 1900, Henry sailed to Britain, and never returned to China. He became interested in forestry, helping set up a forestry school at Cambridge University. Later he became professor of Forestry at the College of Science in the University of Dublin, and led the campaign to reforest Ireland's green land. Back in China, the 'new boy' was Ernest Henry Wilson and, more interested than Augustine Henry in getting living plants back to Europe, he has had more impact on our gardens and how they look than any other collector.

E. H. Wilson was born in 1876, in a modest cottage in the picturesque village of Chipping Campden in Gloucestershire. Apprenticed to a nursery in nearby Solihull, he found his vocation instantly. He fell in love with plants. He was working at Kew Gardens by 1897, and was determined to become an academic botanist. He allowed himself to be diverted from this aim by going to work for Veitch's nursery. The lure was the offer of a well-financed collecting trip to China. He set off westwards, sailing from Liverpool on April 11th 1899, on board the Pavonia, arriving in New England on April 23. The Arnold Arboretum was his first stop. Sargent was interested but, as yet, made no move. Wilson went on across the US, and sailed for China from San Francisco on May 6. Augustine Henry was now in Yunnan Province, a thousand miles inland from Hong Kong. It took Wilson four months to reach him. He spoke no Chinese, and found travelling very difficult. Once he began to learn, he discovered that he could very easily develop a rapport with the native people he met.

Wilson's route to Szemao required that he travel southward from Hong Kong to Tonking in French Indochina. He got to Yunnan aboard a small steamer that took him up the Red River to Laokai (Lao Cai), a jungle town on the Chinese frontier. From there he got a small native boats to Manhao, then assembled a caravan of mules and sedan chairs to reach Szemao. In later trips to China, he usually bought his own boats to make travel easier and much more comfortable, even if, as it turned out, no less hazardous.

After two trips for the Veitch nursery, which brought many wonders into the garden, Charles Sprague Sargent finally got fed up with waiting. During the winter of 1905-1906 Sargent meant to investigate the temperate flora of Peru and Chile. Once there, he changed his itinerary, and determined to return to Boston via England. He wanted to meet Wilson face-to-face. Wilson was guarded. Once back in America, Sargent wrote to Wilson on June 28, 1906, urging that he give 'serious thought to the proposition for another journey to China and that you will come to see your way clear to doing this. I am more than ever convinced of the importance of further botanical investigation in western China and of the fact that you are the only man to undertake this work with the prospect of carrying it out successfully. I think that the financial part of it can be managed here if you are willing to undertake the work…' Wilson signed on the dotted line later that year. Sargent had signed up one of the greatest plants collectors of all time.

Wilson was by now married, though his wife was usually left behind with friends in Britain rather than in America, when he was in China. She complained bitterly, but accepted that she couldn't go with him. He didn't give himself an easy time. In spite of ocean liners, the first motorcars, and other civilised advances, collecting in remote places was still dangerous. Wilson seems to have had, like a cat, nine lives. He wrote of one trip 'I noticed my dog suddenly cease wagging his tail, cringe, and rush onward, and a small piece of rock hit the path and rebounded into the river some 300 feet below us. I shouted a order and the bearers put down the chair. The two front bearers ran forward and I followed suit. … a large boulder crashed into the body of the chair, and down to the river it was hurled. I ran instinctively, ducked as something whisked over my head and my sun hat blew off. Again I ran; a few yards more and I would be under the lea of some hard rocks. Then feeling as if a hot wire passed through my legs, I was bowled over, tried to jump up, found my right leg was useless, so crawled forward to the shelter of the cliff, where the two scared chair-bearers were huddled…. The pigskin puttee on my right leg was cut slantingly as if with a knife and forced round my leg; the toe cap of my boot was torn off and with it the nail of my big toe; the right leg was broken in two places below the knee…

…with the legs of my camera tripod I improvised splints, and while these were being bandaged to my legs the mule-caravan [that we had] passed in the morning loomed into view. The road was too narrow for them to turn back and they dared not stand still until I could be moved forwards since we knew not when the rock slide would recommence. There was only one thing to do. I lay across the road and file of mules stepped over my body. Then it was that I realized the size of the mule's hoof. There were nearer fifty … of them and each stepped clearly over me as if accustomed to such obstacles. Nevertheless, I breathed freely when the last was over!' As this trip had resulted in the collection of *Lilium regale*, he henceforth referred to his 'lily leg' when the pain of the wounds sometimes returned.

His collecting trips had many such moments, yet his ninth life was spent not in China, but in Boston, Massachusetts. By this time, Sargent was dead, and the humble boy from Chipping Campden became director of the august Arnold Arboretum. In spite of his success in America, in spite of the comfortable collecting trips, now with his wife, to Japan and Korea, in spite of the success of his many books, he still dreamt of retiring to the enchanted golden valleys of his native Gloucestershire. By 1930 his plans were fairly advanced, and he and his wife decided to drive over to see their newly married daughter. They were killed in a car accident.

Wilson's plants covered the entire spectrum of gardening. Even on his last Asian trip to look at the little-explored flora of the Korean peninsula, he found lovely things like the Korean forsythia (*Forsythia ovata* Nakai). He found that at the Diamond Mountains, a beautiful part of Korea, where waterfalls crash noisily from misty cliffs and the slopes are thick with maples, birches, and oaks. In our imaginary water and bog garden, let us pan the camera up from drifts of his lilies and ligularias, away from the clumps of rodgersias and golden primulas. Let's back the pool with his forsythia, or some of his other favourite plants of his own collecting: maples like the paperbark (*Acer griseum*), its trunk wrapped in fluttering sheets of translucent mahogany-coloured bark, or his hardy variant of the Silk Tree (*Albizia julibrissin*), or the amazing Dove Tree (*Davidia involucrata)*, or the tea crabapple (*Malus hupehensis*), with its drifts of scented spring flowers, and clusters of golden apples in autumn. Perhaps they could have an underplanting of thickets of the rosy dipelta (*Dipelta floribunda*), or the beautybush (*Kolkwitzia amabilis*), or the sumptuously coloured Korean *Stewartia*. Wilson's plants will have a place in our gardens for as long as we make them. Something like three thousand species used him as a way of colonising the furthest continents.

Chapter 10

The Counter Revolution

David Stuart

COUNTER-REVOLUTION

The great wave of new plant introduction in the sixteenth century was exciting for gardeners who wanted the best and the most beautiful novelties in their gardens. It had its casualties too. Old garden plants, often inhabitants of the garden for many centuries, seemed dull in comparison. They were thrown out. Even John Parkinson, at the end of the seventeenth century bemoaned a few old familiars in the garden he thought were lost. Philip Miller, in the 1750's, wrote that he knew of at least eighteen lost variants of lily. He hoped that 'when they are once fix'd in a Garden, they are not very subject to decay…therefore from such places there may be Hopes of retrieving those flowers again.' His 'such places' were old gardens in the distant countryside.

The wave of new plants in the 19th and early 20th centuries was far larger, and far more turbulent. It created entirely new sorts of gardens and whole new markets for plants. It caused equally huge casualties amongst older garden plants. The sense of loss felt by Parkinson and Miller became, in the nineteenth century, a flood of sentimental nostalgia. It affected all but the most hardened plant collectors. Even the deeply unsentimental William Robinson wrote, in 'The Wild Garden', that 'Some are looking back with regret to the old mixed-border gardens; others are endeavouring to soften the harshness of the bedding system by the introduction of fine-leaved plants, but all are agreed that a great mistake has been made in destroying all our sweet old border flowers..' An anonymous writer wanted once more the gardens of 'quiet country villages where sweet-scented jasmine and Woodbine, purple Clematis and monthly Roses fight longingly for a place beside the rustic porch; while the little plots in front of white thatch-roofed cottages afforded a variety of bright blossoms for the nosegay of the past', rather ignoring the fact that the purple *Clematis x Jackmanii* had only been in cultivation for about twenty years.

Soon, a whole section of the gardening public was transfixed by the supposed simplicity and ease of old country gardens. New flower arranging 'stars' like Mrs Oliphant and Miss Hope collected and publicised old fashioned flowers. Writers and gardeners like Miss Willmott, Mrs Ewing and Miss Jekyll studied the already vanishing ways of the countryside whilst raiding cottagers' gardens for nice, and preferably long forgotten, plants.

Even the forward-looking United States of America proved not immune to the worship of some 'golden age' of gardening, a horticultural counter-revolution, a time before exotics had burst in through the garden gate. Nurseryman, banker and writer George Ellwanger, in 1896, brought out a book called 'The Gardens Story'. Designed especially for the new American market, he wrote: 'The prim modern garden, too, almost always lacks a pleasing feature of the ancient garden when rightly carried out; it has so few spots to lounge in. There is a dearth of garden-seats, niches, and benches, and vine-draped arbours and cloistered summerhouses. And where has the old sun-dial disappeared, that used to count the time so leisurely and shadow the passing hours?' He goes on to proclaim how much he misses the old farmstead gardens that once grew all sorts of lovely sweet-smelling things that could no longer be found, or would no longer grow, 'in our gardens today'. Ellwanger's old-fashioned flora included snowdrops, daffodils, imperials, muscaris, larkspurs, campanulas, bachelors buttons, monkshoods, double white poppies, sweet clover, snow pink (this was, and is, *Dianthus plumarius*), white phloxes, dicentras, sweet williams, tall yellow tulips, sword grass and ribbon grass, tradescantias, sweet peas, valerians, madonna lilies, white and purple stocks, lily of the valley, brier rose, white day lily [he probably meant *Hosta*], tiger lilies, dahlias, hollyhocks, sunflowers, and all the European herbs. It was very much the same flora that the first American garden designer A. J. Downing had been recommending as recently as 1849.

Ellwanger was an interesting and influential man. He became fascinated by fruit trees, and started collecting them. His prescience in this was taken up a few decades later by the United States Department of Agriculture, an arm of government that financed two later collectors in this chapter. Ellwanger was born on December 2, 1816, at Gross-Heppach, in Wurtemberg, then an independant principality, now part of Germany. The 'Rochester and Post Express' devoted a biographical article to him in 1895, and it goes on to record that Ellwanger's father had some vinyards, but that the Napoleonic wars and a long run of bad seasons had kept the family poor. The young George dreamt of living in America, and to that end, joined a florist and nursery business in Stuttgart. Once he'd learnt the trade, he set off across the Atlantic in 1835, and after sixty-two relatively easy days, 'saw Staten Island in the full glory of its June foliage'. He had relatives already established at Tiffin, Ohio, and set off to join them. He also had to learn English. Finally he settled in Rochester, prospered, and in 1839 began business for himself. The region was expanding fast, and he realised the new settlers would need fruit trees. He bought out the establishment of Reynolds & Bateham and also purchased eight acres of land on Mt. Hope Avenue.

In 1840 he went into partnershipwith Patrick Barry, a young Irishman who edited a newspaper called the 'The Genessee Farmer', and eventually took over A. J. Downing's 'The Gardening Magazine' when Downing drowned in 1852, aboard the paddle steamer 'Henry Clay'. Their new partnership ended up owning one of the largest nurseries in the US. They worked hard. At first, they lived in the sheds behind the glasshouses, but when those burnt down in August, 1841, they took to the road, peddling their undamaged plants through western cities and villages in order to raise funds with which to rebuild and expand. Their importance, though, lies in their passion for collecting. Most new settlers bought their fruit and vegetable stock from drifting peddlers whose cheap seeds and plants were often useless, even if they grew. Ellwanger and Barry ordered named saplings from Boston and New York, often of the stocks originally brought in by the first European settlers. Gripped with enthusiasm, in December, 1844, Ellwanger went back to Europe in order to find even more. Journeying through England, France, and Germany, all countries then busily breeding new fruit varieties, he bought hugely. The diligences and stagecoaches in which he traveled must have looked strange topped off, as they were, with bunches of young peach and apple trees, bundles of vines canes and raspberries, and hampers of strawberry plants. Once home in New York state, he sold on some of the material, and used the rest to breed varieties that suited their new conditions. The site of his labours still exists at 625 Mt. Hope Avenue, Rochester, New York, and can be visited.

Though Ellwanger's fruit collections are important later in the chapter, he also began to sell flowers associated with the new nostalgia. It turned into a big market, for the passion for old flowers and old fruit coalesced into a whole new movement in gardening, and a new sort of garden was born: the cottage garden. To find its flowers, amateurs in all walks of like, though mostly middle class, set off into their own countryside and peered hopefully over the garden gates of tumbledown cottages, or urban shacks. Some advertised in the garden press for old sorts of carnation or auricula. In Britain, the energetic Mrs Ewing founded the Parkinson Society in the 1880's, for members who wanted to grow John Parkinson's plants, or at least those about which they could feel suitably sentimental, or which proclaimed their radical disinterest in bedding plants and the very latest high-bred delphinium.

Nowadays it is hard to realise that then even parts of the English home counties were remote and undisturbed, the natives speaking impenetrable dialects, having distinctive modes of dress, and living in conditions that looked extremely primitive from the perspective of London suburbanites. However horticulturally interesting their quest, conditions weren't quite as dangerous as they were in Amazonia or Yunnan, and so explorers of gardens of the past couldn't write gory or dramatic tales of their adventures. The movement didn't really produce famous collectors, though it did spawn minor characters like the wealthy Reverend Henry Harpur Crewe, rector of Drayton Beauchamp. Most active in the mid-century, he found some lovely things, most especially the delightful double-flowered form of the wild golden yellow wallflower (*Cheiranthus cheiri*). The plant he found, now widely grown, may perhaps have been the same plant admired by Parkinson, though may equally be a double form thrown up by a wild population in more recent times. He also found a hybrid Leopards Bane (*Doronicum x excelsum*) that bears his name.

The great garden designer Miss Gertrude Jekyll became a noted collector too. It is a pity that the images usually associated with her, a plump grumpy old woman wearing run-down and misshapen old boots, are at such odds with her handsome and energetic youth. She was both talented and adventurous. She travelled around the Mediterranean, painting, studying the local crafts, and looking at local plants. No mountain or desert blunted her determination. She described her practices as follows: 'As the collection increased I began to compare and discriminate, and of various kinds of one plant to throw out the worse and retain the better and to train myself to see what made a good garden plant'. She was confident enough of her taste to send specimens to the Royal Botanic Gardens at Kew, to improve their chances of conservation. When she became famous, notably through her connection with the society architect Lutyens, she even exported her style of design to America. It wasn't always a good union. She was asked to provide designs for the garden of the Glebe House in Woodbury, Connecticut. By 1926, what was a pretty but modest eighteenth century farmhouse had become a museum. It's trustees wanted a garden that would, more or less, echo a garden of right sort of period. Gertrude Jekyll gave it an astonishing six hundred feet of classic English style herbaceous border, a planted stone terrace and an intimate rose 'allee'. Too much in the 'grand manner', it was never built. The plans were rediscovered in the late 1970's, and Jekyll's present fame has ensured that it is now being completed according to the original plans.

However much romaticised, even inflated, it has sometimes been, the cottage garden is still a popular garden ideal. Discovering and preserving old garden plants has become a widespread and important aim. In Britain, the National Council for the Conservation of Plants and Gardens was set up in 1982. It now looks after many hundred of National Collections, publishes an annual directory of those collections' holdings, and has around 10,000 members. North America has The Garden Conservancy, an organisation that preserves notable gardens, but also has 'The North American Plant Preservation Council' which concentrates on plant preservation.

Some gardeners, though, have a more radical agenda still. Why stop with garden plants of the nineteenth, or even the sixteenth, century when many a country's original native flora is at such risk of disappearance? Many gardeners now want gardens that look like their idealised native meadows, or its prairies, or even its rain forest. The movement is, of course, most important in regions where the flora is extremely rich, not already well explored, and at risk from the pressure of an expanding human population. Brazil, in spite of all the collectors in this book, of the hundreds who have been left out, and of the many botanist still collecting there, is a perfect example. Gradually, the Brazilian state has come to realise the extent of its native flora, and the asset that it represents. That is has has needed the pleas and advice of botanist and naturalists is clear, but the Brazilian flora has also needed a collector-publicist. In Roberto Burle Marx, it found it.

He was born on August 4, 1909, into a wealthy Brazilian business family, with a house on a grand boulevard in São Paulo. The family moved five years later to Rio de Janeiro, where his father was closer to the political centre, and his mother, who was an accomplished opera singer, would feel more at home in its sophisticated circles. Roberto, with terrible eyesight, was kept out of formal education. However, he was insatiably curious about the world, could sing, and, using his eyes, soon wanted to be a painter. He studied art at the Escole de Belas Arte in Rio de Janeiro, but Europe was then the centre of innovation. He was soon in studying in Germany. It was there that he had his personal revelation. Around 1928, he became interested in plant form. He started looking at the tropical plants at the Dahlem Botanical Gardens, and was overwhelmed to discover that many of the most beautiful grew sometimes not that far from the family home in Rio. His direction was set; after his return to Brazil in 1930, he surrounded his own new home there with gardens packed with thousands of rare species from Brazilian forests and swamps, especially those of his great loves: orchids, palms, water lilies, and bromeliads.

An artist, a designer, a plantsman, well-connected, landscape design was a natural synthesis of his talents, and he was soon landing exciting and important commissions. His own eyes now opened, he helped to open the eyes of other Brazilians by using using only Brazilian plants in his schemes. He had plenty to choose from. With nearly 55,000 native species, Brazil is now known to be the country with the richest flora on the planet. Humboldt and Bonpland were right to be overwhelmed. Burle Marx's collection, and his passion for collecting grew so fast that Burle Marx bought an old estate in Barra de Guaratiba in 1949. With several hundred acres, part steep hillside, part mangrove swamp, it had an old house with marvelous views, a tiny sixteenth century chapel, and masses of potential. Marx set about turning the estate into garden, plant nursery, and nature reserve. The plantings covered the major ecological regions of Brazil, from its rainforests to the strange watery Pantanal. He gave the garden structure by building walls made out of carved stonework salvaged from Rio's eighteenth and nineteenth century buildings. He built fountains, pools, water shutes. All were draped with orchids and bromeliads, clambering philodendrons. There were banks of the beautiful bougainvillea native to Rio de Janeiro, and collected by Philibert Commerson and Jeanne Baret so long ago. There were banana plantations as well as carefully preserved fragments of the state of Rio de Janeiros fast disappearing 'Atlantic forest'.

    Hugely influential as an artist and architect, and with an exceptionally expansive personality, the Brazilian flora had found a major and, more importantly, local, advocate. He constantly entertained Brazil's rich and influential elite, his lovely house and its courtyards flamboyantly decorated with Brazil's most extraordinary plants. He tried to show everyone, amidst the lavish hospitality, how marvellous the flowers of the country were, how much they were endangered, and how much they were worth preserving.

Sometimes his expeditions to collect them seemed merely extensions of the partying, and with a shout, perhaps even a whole aria, of 'Come, all my beautiful children, my beautiful crazies,' he would set off with a throng of clients and friends, loaded with cameras, insect repellent, and broadbrimmed hats, into the tropical forests. If Brazil now begins to lead the way in the preservation of the vast diversity of the South American flora, the movement owes a great debt to the plump, ebullient man commemorated in dozens of plants, running from begonias like the crinkly-leafed *Begonia burle-marxii*, to astonishing pieces of botanical engineering like *Heliconia burle-marxii*. Currently about seven percent of the Amazon region is 'preserved' as much as is possible, and the 'indigenous areas' add another twenty four percent. The other regions, further south but almost as species rich, are in a less good state, with less than one percent under official protection. That there is anything at all is due, in good part, to him. In 1985, he gave his estate to the National Institute for Cultural Heritage, who now open it to the public. He died on June 4, 1994.

But for the last two collectors, and their plants, let's return to George Ellwanger in Rochester. His thorough-going approach to old or historic varieties of plants interested people far beyond his own neighbourhood. By the early twentieth century, the United States Department of Agriculture was beginning to think of trying big breeding programmes on almost any plant that could be of commercial use to American farmers. Most of the fruit species brought to America by the European settlers, and which were now commercially important, had not first originated in Europe. They had been domesticated further east: Turkey, Armenia, Northern India, China. They wanted to explore the variants of these crops that still existed in those countries to see if they had characteristics, perhaps disease resistance, or tolerance of cold, that would be useful crossed into new varieties for the American grower. But first they wanted a sure-fire winner, a medicinal plant. A tree whose crushed seeds yielded 'chaulgmoogra oil' was one of their most important projects. In legend, chaulmoogra oil had been revealed in a dream to an ancient king of Siam. It would cure his leprosy. It had certainly been used against the disease for more than a thousand years. The tree, *Hydnocarpus kurzli* (now sometime put in the genus *Taraktogenos*), is rare. It is also poisonous, and its oil, when swallowed, made patients seriously sick. Some American doctors were trying to inject it, but it caused terrible ulcers. The oil wasn't available in sufficient quantities to see if it

could be refine in any way. Seed was required. The USDA needed a
collector, someone who was a tough traveller, someone who knew enough
botany to recognise the tree when he saw it, and also someone who spoke
Chinese. They were't expecting anyone particularly remarkable. The man
they got was Joseph Rock.

Let us meet him, probably as he would have most liked, riding with his
retinue through the hills of China. He's preceded by a group of unruly, half
destitute soldiers, some of their guns held together with wire. Then come a
dozen or so Nakhi coolies, themselves and their pack animals heavily laden.
Much of the baggage consists of Rock's personal belongings. He cannot
travel without all the materials for a smart Viennese dinner: tablecloths of
linen damask, napkins, silver cutlery, elegant glassware, and books so that his
cook could make proper Austrian meals. He is obsessed with his personal
hygiene, and so needs a folding bath made by Abercrombie & Fitch. He also
travels with a large wardrobe filled with suits and expensive shirts so that he
will never lose status when visiting even the most insignificant of chieftains.
He is eventually reputed to travel with a dinner service of purest gold,
making him a natural target for the sort of people of whom he is most
terrified.

The expression on his face gives nothing away. Inside, he's terrified of
the bandits rumoured to be following him in the hope of rich pickings. He's
quarreled with the soldiers and now can't trust their loyalty. He suspects his
carriers have some opium, even though he carefully sniffs at each man first
thing in the morning to check that they haven't been smoking it. He broods
on what he sees as a snub by the hostess at a Boston dinner party six months
ago. He has written in his diary: 'Personality cannot be developed in
solitude.... It must be surrounded by other living beings to make itself felt.

What we often call personality is the power to perceive the weakness in others in a twinkling of an eye and thus dominate by sheer arrogance and self-forwardness like a rooster charging a council of hens among a few grains of wheat, scattering them, and then picking up leisurely the rest. The hens look on with cowed heads.'

In the roar of the river far below, he hears his father's voice intoning the last rites, except that his father was not a priest, but a humble pastry cook working in the kitchens of Count Potocki's winter palace in Vienna. Alas, as well as a pastry cook, he was also a terrifying, anger-filled, religious maniac who'd constructed a tiny altar in his drab apartment, and got his children to play the role of his priestly acolytes. Joseph's mother had died in 1890 when he was six. With the body lying in state, his father insisted on him placing flowers in her chilly hands. Two weeks later, Joseph's only other source of comfort, his grandmother, died too.

Joseph first ran away from home when he was eight. He was hoping to reach his dead mother's relatives in Hungary, and with whom he was happy. He got no further than the outskirts of Vienna before he was robbed of his few pennies, and the food he had taken from his father's larder. He ran away from school often. Truanting, he visited his mother's grave, or wandered, fascinated, amongst the exotic fairground performers of the Prater. He became a regular familiar of fire-eaters, jugglers, sword swallowers, and story tellers. He discovered he had a talent for tongues; he began to learn Arabic and Chinese. His pockets were full of scraps of card with Chinese characters printed on them. He began to dream of running away to Peking and Lhasa. When he was at school, he so wrapped himself in ideas of grandeur and mystery, that his fellow pupils called him 'the Count'.

Finally, in 1901, he begged his father to let him join the Austrian Navy. His father had determined he should be a real priest, and swore that it was the seminary or death. Joseph left home forever in 1902. Taking menial jobs as a tourist guide, or working as a seaman, he travelled around Europe and North Africa. He only went back to Vienna when his father died, and lived briefly with his sister Lena. Soon, Joseph left for England, but in its damp climate soon discovered that he had tuberculosis. Panicking when he began to cough blood, he rushed back to Lena. Vienna was worse than London, and he headed south to Italy, then to Tunis, and wound up on the island of Malta. Dreaming of warmer climates still, he soon recovered enough to work his way to the Orient. Finally, almost by chance, he drifted to the shores of

Hawaii. He became interested in its plants, began teaching others about them, and remained on the island between 1908 and 1919. Having drifted and dreamed for so long, his destiny was slowly being forged. He saw the advert place for a botanist-explorer place by The Office of Foreign Seed and Plant Introduction of the U. S. Department of Agriculture. He got the job.

On February 11, 1922, Joseph Francis Charles Rock finally entered his dream-land, and reached the far western border of China. He had with him two medical missionaries, six carriers, two guides and a cook. One of the missionaries was the Scottish Dr. Ernest Muir who passionately believed that the oil from the chaulmoogra tree offered real hope to lepers. The expeditions stores, and Rock's folding bath, were carried by fifteen horses. The party had been inching its way into the mountains from Siam for three months. Passing from one tribal region to another, often being chased by bandits, it had now had reached a small Chinese outpost in remotest Yunnan. Rock wrote: 'the moon rose shortly before our arrival... and the sun was just setting, and the hills in the distance were purple. The sky was slightly hazy, and the full moon gently riding on the pale lilac haze, herself a pale silver disc, with the land masses clearly showing... A much-faded Chinese flag was implanted almost in the center of the road. To the left of it was a bamboo wooden shanty where the Chinese official, a small dirty fellow with a kindly smile, gave us a rather nice reception. Several Chinese were sitting about dressed in blue.... and entered into a lively conversation.' They passed over the border, and were shown the way on to Chieng Law.

He found the chaulmoogra tree, and sent back large quantities of seed. Some of it was to the University of Hawaii, where twenty seven acres of it were planted at Waiahole, Oahu, and where the oil's essentials were first extracted. Sadly, they were found to be too toxic to use, and probably useless anyway. Sulphonamides and their derivatives also appeared at much the same time, so whether chaulmoogra oil was of any real use was never finally tested. Nevertheless, the trip made him. He was commissioned by the editor of the National Geographic Magazine, Gilbert H. Grosvenor, to write about the south Asian chaulmoogra oil plant as a possible cure for leprosy. He did, and took the photographs too. The article was such a success that he went on to do a further nine for the magazine, with romantic titles such as 'Experiences of a Lone Geographer: An American Explorer Makes his way through Brigand-Infested Central China'. With his need for self-dramatisation, they made exciting reading. On his trips back to America, he was lionised, but that made him only more difficult and paranoid still. He retreated. From 1922 to 1949 he lived almost continuously on the road in China. The natives knew him as 'Hef', and thought him a man of quick and violent temper, eventually so stocky that he commissioned local carpenters to build special chairs and a desk to accommodate his size. He collected some 60,000 plant specimens for American institutions, mostly the Smithsonian. He also shot 1,600 bird specimens given to American ornithologists. He became an anthropologist too, becoming fascinated by the ancient culture of his Nakhi bearers. He collected hundreds of ancient heiroglyphic manuscripts, sometimes giving the material to American libraries, sometimes selling them to private collectors. Many he had translated by local wisemen who understood the ancient language. He wrote about them too, notably in books like 'The Ancient Na-Khi Kingdom Of Southwest China', and the grandly titled 'Lamas, princes, and brigands : Joseph Rock's photographs of the Tibetan borderlands of China'. He himself died in Hawaii in 1962. His many splendid photographs are in the archives of the Royal Botanic Garden, Edinburgh

The USDA. only financed his first trip. He was poached on his return by another influential, and rather more prestigious American organisation, the Arnold Arboretum of Harvard. The USDA was not pleased. It had became more and more intent on copying the English king Henry VIII, sending collectors abroad to discover new varieties of good things to eat. It therefore needed another collector to explore China. It found Frank Meyer. Meyer's story goes like an arrow.

    Unlike Rock, he knew he was a gardeners and plant collector even when he was still almost a child. He was born, Frans Meier, on November 29, 1875 in a small house in the docklands of Amsterdam. He was a bright child, but poverty gave him little prospect. At fourteen, he became a jobbing helper, and later a gardener, at the Amsterdam Botanical Garden. Its director, Hugo De Vries, recognised the boy's enthusiasm and intelligence, and began to train him to be his laboratory assistant, teaching him French and English as well as botany. Frans was restless and wanted more still. He began to explore Holland. With almost no money, he often walked the fifty miles to the dunes, sleeping outdoors all night. He made a herbarium, studied more languages, mathematics, science, and drawing. He kept studying botany. He left home to live in a boarding-house in Amsterdam. He went to concerts, became interested in Buddhism and theosophy, read Schopenhauer. He became fascinated by the idea of an ultimate and irrational will, and he learned from his acquaintances that he wasn't the only man in the world who suffered from depression. For a while, when he was twenty-three, he joined a Utopian colony founded by the Dutch poet Frederick van Eden, and based on the ideas of Thoreau. The colony was called Walden, and operated on the principle that all would share in the work and in the fruits of their toil. He didn't stay long. It was too restricting. He wanted to set off on his travels, get away from the pearl grey skies of Holland, away to see the lemon and orange orchards that were so vivid in his dreams of Italy and blue-shadowed sunshine. To do this, he simply bought a map and a compass and started walking south with no attention to roads or to the useful tracks of others. In one alpine pass, he nearly lost his life in a blizzard. Descending into the foothills in Italy, he had startled a farmer who asked where he had come from. "Across the mountains," replied Meyer. 'Impossible,' the farmer objected, 'there are no roads.' There weren't.

Frank ended his days in Europe working in commercial nurseries in England. At last, he had enough money to get to America. On October 12, 1901, he left Southampton on the 'S.S. Philadelphia'. He wrote to friends in Amsterdam: 'I am pessimistic by nature… and have not found a road which leads to relaxation. I withdraw from humanity and try to find relaxation with plants. I live now in expectation of what will come.' There was to be plenty.

He found work readily in nurseries and botanic gardens where his skills were always of use. He wandered and wandered. He hiked for hundreds of miles through Mexico. Then, wanting to see the World Fair in Saint Louis, he made his way there on foot. He rapidly found a job at the Missouri Botanical Garden. He was fascinated by the World Fair. His boss, Dr. William Trelease had invited de Vries over from Amsterdam to give some lectures, and was astonished when de Vries and his best propagator, now renamed 'Frank Meyer', turned out to be old friends. Things were setting fair. Suddenly the miracle happened; the dream of his youth came true. On March 10, 1905, a telegram from Adrian J. Pieters of the USDA arrived. Meyer was offered the chance to go searching for the cultivated plants of China. Frank telegraphed back immediately 'Great thanks for your offer. Accept it. Will be ready any time but would like to stay here a few weeks yet.' He telegraphed his mother 'I have big news…' but he didn't quite yet believe it, for he added that 'the offer is a beautiful one even if it does not go through.'

It did, and he ended up making four great trips to Asia, collecting immense quantities of plant material, travelling very simply and cheaply, worrying as much about filing his expenses from places where the currencies themselves varied constantly in both nationality and value, as about bandits and the sheer physical dangers of plant collecting. He bought gifts for his friends, friends mostly drawn from the place where he worked. When travelling he wrote them letters. He often expressed loneliness and depression, even a curious sense of incompleteness. 'Loneliness hangs always around the man who leaves his own race and moves among an alien population," he acknowledged, and tried to believe Ibsen's false statement that the strongest man is he who stands alone. However, he also often wrote of the thrill of finding new plants, and the beauty of the places where he found them. He even sent his recommendations for his superior's new garden back in America. He'd heard that they had ordered over a hundred flowering cherries from Suzuki's nursery in Rokohama, Japan. Frank

thought that sounded lovely, and replied: 'If you plant cherries as a spring
delight, do not fail to plant Japanese maples for fall effects. Have you a
brook? If so, plant *Iris kaempferi*. There are dreams of beauty among them.
Do you love weeping trees? The Weeping Pagoda Tree is delightful. Plant
also a few clumps of the Chinese tree peony and have some big Chinese
porcelain vessels in which you can plant lotus. Have also a few clumps of
magnolias. They are so noble in the early spring. Have some white-barked
birches, the most elegant of all northern trees. If you can get a specimen of
the *Davidia involucrata* sent to England by Wilson, do try it.' The garden
was called 'In the Woods', and on his trips back to America, when he worked
on his collections, it would become much loved place.

America had become 'home'. He didn't visit Holland again. In 1918, he
was back in China. Laden with material, though with some unspecified
ailment of his innards, he dreamt of returning to a settled life. He wrote that
he expected to take a steamer down the Yangtze, possibly stopping at
Kiukiang (Jiujiang) to inspect tung oil plantations. A week later Meyer told
his family that he wasn't really enjoying looking at the Yangtze Valley in
June. It was too hot. He had become less able to tolerate being
uncomfortable. Sleep was difficult. His appetite wasn't good. He was
worried about China's political instablity, about the teeming insects, about
the diseases that surrounded him. He was tired out. He wanted to visit his
family in Holland. He was worried for them, yet, from China, it seemed as if
the First World War was still raging. He commented, bitterly, that traveling
might seem a pleasure to someone who stayed at home; however, a traveler
often longed to have a home and a garden, and never to have to move on.

He stopped off at the town of Hankow, and having 'stomach trouble
accompanied by vomiting', he stayed at a comfortable hotel for Europeans.
It was noisy. Western naval officers kept insisting that he come to have a
drink with them. Intestinal infections often make the sufferer desperate for a
darkened room and silence. He and his servant-guide moved to a cheaper
'native' hotel where he wouldn't be bothered, and after a few days he seemed
better. His servant Yao-feng Ting thought that he looked thinner even than
when they left Ichang.

On Friday, May 31, Meyer and Yao-feng boarded a Japanese riverboat,
the 'Feng Yang Maru', under Captain Inwood. It was to take them down the
Yangtze to Shanghai. Practically all foreigners except missionaries traveled
first class. Meyer, modest as usual, or perhaps still thinking of the Hankow

Hotel, chose the cheaper Chinese variation of first-class accommodation. The next day, he still wasn't feeling well enough to visit the tung oil plantations as he had planned. Worse, a British insurance man, Islay Drysdale, boarded the steamer at Kiukiang. For some reason, he too wanted to use the Chinese first-class, and so had to share Meyer's cabin. They seem to have spent most of the day talking as the boat sped downstream through the surging currents. Drysdale left the riverboat at Anking at 4:00pm. Soon after, Captain Inwood looked in to see how Meyer was doing. Frank replied that he was well except for a headache. That evening he ate a full Chinese dinner. Yao-feng Ting served tea in his master's cabin. Meyer was better.

About 11:20pm., Meyer left his cabin, wanderd up on deck. He had been seen by the deck steward. It was a clear night. The 'Feng Yang Maru' was passing the light-boat off Barker Island. The river swirled past. Forty minutes later the cabin boy reported to Captain Inwood that he could not find Mr. Meyer. Inwood started a search. The boat wasn't large. Frank Meyer was not on board it. The officers searched along the guards and rails. Meyer's disappearance had left no trace.

But let us leave him here, on this June night, the lights of the 'Feng Yang Maru', and the pulse of its engine, vanished in the darkness. His body, arms akimbo, is tumbling over and over in the rough embrace of the river. He will drift ashore four days later and be found by a local fisherman. There will be enquiries. Islay Drysdale will be interviewed. Chinese passengers will be suspected. Nothing will be discovered, and no explanation found.

In his cabin trunks are seeds that are still influencing our lives, and which are increasingly finding their way into the breeding programmes of a huge diversity of garden plants. His materials can be found in the tough *Zoysia* grasses that will make green the lawns and fairways of California, Oklahoma and Texas, in drought and wind resistant elms, in disease resistant chestnuts, in mildew resistant spinaches. Amongst other material that he has sent back to America are sumptuous seedless persimmons only now finding their way into commerce, hawthorns with fruits as big as crab apples, fast-growing Chinese cabbages, splendid decoratives like the tough yellow rose (*Rosa xanthina*), and the tiny and delicious lilac so long in Chinese gardens that it relates to no known wild species (*Syringa meyeri var. palibiniana*).

There is also an unusually hardy lemon, one that will go on to make a fine backyard plant in all the warm states of the US, make huge commercial plantations for juicing fruits in Florida, Texas, South Africa, and New

Zealand. Even in northern Europe, it will go on to become a popular garden centre citrus, its fragrant flowers standing out in brilliant white amongst the glossy leaves and young green fruit: Meyer's lemon.

****

ENDPIECE

Now, of course, plant collecting is very different. Much more of the planet is opened up. Collectors can arrive on site by helicopter or jeep. They can transmit pictures of plants growing live in the remotest places of the globe to experts in London, Paris, Edinburgh, Boston, Vienna, with libraries and herbaria to hand. A plant can be determined as 'new' almost instantaneously. A market for it can be created soon after. However there are also new barriers between a plant in the wild, and the distant gardeners who might grow it. The 'Convention on Biological Diversity', signed during the Rio Earth Summit held in Rio de Janeiro, Brazil in June 1992 is a legally binding agreement for the conservation and sustainable use of biodiversity. It came into force on 29 December 1993, and while attempting to protect a country's botanical assets so that it can get some financial return if its plants turn out to be desired by gardeners, or to contain a pharmacological bounty, it does sever the easy link that existed between plant and gardener. A new species cannot get into commerce without the agreement of the country in which it was found. However, the Convention is almost impossible to police, and is not retrospective. After the great age of plant collecting that finished in the mid-twentieth century, it seems very much an attempt to bolt the treasury door long after much of the treasure is freely available to whomsoever wants it.

Yet contemporary plant collectors, in areas like Bhutan or the Cerrado regions of South America, say that almost certainly huge numbers of species still await discovery and liberation. However many expeditions there have been up the Yangtse, or the Amazon, or over the crunching gravel of the Karroo desert, there are still seasons that haven't been covered, still inlets or valleys not yet traversed. Gardeners will see.

Meanwhile, there is a colossal flora available to every gardener who wants to explore it. If you garden, let your collector's instinct loose. Let plants in all their fantastical diversity pour themselves into your garden. Diversity is all. Gardeners can preserve it. Plant breeders and hybridists can increase it. So many species have arrived so recently in the garden that the genetic potential of the mix has hardly been tapped. Contemporary gardeners seem to be in an extraordinary position: at any moment, a new plant discovery, or the development of a group of plants by an unknown gardener or nurseryman, might turn out to have the potential to transform our gardens all over again. So, don't dead head. Let seed pods form. Sow what you get; each seed in the packet, or at the bottom of the crumpled and dusty envelope. You might find nothing new, or, if rarely, something far more beautiful than the plants you already have. Even better, you might create a wonder, something that starts us all off in a new direction. And even if you don't, at least sow each seed. Each seedling, however small, is a part, as we all are, of the glory and abundance of the world.

END